HENRI BENDEL

ISBN 13): 978-1-959569-05-3

http://ulpress.org
University of Louisiana at Lafayette Press
P.O. Box 43558
Lafayette, LA 70504-3558

cover art: *Spring Sale at Bendel's* (1921) by Florine Stettheimer
Philadelphia Museum of Art: Gift of Miss Ettie Stettheimer

Printed in the United States

Library of Congress Cataloging-in-Publication Data

Names: Allis, Tim, 1961- author.
Title: Henri Bendel and the worlds he fashioned / Tim Allis.
Description: Lafayette : University of Louisiana at Lafayette Press, 2024.
   | Includes bibliographical references.
Identifiers: LCCN 2023043156 | ISBN 9781959569053 (hardcover)
Subjects: LCSH: Bendel, Henri, 1868-1936. | Henri Bendel (Firm)--History. |
   Department stores--New York (State)--New York--History. |
   Merchants--United States--Biography.
Classification: LCC HF5465.U64 B45 2024 | DDC
   381/.141097471--dc23/eng/20240129
LC record available at https://lccn.loc.gov/2023043156

HENRI BENDEL

AND THE WORLDS HE FASHIONED

TIM ALLIS

UNIVERSITY OF LOUISIANA AT LAFAYETTE PRESS
2024

For Jeffery

"You're a Bendel bonnet
A Shakespeare sonnet
You're Mickey Mouse!"

   —"You're the Top," from Cole Porter's musical *Anything Goes*

"Bendel's clothes, hats, lingerie, and accessories exhausted all my superlatives long ago."

   —"Shophound's Advice to the Shop-Worn," *Vogue*, 1935

"Dressmaking like all art is autobiographical."

—Henri Bendel

TABLE OF CONTENTS

CHAPTER 1

FULL TILT

In the crimson and blush-pink tableau of Florine Stettheimer's whimsical 1921 painting *Spring Sale at Bendel's*, which lives in the Philadelphia Museum of Art, the figure in a black morning suit and spat-top shoes pulls your eye, even as he's tucked to the side. He's got one hand on a velvet stanchion at the bottom of a grand, red-carpeted staircase and is the only character who faces the viewer, placidly meeting our gaze. He's a calm, knowing counterpoint to the score of jewel-hued ladies of fashion who are too absorbed in shopping, too intoxicated, it seems, to look up. They primp and prance, slipping into and contorting themselves out of frocks and frippery, one over-eager woman diving into a pile of dresses, another almost falling off a balustrade to snatch a scarf. It was a clearance sale, after all, a concept Henri Bendel had pioneered—every gal for herself! Meanwhile, the natty ballet master overseeing this farcical dance—Henri—remains unruffled amidst the mayhem.

Sober, restrained, fussily *correct*, Bendel would never show it publicly, but despite his feet being properly planted in Stettheimer's lark of a painting, he was, in real life, flying as high as her leaping lady. As the 1920s roared in, Henri, at fifty-two, was approaching his professional zenith. And unlike the mild-faced little man in the painting, he was imposing, robust, hardly off to the side of anything. Indeed, he had made himself the center of fashionable life in New York City and beyond. Setter of style. Game-changing merchant. A French fashion ambassador who wasn't French.

"The great New York house of Bendel," said *Vogue* magazine, is "now probably the largest importer of Paris frocks in the world."

Yet in an act of having his brioche and eating it too, Bendel simultaneously sounded a battle cry for liberation *from* Parisian style. "I think it's high time American designers were thinking for themselves," he had declared a few years earlier. Now, even as he shipped in and touted the most important labels from Paris—including Lanvin, Worth, Paquin, Callot Soeurs, Doucet,

Opposite: *Spring Sale at Bendel's* (1921) by Florine Stettheimer

1

Molyneaux, and Chanel, the last of which he introduced to this country—he was creating and selling original designs—American designs—to stand toe-to-satin-toe with the French.

From the drowsy bayou country of southern Louisiana to the dazzling vortex of Fashion and Commerce lampooned in Stettheimer's painting, Bendel's trajectory was anything but likely. Born in Vermilionville—now Lafayette—not long after the Civil War, he had parlayed his talent, taste, and drive—along with a skill for merchandising imparted by his family—into a career that began with dry goods, segued into millinery, and rapidly grew into a full-scale ladies' emporium that garnered wide acclaim and made him rich and famous. His multi-level store on West Fifty-Seventh Street, off Fifth Avenue, was a magnet for women of taste and discernment. Bendel had figured out how to meet a fashionable woman's every fashion need under one gilded roof. The finest dresses, gowns, coats, furs, millinery, accessories, lingerie—all appeared in bounteous variety. A corps of crisp and accommodating salespeople stood ready to help shoppers navigate the wonderland.

And Henri created a few fashion needs said shopper didn't even know she had. Bendel was one of the earliest dress merchants to practice branding, first by launching a line of house-label soaps and perfumes, most concocted in Paris, a city he adored. Un Peu D'Elle was his original signature scent, and there would be many more to come. Beyond clearance sales, Bendel was among the first to stage in-store fashion shows and to have models moving about the floor. Even with such elite flourishes, he crafted a nuanced balance between accessibility and aspiration. The well-turned-out tourist from Des Moines could grab a pair of stockings; a Manhattan matron of means could procure an evening dress and companionable scarf; and the Prince of Wales could warehouse a tuxedo in the refrigerated fur vault, as in fact he did.

When Fifty-Seventh Street had been strictly residential, Henri was the boundary-busting outlier, the trailblazer of "the Rue de la Paix of New York" as that section of the thoroughfare would come to be called in a nod to Paris's fabled street of couture ateliers. And his success transcended profits and retail might. Over the previous decade and a half Bendel had earned respect from all quarters. He was, according to fashion historian Caroline Rennolds Milbank, "universally acknowledged as a genius of taste and style."

And of marketing. Beyond his and the store's near-constant presence—in both ads and editorial spreads—in *Vogue, Harper's Bazaar,* and other leading fashion publications of the day, Bendel's name appeared regularly in Broadway playbills, as costumer to the top-billed star. It could also be spotted, though less frequently, in film credits, for dressing the likes of such screen icons as Billie Burke and Lillian Gish. Offstage some of these high-profile actresses, including Ina Claire and Tallulah Bankhead, appeared in promotions for the store, as did Miss Gish and Bendel's friend Geraldine Farrar, an opera singer and silent film star.

Colored organdie plays a new rôle when Bendel uses it in a rose shade to make the waistcoat of a black satin tailleur with side godets. The Lanvin hat is fringed with ostrich.

The gown with cape to match is greatly liked. Black and white striped serge, the stripes outlined with ciré ribbon, fashions a three-piece model. The loops on the hat are gray.

Yellow organdie lines a long coat of white serge, and makes the deep sleeve frills. Tassels and embroidered motifs in scarab design ornament the coat. Purple plumes trim the tagal hat.

Blue and white foulard and blue taffeta are combined in a trotteur from Bendel. A touch of red appears on the girdle. Crêpe in the new yellow faces the hat. The collar is organdie.

PARIS ADVOCATES GAYER COLORS
AND LENGTHENS HER SKIRTS

By

Henri W. Bendel

New York.

DURING my recent stay in Paris, where I visited all of the *grandes maisons*, I was strongly impressed by the effort the couturiers are making to meet present conditions. Prices are lower, not a great deal to be sure, but the difference between this season's prices and those of last year is appreciable. And this lower tendency is noticeable in the shops; that is, excluding those devoted to jewels. The cost of jewelry is simply staggering, but so far as hats, gowns and wraps are concerned, while the prices are still too exigent for the French woman, there is no doubt that the American woman is finding it easier to do her shopping in Paris.

And further, the couturiers are making a real

A Bendel-penned fashion article in *Harper's Bazar* (the magazine's original spelling) in May 1921

As a merchant, Bendel in the early '20s now stood on equal footing with leading dress merchants John Wanamaker of Wanamaker's and Edwin Goodman of Bergdorf Goodman. One publication dubbed Henri "the genial dictator of American fashion." But those other men kept themselves back-of-house for the most part. In his somewhat unassuming manner Henri had claimed a place in the spotlight, pitched his voice (without raising it) to a tone somewhere between highfalutin and plain-dealing, and made himself an authority to heed. The last word on all things fashionable. "It's a fact that frills are finished in New York," wrote *Women's Wear* (later known as *Women's Wear Daily*). "Henri Bendel will have none of them."

Bendel was quoted routinely in magazines and newspapers across the country and by the mid-1920s he'd have his own syndicated column. Though sometimes indulging in the baroque fashion-speak of his day, he more often tended to be direct. "Let me warn you," he wrote, "that your evening and dinner gowns will not be so short as last season—even though an inch below the knee is considered quite enough for a day frock—they are rarely shorter than twelve inches from the floor." Also often bemused: "Paris couturiers are apparently repentant over the meager way in which they doled out color and glitter for so long and are making amends in a lavish manner." Even mock exasperated: "Women make their battle with life much harder when they refuse the cooperation of the very feminine frock," he opined. "It has its time and place in our lives."

If his voice came down from on high, his personage worked the trenches—putting in long hours at the store, constantly switching between his business hat and his artist hat: guiding in-house designs, scouting imports, tracking trends, overseeing the staff and the books, planning for the future. And busy as he was, the one-time decorator of church altars was not above helping to style a window display, greeting shoppers, or even wrapping a

LEFT: Over the decades the Bendel logo treatment has morphed many times, a testament to the power of the name itself.

> "To have a gown with a Bendel label is something that women the world over aspire to, but only a fortunate few may possess."
> —*the* North Side Tribune *(Great Neck, NY)*

customer's package. As a 1920s newspaper profile put it, "There is not a gown leaves the shop but has been examined by Mr. Bendel."

Sanctuary from his bustling work came in the form of an eighteen-room beaux arts mansion at Kings Point, New York, a lush enclave of Great Neck, on the pristine Long Island Sound. There, surrounded by fine antiques and near-priceless tapestries procured abroad—and supported by a large live-in staff—Henri could catch his breath. It was amid this dramatic yet serene luxury that he was growing and nurturing a most unorthodox family: his niece

A rear view of Bendel's mansion at Kings Point, Long Island. By one account he dubbed the beaux arts waterfront estate Henriour. Eventually he would sell it to auto magnate Walter Chrysler.

and nephew, Florye and Benjamin, over whom he had guardianship; their mother, Emma, who was Henri's half sister; plus his longtime companions, John Blish, a former buyer from Altman's, thirteen years Bendel's senior, and Abraham Beekman Bastedo, a church organist who was a decade younger than Henri. On the 1920 Census form, Bastedo and Blish were listed as "boarders." At the store they had official titles as buyers and vice presidents. The true nature of the relationships was . . . more complex.

Understanding the nuance of these relationships and getting to the deepest heart of Henri—the private man, at an intimate level—is daunting. He left little behind, at least that this writer has found, in the way of private writings: no memoir, no diaries, and even most family-and-friends correspondence is lost. This may be owing to the passing of time and the flipping of generations—anyone alive today who might actually have met him would have done so as a young child.

And a paper trail may be elusive, in part, because perhaps Bendel wanted it that way. Furthermore, did heirs and friends cover his tracks? The idea of letters tossed in the fire does not feel like a stretch of the imagination. And later, did journalists and academicians who wrote about him do their part to elide or play down his whole story, adhering to old codes of what was socially palatable? Still, clues abound. And we have a trove of his public proclamations; Henri Bendel was hardly in hiding.

But as prominent a voice as he had, and as passionate as he was in speaking and writing, can we take everything he uttered at face value? "Henri Bendel lent himself to the creation of myths," delicately noted his friend Morris De Camp Crawford, editor of the fashion trade paper *Women's Wear*. Was he on occasion the proverbial unreliable narrator? Every time he said business was booming, was it? When he got his dander up over short skirts or, God forbid, pants on women, was he as appalled as he sounded, or going for the dramatic effect? He certainly knew how to market trends, whatever he might think of some of them privately.

Seeking Henri Bendel requires imagining Henri Bendel and reading between the brown and white stripes of his legend. Also to marvel at his range and take note of his contradictions: an obsessive devotee of antiquities who profited from the new and the now. A southerner who found his footing and fame up north. A Jew and

A sketch of a Coco Chanel dress of 1921, from the Bendel Sketch Collection at the Brooklyn Museum in New York City. It's one of more than seven thousand sketches bequeathed to the museum by the store in the 1950s.

A charcoal sketch of Mr. Bendel, which the store used on its website.

an Episcopalian. A once-married man who reconciled his homosexuality. And an artist equally adept at business. No one is ever one thing, but Henri's polarities are striking. Still, in many ways he was exactly who he appeared to be: unshy in his opinions, cheerful but firm in his daily dealings, robust in his passions. Indeed, he wore his passion on his sleeves—and in the cut of the gowns he sold, in the ribbons on the hats he crafted.

And he showed no deeper passion than his devotion to all things French. "Paris couldn't stop creating," he said. "It's bred in the bone and blood of her, and to her tiptoes she is art." But as early as the mid-nineteen-teens, between his copying Parisian dresses and having his in-house designers create

Acclaimed photographer George Platt Lynes shot more than one artful editorial spread featuring Bendel fashions, this one for *Harper's Bazaar* in 1938.

• The black crepe cocktail dress, full skirted for the rhumba,

which you will wear out dining and dancing these February nights. Henri Bendel.

Gold and diamond cactus leaves from Paul Flato.

GEORGE PLATT LYNES

8 8

new looks, he was starting to tip the scales. A dramatically composed piece of reportage in a theater journal of the era, describing the style scene at Long Island's tony Belmont Park equestrian track, suggests just how much Henri was helping society clotheshorses avoid transatlantic fatigue:

> Now let me whisper a secret. Not my secret, but that of Mrs. Oelrichs and her sister 'Birdie' Fair Vanderbilt: It is New York, not Paris, which has turned out the delicious frocks that the Harriman girls, the Vanderbilt matrons, the brides of the year and the Astors and Goulds are wearing. "Bendel, my dear," said Mrs. Oelrichs and her sister in

a breath, as the former waved her Chinese umbrella of old green with a marvelous jade dragon for a handle, in the direction of Lady de Bathe, who was strolling across the club house lawn with a train of cavaliers at the last day of racing at Belmont Park.

Impressed as they may have been, neither Mrs. Oelrichs nor Lady de Bathe could begin to imagine how Bendel's influence would soon radiate out from their snug (not to say smug) social milieu and touch the lives of millions of women across the country for many decades ahead. That Bendel would be at the vanguard of promoting American fashion, craft new ways of shopping and marketing, conceive of satellite stores in other cities, and startle the business world by offering generous profit-sharing for his employees, all while upholding a kind of old-fashioned decorum and adherence to quality and personal service that the women at Belmont Park would demand.

The New York flagship store in its final location at 714 Fifth Avenue

Nor could they foresee that the shop that bore his name would, long after he was gone, continue setting the pace—especially under an extraordinary woman named Geraldine Stutz who took over in the late 1950s when a female president at the helm of a department store was virtually unheard of. In the '60s and '70s she would recast Bendel's as a magical bazaar of boutiques that revolutionized fashion retailing, and she would launch or give critical early boosts to some of the most influential designers of their generation, from British bright light Jean Muir and the French "queen of knits" Sonia Rykiel to domestic supernovas Perry Ellis and Ralph Lauren, and the pioneering Black American designer Stephen Burrows. And that the store would become a magnet for fashion fanatics and au courant celebrities, popping up in novels, movies, and TV shows.

That the name Henri Bendel, and his signature stripes, would resonate across three centuries.

Mrs. Oelrichs and the strolling ladies at Belmont Park didn't have a clue.

Could even Bendel himself have envisioned it—the gentle-looking fellow on the stairs in the Stettheimer painting who had come so far from where he began?

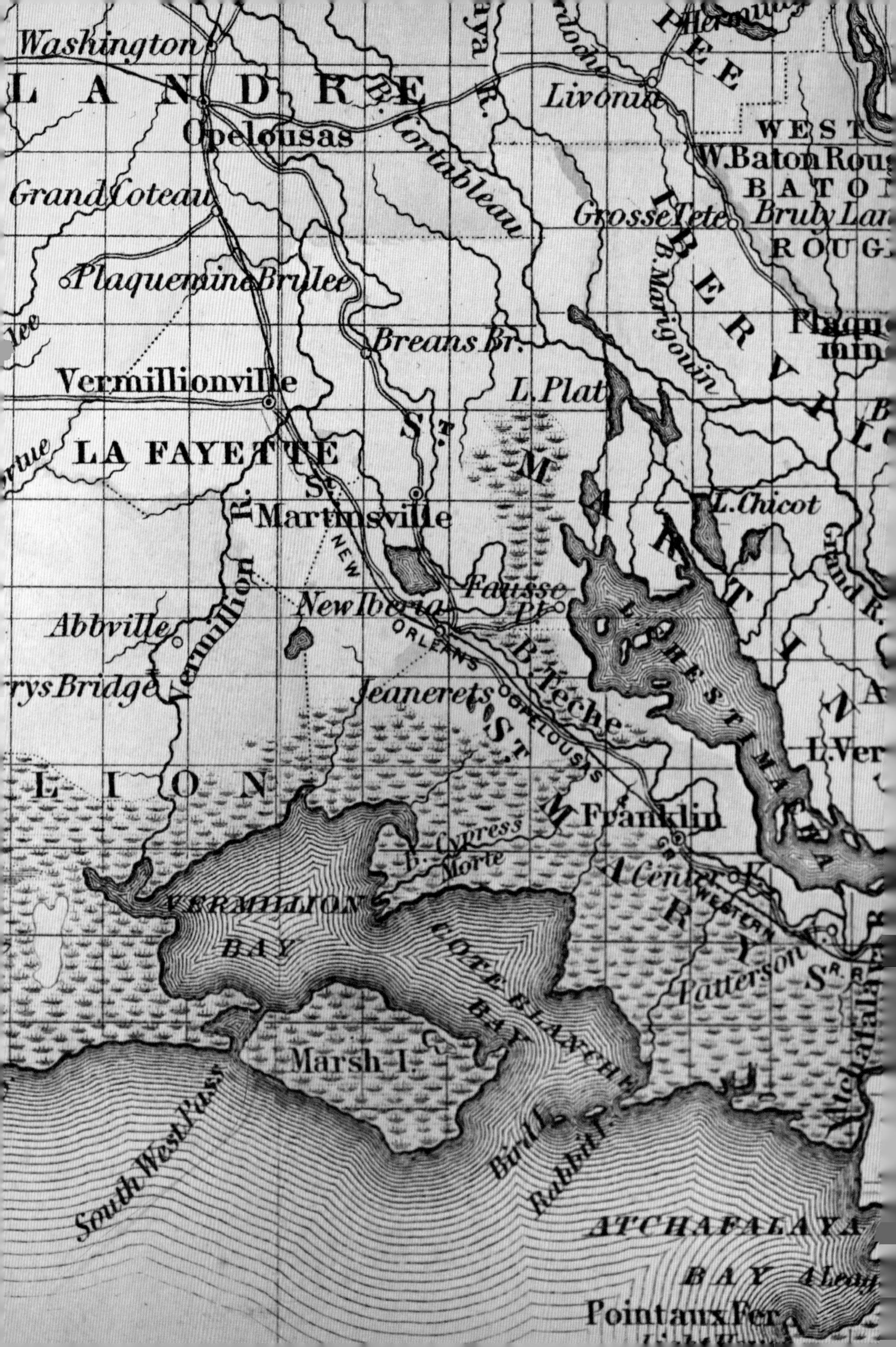

Washington

LANDRE

Opelousas

Livonia

WEST

W. Baton Roug

BATO

Grand Coteau

Grosse Tete

Bruly Lan

ROUG

Plaquemine Brulee

Plaque

min

Breans Br.

L. Plat

Vermillionville

L. Chicot

LA FAYETTE

St.

St.

Martinsville

Fausse
Pt.

Abbville

New Iberia

Grand

rys Bridge

Jeanerets

L. Ver

B. Teche

LION

Franklin

Center

Cypress
Morte

Patterson

VERMILLION
BAY

BAY

Marsh I.

South West Pass

Bird

Rabbit I.

ATCHAFALAYA

BAY

Point aux Fer

CHAPTER 2

A FRENCH INFLECTION

$\mathcal{S}$OME ARDENT NEW YORKERS say that they never knew home until they arrived there. As if the great metropolis was their natural, rightful place in the world, which they reclaimed in some cosmic sense after overcoming the inconvenience of having been born and raised someplace else. Henri Bendel might have been inclined to such feelings. The city's dynamism, ambition, and dedication to style, art, and gracious living fairly matched his own. And traits and passions that may have made him an outsider in little Vermilionville, Louisiana, in the nineteenth century would've been tolerated and even embraced in cosmopolitan New York City. Henri eventually grew enraptured by Europe too, especially Paris, where his Louisiana-acquired French lubricated his entrée into the rarefied salons of *haute couture*. Over the years he collected so many fine antiques and tapestries from his many trips abroad and gushed so about the appeal of Continental style and customs, one might conclude that he felt even more like a *European* than a New Yorker.

But no. After decades of living and working in New York, running an empire of his own imagining, Bendel never lost sight of, or affection for, where he came from. Nor did he cut ties to his birthplace or his family there—several of whom eventually came north to work for his store, and in the case of his half sister and her children, move in with him. Henri returned to the South frequently and eventually built a winter retreat right outside of town. "I [just] had a mighty fine visit with relatives and friends here," he told the local *Daily Advertiser* in 1925, "and I always enjoy getting back to Lafayette which I still feel is my home."

Even today, many imagine that designer and ladies' dress store founder Henri-with-an-*i* Bendel must have been French and are surprised to learn of his real provenance. He was called Henry with a *y* growing up and may in fact have been born with that name—no birth certificate survives—but any way you spell it he was, and remained, a Louisianan at heart.

OPPOSITE: Louisiana map detail, 1855

"When Mr. Bendel first saw the light of day in the little Southern town of Lafayette who was to know what importance that infant was to gain and what he was to accomplish," gushed a 1925 newspaper columnist in Great Neck, New York, where Henri had built his first mansion along Long Island's Gold Coast. "Mr. Bendel is proud of the place of his birth and makes a trip to his boyhood home whenever business conditions will permit. And Lafayette is equally proud of her son."

To the end of his life, he would sing the praises of Cajun Country, as it's called. "I talk of Lafayette wherever I go," he told the *Advertiser*, while on an extended visit in 1929, "and I am going to bring my friends here from the East and other parts of the country and show them what they are missing."

Bendel's particular nook of Louisiana, a sticky-sweet lowland of barely moving bayous and sprawling live oak trees, not to mention mosquitoes, snakes, and stifling summer heat, was a fairly unique place to grow up. Its charms and challenges, and the character of the people, inevitably shaped who he would become. Located on prairie land adjacent to the estuaries and swamps of coastal Louisiana, about 140 miles west-northwest of New Orleans, the town of Vermilionville (named for the nearby reddish-brown Vermilion River) was, like much of southern Louisiana in the mid-nineteenth century, still something of a frontier. Hard to reach and plagued by those natural adversaries mentioned above, it had taken tough, determined souls to call it home:

A typical Acadiana landscape with a moss-drenched oak alongside a bayou

Downtown Lafayette in the early 1900s, not long after it changed its name from Vermilionville

first the Atakapa-Ishak and Opelousa Indian nations; then French and English trappers and traders; and next the exiled Acadians, who settled there after the British expelled them en masse from the French colony of Acadie (now Nova Scotia, New Brunswick, and Prince Edward Island) starting in the 1750s, over fears of their allegiance to France. After Spain took possession of Louisiana in 1763, land grants offered a reunification opportunity for the Acadians dispersed throughout other parts of the country and abroad. As they made a new homeland on the fertile soil, the Cajuns, as they came to be called, leaned on their farming, fishing, and trapping know-how, and invested the area with their French language and earthy, piquant cast-iron pot cuisine, plus their devout Catholic faith and seemingly bottomless fortitude.

The 1800s saw the expansion and industrialization of sugarcane harvesting there, and, to a lesser extent, cotton farming. Lucrative as these crops were, the ravenous pursuit of them came at too high a moral price, engendering the wide proliferation of slavery, which had begun in the early 1700s and by the mid-1800s had exploded throughout the South. At the start of the Civil War in 1861, more than 330,000 African Americans were enslaved in Louisiana (there were also some 18,000 free people of color, many in New Orleans). For most formerly enslaved people, the post-war transition to freedom starting in 1865 was, despite Reconstruction, still a harsh condemnation to field work and hard manual labor, a continued consignment to second-class citizenship. Yet as African Americans helped power the economy and strived toward fuller freedom, their language, music, and cuisine seeped into the wider culture, as did influences from other groups, such as Haitians and Germans.

Into this mix came another wave of enterprising immigrants in the early and middle 1800s: Central and Eastern Europeans fleeing national instability, financial hardship, or poverty, and in some cases ethnic discrimination in their

Henry's mother, Mary Plonsky Bendel Falk

volatile homelands. Some had been fairly established in the old country but were seeking a shot at a better, safer life. Many were Jewish, including Henri's parents.

His father, William Louis Bendel, was born in Vienna, Austria, in 1837. He'd come to the United States after serving as an officer in the British navy. Mary Plonsky, Henri's mother, was born in Golub, Prussia, in 1839 and had been living in the Alsace-Lorraine region of eastern France before she immigrated with her parents and siblings to Louisiana. Mary and William met in New Orleans and married there in 1863, staying long enough to have their first two children—Samuel and Fanny. Mary's sister, Frimmit, and her husband, Lazarus Levy, apparently were already living in Vermilionville—they had likely been drawn by the French-language culture—making a go of it in mercantilism, the trade they knew from their homelands. The Bendels joined them, acquiring land in the center of town across the street from the Levy's property. Here they opened a general merchandise or "dry goods" store on the first floor of their two-story home. In time, hard work and vision would allow the business to expand considerably.

Henry (or perhaps Henri) Willis Bendel was born on January 22, 1868, three years after the end of the Civil War. Mary and William had three more children in quick succession—Isaac, Lena, and Rose—before tragedy struck. On a buying trip to New Orleans in 1874, William Bendel suffered appendicitis and died. Mary was pregnant with their seventh child, a daughter to be named Louise. Henry was six years old.

A few years prior to this, the Bendel, Plonsky, and Levy families sponsored a young man to emigrate to the United States from Russia. Benjamin Falk, just eighteen when he came over, took up work at the Bendels' store, proved his proficiency at selling and grew to be a part of the Bendel and Levy extended clan. When William died suddenly, with Mary seven months pregnant, Falk stepped in to run the business until she was able to resume her duties. Benjamin was "a great admirer of [Henry's] father and well-loved friend of all the children," according to family notes compiled by Henri's nephew,

Henry's stepfather, Benjamin Falk

Leon Bendel Schmulen, in the article *Henri Willis Bendel, 1868-1936, An Appreciation* by Frances Anderson. Indeed, he quickly took a fatherly interest in Mary's brood of seven, and eventually an amorous interest in Mary. They married in 1876 despite their fourteen-year age difference.

In later years Henry's brother Isaac—called Ike—would recall a humble home across the street from the courthouse. Nevertheless, as a newspaper retrospective article put it, Falk "tended his ready-made flock well, although their means were limited."

"Benjamin Falk was a rare personality," writes Anderson. "He took the seven young Bendel children to his heart as if they had always been his own, and together with his indefatigable wife guided their tender adolescence, sought to fill their impressionistic years with charm and learning, aimed to unfold special endowments." According to *Henri Bendel: From Louisiana Obscurity to Fame as Fashion Authority and Bon Vivant Icon*, a published 2013 lecture by historian Sally Robbins, "Benjamin was a loving and indulgent stepfather; his big heart and generous character probably helped to shape Henri's lifelong traits of generosity and family feeling."

Early on, young Henry showed a strong artistic streak. "As a child [he] liked to play . . . with things cut out of paper—paper dolls," according to Elisabeth Denbo Montgomery, a family friend. "He created [them] and dressed them up, and the children used to tease him because they thought he was so feminine. But from the time he was young, he created beautiful arrangements." It's unclear what exactly Mrs. Montgomery meant by "arrangements"—her recollections were recorded many years after Bendel had died, when she was elderly. Perhaps it was dioramas, popular in that age, or maybe other handcrafted artworks. His having been teased for playing with dolls, paper or otherwise, no doubt stung Henry. But not enough for him to suppress his impulses or arrest his creativity. Perhaps such childish cruelty, predicated on stereotypes and taboos about masculine and feminine behavior, thickened his skin and spurred him on in defiance.

Henry from a young age gravitated to arts and crafts, including, according to one family friend, paper figures.

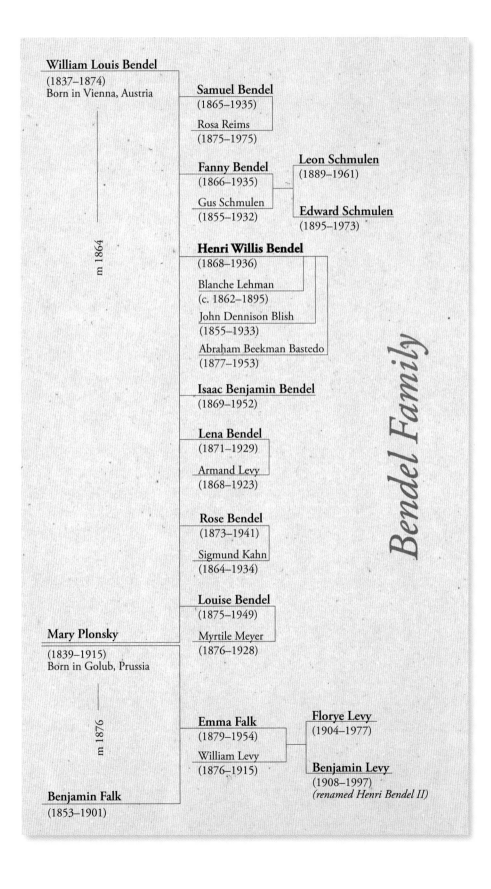

William Louis Bendel
(1837–1874)
Born in Vienna, Austria

m 1864

Mary Plonsky
(1839–1915)
Born in Golub, Prussia

m 1876

Benjamin Falk
(1853–1901)

Samuel Bendel
(1865–1935)
Rosa Reims
(1875–1975)

Fanny Bendel
(1866–1935)
Gus Schmulen
(1855–1932)

Leon Schmulen
(1889–1961)

Edward Schmulen
(1895–1973)

Henri Willis Bendel
(1868–1936)
Blanche Lehman
(c. 1862–1895)
John Dennison Blish
(1855–1933)
Abraham Beekman Bastedo
(1877–1953)

Isaac Benjamin Bendel
(1869–1952)

Lena Bendel
(1871–1929)
Armand Levy
(1868–1923)

Rose Bendel
(1873–1941)
Sigmund Kahn
(1864–1934)

Louise Bendel
(1875–1949)
Myrtile Meyer
(1876–1928)

Emma Falk
(1879–1954)
William Levy
(1876–1915)

Florye Levy
(1904–1977)

Benjamin Levy
(1908–1997)
(renamed Henri Bendel II)

Bendel Family

"Quiet, shy, sensitive, the little boy Henry nevertheless quickly revealed to his devoted parents that his talents were out of the ordinary," notes Anderson. "Eager for the boy's cultural growth, they placed him in the local private school of Madame Columbus Eastin when he was seven." Beyond such expected subjects as literature and history, Eastin also offered her pupils "a thorough grounding in the manners of the court of Louis Phillipe." If that sounds grandiose or incomprehensible, it may hint at the unlikely confluence of cultures—French, Spanish, Catholic, Jewish, old world, new—swirling together there at that time, and in fact Louis Phillipe I, a future king of France, had visited New Orleans and environs during his exile in America. In any case, it was, according to Robbins, "an ambitious cultural agenda for the cosmopolitan life that lay in [Henry's] future."

Anderson reports that Madame Eastin's "favorite pupil was also her most apt one, and at 12 young Henry was ready for college matriculation." In the fall of 1880, his mother and stepfather enrolled him in St. Charles College, a Jesuit boys' school in Grand Coteau, Louisiana, about fifteen miles north of Vermilionville. His older brother, Sam, was already a student there, and later his younger brother, Isaac, would join him. "Henry really spread his wings at college," writes Anderson. "Here, under the ancient oaks of Grand Coteau, the sensitive youth responded well to planned tutelage." He had been bilingual since infancy. Now he was gaining exposure to German, Latin, and Greek. And his enthusiasm for art and drama were encouraged by the Jesuits. He won academic prizes, sang in the choir, acted in plays, and, owing to his flair for all things artful, he was invited by the priests to decorate the altar at Christmas, Easter, and other feast days.

As a teen Henry attended St. Charles College, a Jesuit school in Grand Coteau, Louisiana, about fifteen miles from Vermilionville, which had opened in 1838.

He also tended to the Jesuits' ecclesiastical vestments. According to Morris Crawford, the *Women's Wear* editor to whom Bendel, later in his life, shared stories of his upbringing, young Henry "saw for the first time those fine fabrics . . . which were to be a lifelong interest." At home Henry would sew dresses for his sisters, whom Robbins says "looked to him as a style authority." A great-niece recalled family lore about how he once disapproved of a hat that his sister Lena was about to wear to a party; apparently, he all but ripped it off her head, soaked the crown in water to make it malleable, and refashioned it into something he considered suitable. According to Anderson, Henry's siblings "soon accepted the fact that in matters artistic, [their brother's] judgment was not to be disputed."

When he was home on weekends and longer school breaks, Henry helped out with his mother and stepfather's growing business fiefdom. Mary was "quite a businesswoman," according to her great-niece, Flora Levy (not to be confused with Henri's niece Florye) and in relatively short order she and Benjamin grew rather prosperous, having widened their assorted enterprises to include not only the dry goods store, but also a clothing business, a furniture store, a funeral parlor, and, above their furniture shop, Falk's Opera House. Though rustic and not very large, the hall became the premiere venue for local and touring entertainment, apparently everything from Saturday night dances to recitals, vaudeville acts, and theatrical productions. The Falks also raised

Falk's furniture store (downstairs) and opera house (upstairs) on Washington Street

> "His artistic ability was encouraged by the Jesuits who called upon him to decorate the altars for Christmas and Easter."
>
> —*Adrienne Mouton*

and sold horses and mules, which were in high demand for farming and transportation. In time their home and various businesses came to occupy much of both sides of a prominent city block on Washington Street. (Their family grew as well: in 1879 Henry and his siblings acquired a new half sister with the birth of Emma Falk, whose life would one day be more entwined with Henry's than that of any of his Bendel brothers and sisters.) So, while teenaged Henry—in addition to learning languages and history and science—was nurturing his creative impulses at school, at home he was getting an advanced degree in the art of selling. And it was the merging of these two often at-odds aptitudes that would in time define his career: Henri Bendel, designer *and* merchant. An artist/aesthete who came to excel equally as a businessman.

Disciplined and focused as he was, young Henry was also happily co-cooned in his tight-knit clan with siblings who "were full of fun," as Sam Bendel's daughter Elyse Goodman would years later report to her grandson John Goodman. "She had heard from her mother," says John, "that they used to dress up and attempt to fool each other by masquerading as someone else." Such hijinks and play balanced the parents' expectation that the children apply themselves to serious study and daily chores. The Falks were also deeply committed to their Hebrew faith and to their community. The Plonsky and Bendel families "were among the early members and benefactors of Lafayette's Congregation Rodeph Sholom," the first formalized synagogue in town (prior to that, Jewish worship had been performed in private homes), according to Alvin Bethard, in his article "Henry Bendel 'Connoisseur of Style'" in the *Attakapas Gazette* (1991). Over the

In 1882 Henry's stepfather, Benjamin Falk, aided in building a new temple for the Rodeph Sholom congregation of Lafayette.

To Builders.

SEALED proposals will be received for the building of The Jewish Synagogue, in Vermilionville, parish of Lafayette, during the next twenty days. Plans and specifications to be seen at the store of L. Liberman, in Vermilionville. Communications to be addressed to L. Liberman, President Rudoph Sholom Congregation.

The committee reserve the right to reject any and all bids.   E. PHILLIPS,
    B. FALK,
    L. LEVY,
Jan. 14, 1882.   Committee.

coming decades the Bendel-Falk family would be among the most distinguished in what grew to be a robust Hebrew community in town. In later years Benjamin Falk would be remembered as a great civic leader, "an assistant fire chief and city alderman [who] helped establish the Lafayette Improvement Association (forerunner of the Chamber of Commerce), the first high school, and first synagogue," according to American National Biography Online. "His parents' prominence contributed to Henri's drive, business acumen and dedication to his hometown even after he moved away."

By age sixteen, Henry (with a *y*, as he spelled it then) had graduated from St. Charles College with a two-year degree. He easily could have taken on a role in the family's businesses then, but, writes Anderson, "his mother recognized her precocious son's restlessness, and urged the zealous boy to go forth on his own." As was her custom with each of her children as they left the nest, either to marry or seek work outside Vermilionville, Mary Plonsky gave Henry $1,500 to help set him on his way—about $43,000 in today's money. Armed with generous funding and natural gumption, he struck out for Raceland, Louisiana, about 140 miles east-southeast of Vermilionville, where, likely through family connections, he got on as clerk at a plantation store. By at least one account, the plantation store's name was Hiller but may actually have been the large plantation store of Simon Abraham, which served the vast Godchaux sugar plantation. The Godchaux family—Alsatian Jews who

New Orleans department store D. H. Holmes, circa 1882-1887

had started out as dry goods merchants in New Orleans before expanding into sugarcane cultivation and eventually clothing merchandising too—may well have been acquainted with the Plonsky, Bendel, and Falk families of Lafayette. If it was in fact the Abraham outfit, this would have given Henri his first experience working with a large quantity of diverse merchandise and a heavy flow of customers.

After no more than a couple of years in Raceland, he headed to New Orleans, then one of the largest and most cosmopolitan cities in America. Little is known of his year or so there, but he likely clerked at a store of some sort, possibly Godchaux's Crescent City outfit (which would later relocate and transform into a large department store and local institution). He certainly would've visited the established department stores along Canal Street, such as Maison Blanche and D. H. Holmes—a crucial early exposure to the sort of large-scale, deluxe

Interior view of the D. H. Holmes department store on the floor where fabric was sold, circa 1882–1887. Henry–photographed by noted portraitist Theodore Lilienthal (BELOW)–likely visited the store.

retailing that he would one day elevate to new heights. He must have soaked up their grandeur and studied what made each business unique—their display techniques, packaging, window dressing, the way salespeople comported themselves— every detail, as he took mental notes.

One extant artifact shines a little light on Bendel's New Orleans stint. While there he paid to have the renowned photographer Theodore Lilienthal make his portrait. The sepia image captures a mustachioed Henry in waistcoat, vest, and a large-knot, floral-patterned tie, looking about how he must have perceived himself—youthfully fashionable yet proper, of solid social standing, stalwart, ready. With bright eyes trained in the distance on something he alone could see.

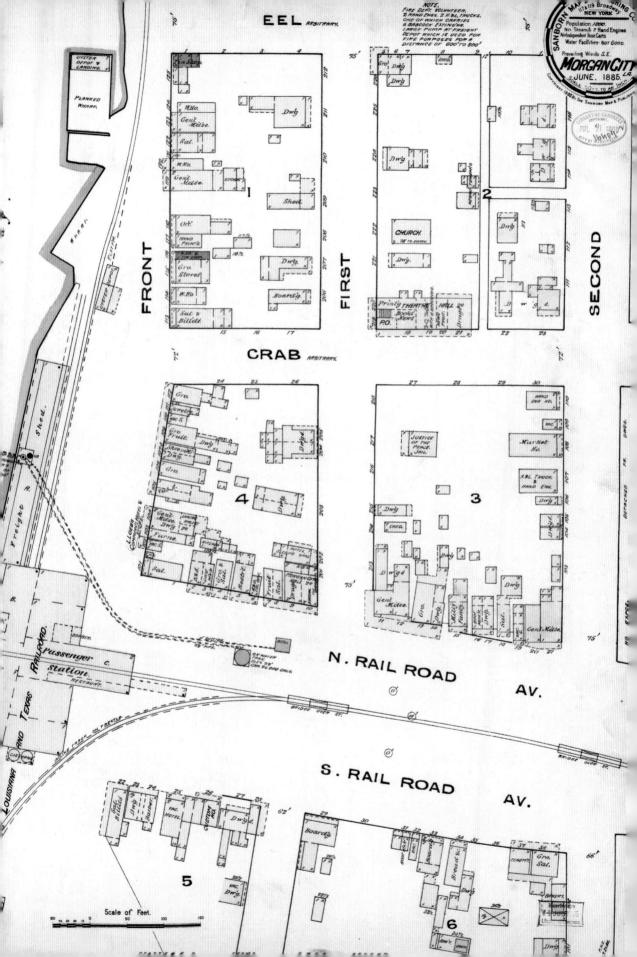

EEL ARBITRARY.

SANBORN MAP & PUBLISHING CO.
117 & 119 Broadway
NEW YORK

NOTE.
FIRE DEPT. VOLUNTEER.
2 HAND ENGS. 2 H.&L. TRUCKS.
ONE OF UNION CARRIES
6 BABCOCK EXTINGRS.
LARGE PUMP AT RESIDENT
DEPOT WHICH IS USED FOR
FIRE PURPOSES FOR A
DISTANCE OF 600' TO 800'

Population 1800.
No. Steamers & Hand Engines
No Independent Hose Carts
Water Facilities: Not Good.
Prevailing Winds S.E.

MorganCity
JUNE. 1885. LA.

CRAB ARBITRARY.

FRONT

FIRST

SECOND

CHURCH

Dwg

Dwg

Dwg

THEATRE
HALL 2°
P.O.

OYSTER
DEPOT &
LANDING.

PLANKED
WHARF.

WHARF.

JUSTICE
OF THE
PEACE.
JAIL

MARKET
Ho.

H.&L. TRUCK
& HAND ENG.

Gent.
Mdse.

Dwgs

N. RAIL ROAD AV.

Passenger
Station.

Railroad.

Louisiana and Texas

S. RAIL ROAD AV.

CUSTOM HO.

Boardg

5

6

Scale of Feet.

CHAPTER 3

FIRST STEPS

$\mathcal{A}$s instructive and aesthetically stimulating as New Orleans must have been—Henry's finishing school, as it were—and for all its commercial vitality, the Crescent City would have been hard to crack professionally for a man so green, not to mention for one from the hinterlands of South Louisiana, at least in the eyes of gentrified, socially guarded New Orleanians. Not an easy launchpad for someone of Henry's ambition, looking to move up quickly. New Orleans gave him a generous taste of sophisticated urban living, but in order to really feast on such a life he would first have to pay his dues in a humbler setting.

Still fortified with the money his mother had given him, Bendel considered his options and cast his eye not so far from his first job, in Lafourche Parish. Some forty miles west of Raceland, about eighty miles west-north-west of New Orleans, Morgan City, Louisiana, was unprepossessing but it had several things going for it that made it rich with opportunity. Foremost, its adjacency to water. With the immense and resource-laden Atchafalaya Basin above it, the Atchafalaya River running through it, and the Gulf of Mexico nearly lapping at its feet, the town, straddling St. Mary and St. Martin Parishes with a population of just 1,800, had for years been a trade nexus for river and Gulf commerce, with steamships coming in from the Gulf and all manner of boats and barges sailing up and down the Atchafalaya River, ferrying a wide array of products.

Originally named Brashear City, the hamlet got a critical boost in 1857 when Charles Morgan, an industrialist who had dredged Berwick's Bay, purchased and upgraded the Opelousas and Great Western Railroad, effectively connecting Texas to southern Louisiana (including New Orleans and Vermilionville) and points further east by railway. At the time, that was considered a near-impossible feat. "Built in defiance of the adverse opinions of eminent engineers, [the railroad] has had to overcome almost insurmountable obstacles," reported the New Orleans *Times-Democrat* in 1887, "and for many years after it seemed as if the swamps, floating prairies and floods would

OPPOSITE: A map of downtown Morgan City, Louisiana

23

triumph after all." Yet after years of such floods and hurricanes, requiring numerous fixes and fortifications, by the time twenty-year-old Henry arrived in 1887, the railroad had prevailed, trade had swelled, and the town and its environs, according to the paper, "are well worthy of the attending of capitalists and new settlers."

Morgan City wasn't New Orleans, but it wasn't a backwater village either. It boasted several attractive residential blocks with some stately homes, as well as rooming houses, numerous churches, and a synagogue, Congregation Shaarey Zedek. The town also had a grocer, a bottler, a printer, a tinsmith, and a boots and shoes store. Masons, Knights of Pythias (a fraternal service organization), American Legion of Honor, and Knights of Labor all had chapters, and there were two weekly newspapers, the *St. Mary Review* and the *Free Press*.

Beyond being a trade and transport hub, Morgan City flourished too on account of its native commodities, including sugarcane, oysters (hundreds of thousands were shipped each year to Texas alone), catfish, and lumber. And then there were exports almost unique to the dense, sprawling Atchafalaya Basin estuary—valuable animal hides and skins, such as alligator and beaver, and rare bird feathers. Young men who made a living harvesting oysters in colder months often took to the swamps in the spring and summer in pursuit of these coveted creatures. As it turned out, such feathers—those from herons, terns, and, most prized of all, the snowy-white plumage of egrets—would play a key role in Henry's destiny.

The corner of Front and Railroad Streets
in Morgan City in the late 1890s

Morgan City also beckoned to Henry for a practical reason: he had extended family there and likely a waiting job. His cousin Mose Levy ran the Red Star dry goods store, similar to the plantation store in Raceland and akin to the business in Lafayette that Bendel's mother and stepfather ran. Selling dry goods—which might include everything from household items and non-perishable groceries to clothing—was in Henry's blood and a proven skill. The store sat at the corner of Railroad and Second Streets, a central spot steps away from the wharf, surrounded by other businesses and drinking establishments.

Bendel worked at the Red Star alongside a young man named Albert Coguenhem, three years his senior. Albert's father had immigrated from France and his mother from Germany. (The family name seems to have morphed over the years and various recorded spellings include Gugenheim, Cougenheim, and Cougenhem.) Albert's older brother, Manuel, became well established in Morgan City as partner of the firm of Coguenhem and Lehman, which traded in "general merchandise," as well as oysters, furs, skins, and feathers. Theodore (Theo) Lehman ran the general store, and his brother, Jacques Lehman, was dubbed the Oyster King. The brothers had come to Morgan City from Alsace-Lorraine in 1870 with their parents and another brother, Charles. (The family name was originally spelled with two n's, and some contemporaneous records imply that at various times members indeed spelled it "Lehmann.")

A news and notes column in the July 3, 1886, *Donaldsonville Chief* reported that "nearly $5000 worth of feathers, plumes, bird skins, and alligator hides have been shipped North by Messrs. Coguenhem & Lehman of Morgan City."

At the Red Star, Albert Coguenhem and Henry struck up a friendship that extended beyond work. They socialized and traveled together and in 1890 Albert served as an usher at the wedding of Henry's sister Lena to her cousin Armand Levy—Mose's brother—in Lafayette (as Vermilionville had been renamed in 1884). Later, in 1893, he attended both the wedding of Henry's cousin Hannah Levy in June, and then in November the wedding of Henry's sister Rose to Sig Kahn.

During these years, as Henry honed his talent for merchandising and fortified his standing as a prosperous, engaged citizen of Morgan City, he remained close to his family. In a prefiguring of how he would one day offer positions in his New York fashion store to extended family members, Henry secured a job at the Red Star for a sixteen-year-old cousin, Heyman Plonsky. And he made somewhat frequent trips home to Lafayette and to other corners of South Louisiana as his siblings married and radiated out.

Bustles, bows, pleats, and pain—the state of women's fashion in 1875

Some of Henry's brothers, sisters, and cousins got rave reviews for a play they performed at Falk's Opera House in 1890.

In the summer of 1889, for example, Henry rode by train to Lafayette for his cousin Armand Levy's twenty-first birthday party at the young man's parents' home. The *Lafayette Advertiser* reported that the "collation spread for their enjoyment was choice and sumptuous and met with full appreciation." Henry, who in time would come to be an effusive speaker and writer, made a toast, and "after the repast the party adjourned to Falk's Hall where games and dancing were indulged in until a late hour."

At some point back in Morgan City, Henry and Albert formulated a plan to buy out Mose Levy, with Henry taking the lead role in acquiring the store. By 1893 a large newspaper ad for the Red Star had a sign-off at the bottom:

> *Henry Bendel & Co., Props*
> *Morgan City, La.*

The ad bragged, "We have something for everybody! From the baby in the cradle to the old folks in their dotage."

And it included an intriguing note about hats: "For some time we have made no mention of our millinery department, as we have taken for granted that you know we keep the largest and best selected stock in town. We cordially ask you to come and look at the pretties we have for your selection."

Henry had been interested in women's hats and hat-making since at least his teen years, as his sisters could attest. Exactly when and how he declared himself a milliner is unknown, but if the Red Star hadn't been a purveyor of fashion of any note previously, under Henry's guidance it likely became that. And the ready access to rare feathers would've made his ability to execute original designs, or perhaps to gussy up stock chapeau, that much easier, and open to boundless creativity. It had to be here, then, in little Morgan City, that "Henri Bendel, Milliner" was born.

Henry also would've been keenly aware—from his Coguenhem and Lehman neighbors in business—of who was buying those feathers up north and what they were doing with them. In 1888, an ad for Coguenhem and Lehman taken out in the *Meridional,* a newspaper of tiny Abbeville, Louisiana, a town south of Lafayette with water access to the Gulf, offered "good cash prices" to any trappers and hunters who could provide white heron and egret "skins" and "other plumages." They suggested that anyone who might "have anything" along these lines write to them. Significantly, the firm listed two addresses: Morgan City and 131 Bowery, New York.

The Price of Feathers

Marie Antoinette made feathers high fashion with the *aigrette*, or headpiece spray—aigrette being a variation on the word egret. But the vogue for plumaged hats really took off in the mid-1800s. "A well-dressed woman nowadays is as fluffy as a downy bird fresh from the nest," reported one style watcher. Egret, herons, and ostrich were most prized, but no species was off-limits, including bluebirds, orioles, grebes, tanagers, grosbeaks, warblers, and cuckoos. Not only the feathers: As *Harper's Bazar* explained in 1879, "Occasionally the whole bird is placed in a natural [pose] on the front or side of the hat."

In 1886, ornithologist Frank Chapman of the American Museum of Natural History conducted "field" research on the streets of Manhattan. In two strolls he notated more than forty native species atop some five hundred women's heads, including cardinals, egrets, and quail.

An egret-feathered hat circa 1878

The plume trade was a multi-million-dollar global market; feathers from herons sold for as much as $32 per ounce (more than $1,000 today)—worth nearly twice their weight in gold. In 1892 one London dealer procured 6,000 bird of paradise feathers, 40,000 hummingbird feathers, and some 360,000 feathers of various other species, all from the East Indies. A single well-known "feather foundry" in Hoboken, New Jersey, was reputed to have handled millions of bird skins over a thirty-five-year span; the proprietor estimated that 10 to 15 percent of his stock came from the United States, mainly Florida, Texas, and Louisiana.

But by the mid-1890s, the rage for feathers was turning to outrage in influential circles, such as that of Boston naturalist Harriet Hemenway and her cousin Minna Hall, who persuaded some 900 society women to forgo wearing feathers. The two women founded the first Audubon Society, which became a state-by-state movement. Still, it was a long battle. "No unprotected bird is safe," wrote W. T. Hornaday, chief taxidermist at the Smithsonian in his 1913 book *Our Vanishing Wildlife*. Indeed, many species were decimated, and a few became extinct. Passionate advocacy led to the Weeks-McClean Law (the Migratory Bird Act) in 1913, which made market hunting and interstate transport of birds illegal. Laws regarding international feather trade followed, so by the end of the nineteen-teens, with little supply and receding demand, milliners—including those who worked for Bendel—returned to less lethal embellishments such as ribbon and lace.

A chapeau of ostrich and bird of paradise feathers from Henri Bendel in 1907

An ad in the
*Morgan City Daily
Review* in 1889

On the receiving end of the feathers shipments: New York City, the fashion capital of America. Expressly intended for milliners.

From the same 1887 *Times-Democrat* account of Morgan City's industries: "In birds, as in other things wherein the fair sex are concerned, fashion regulates everything, and continually changes. The bayous, lakes and islands round Morgan City furnish many beautiful varieties. Most valuable is the egrette, a small crane, whose delicate white plumes are greatly in demand."

The article explained that while the white crane was "sale-able," blue cranes were "not at present of any use." It reported a market for least terns, a small sea bird, with fifteen thousand having been shipped north the previous season, whereas blue hawks, worth $3.50 a bird the year before, were no longer desired. The paper estimated that the bird trade of Morgan City amounted to $12,000 a season—about a third of a million dollars today.

Years later, birds would serve as metaphors as Bendel opined about how a lady ought to dress in sync with her natural attributes. "The world of women is composed of peacocks, butterflies and Jenny wrens," he told a fashion journalist, "and they should be costumed as differently as they are in the animal world."

For Henry, learning which feathers were prized in New York gave him a tactile sense of contemporary American millinery-making and styles. And for his own creations, he commanded the best prices. So, he was already somewhat savvy and skilled with hats when the stars aligned to introduce him to a woman who would eventually help him follow the feather trail north. She was five or six years older than Henry and her name was Blanche Lehman.

In the late 1880s another colleague of Bendel's at the Red Star was one Charles Lehman, originally of New Orleans. He may or may not have been a relative of the Morgan City Lehmann/Lehmans. His immediate family had lived in New Orleans where his father, Aaron, had an import house which, like Coguenhem and Lehman, trafficked in decorative feathers.

Around the end of the Civil War the family had moved to New York, "probably to bolster their presence in their most important market, and perhaps to escape a war torn South," says Richard Eisner, a descendant. (In fact, many prosperous Jewish merchants left the South as the war began.) Charley, as he was known, had four younger half siblings by Aaron's second wife, Annette: Blanche, Sarah, Mitchell, and Albert. When the family moved from New Orleans to New York, Charles, who was grown, had stayed behind in Louisiana. He was likely in his midthirties when he moved to Morgan City and got on at the Red Star.

In March of 1889 a social squib in the Morgan City section of the New Orleans *Times-Democrat* reported that "Mrs. and Miss Lehman, of New York City, are visiting their son and brother, Mr. Charley Lehman, and are the guests of Mrs. M. Coguenhem." In other words, Annette Lehman and her daughter Blanche had gone down south for a visit. That they stayed at the home of Manuel Coguenhem points to possible extended family ties between the New York Lehmans, the Morgan City Lehmans, and the Coguenhems (Annette was a Gugenhiem, with a G, but there's no evidence of a direct family connection).

The only known image of Henry's future wife, Blanche Lehman, taken when she was a little girl

Blanche's parents, Aaron and Annette Lehman, and their children, Sarah, Blanche, Albert, and Mitchell

Whatever familial and friendship bonds were in play, this visit by Blanche and her mother could well have been when Henry met his future wife. Charles's half sister Blanche was several years older than Henry, in her midtwenties (no birth certificate survives but she was likely born in 1862 or 1863). She possessed grace and social standing but was perhaps looking to make a fresh start. Blanche had been married previously and her husband, George Silva of New York—himself engaged in the millinery trade selling ostrich and other fancy feathers—was wildly abusive. So much so that she had sued him for divorce on the grounds of "cruelty and abandonment." She claimed that, after the death of her father in 1886, when Silva learned that Aaron had left all his money to Blanche's mother and none to Blanche, his attitude toward his wife took an abrupt turn. As the *New York Times* reported on April 26, 1887, under the headline "A Wife's Plea For Divorce":

> Last May, [Blanche] says, [Silva] went to Europe, and came back in August, and after his return he told her that he was paying attention to another woman; that if she continued to live with him he would make her life miserable, as he intended to live a gay life and come home when he pleased. Once, she asserts, after he had tantalized her shamefully, she asked him how long such treatment would continue, and his reply was, "The end will come when I finish with that," pointing toward a loaded revolver. Then she went to Mr. Silva's father for sympathy. She says that he said to her: "When my son married you he expected to receive a thirty-thousand-dollar home, fully furnished, as a wedding present, but he has got nothing."

To have survived such torment, and then endure seeing her name in the papers about it with all that implied for a young woman in the late nineteenth century, Blanche may have felt on shaky ground. But she met Henry and clearly responded favorably to his gentility and decency. Soon enough, far from the prying eyes of New York society, a courtship ensued, perhaps nurtured in letter-writing over the next few years.

Apparently during this time Bendel had an impulse to expand his enterprises beyond Morgan City. A business item in the *Lafayette Advertiser* of February 25, 1893, reported that "Mr. Henry Bendel left this week for Orange, Texas, where he will assume the management of a large general store." It's not clear from the scant evidence whether that came to pass. The same squib further identified Henry as having been previously "connected with" the Berwick Bay Lumber Co., near Morgan City. These are intriguing reports, but however much he may have been starting to diversify his business, there is nothing to suggest that he either quit or folded the Red Star store.

Regardless, his prospects in Morgan City changed in an unforeseeable instant. Several short histories of Bendel's life reference a catastrophic fire, date unknown, which destroyed his and Albert's store. Fires were common and often devastating—for example in September 1890, on a major Jewish holiday, a blaze consumed a sizable area of downtown Morgan City, burning several residences and businesses, including the offices and stock rooms of Coguenhem and Lehman, Theo Lehman's own residence, and the drugstore of Lucien Lehman. There's no documentation that Henry's store was harmed then, and if it had been, his prominent name would've surely made the papers along with the others who lost property and stock. Moreover, Bendel and Co. was still up and running a couple of years after that famous conflagration. But, apparently, a subsequent fire destroyed Henry and Albert's store, propelling Bendel to Berwick Bay Lumber, just across the river, and perhaps to seek opportunities in Texas.

In any case, throughout this tumultuous professional period, Henry had found a personal anchor, and by the summer of 1894 he and Blanche were pledged to one another.

From the *Lafayette Gazette,* September 15, 1894: "The Gazette has received an invitation to attend the marriage of Miss Blanche Lehman to Henry Bendel, Tuesday evening, September 25, 1894, at 117 East 64th St., New York. Mr. Bendel has lived here, where he is well and favorably known; he is now a leading merchant at Morgan City."

> The Gazette has received an invitation to attend the marriage of Miss Blanche Lehman to Henry Bendel, Tuesday evening, September 25, 1894, at 117 East 64th street, New York. Mr. Bendel has lived here, where he is well and favorably known; he is now a leading merchant at Morgan City.

A *Lafayette Gazette* announcement of Henry and Blanche's impending wedding

But not for long. Through the confluence of the bad luck of the fire that destroyed his business—according to one report the Red Star store was uninsured—and the happy luck of his betrothal to Blanche, suddenly a new world was glinting on the northern horizon.

CHAPTER 4

NEW YORK, NEW YORK

*I*N LATE AUGUST OF 1894, Henry's brother Ike and their mother, Mary Falk, left Louisiana by train for the long trip north for Henry's wedding. A social squib in the New Orleans *Times-Democrat* about their impending departure refers to Henry's bride-to-be Blanche Lehman as "an accomplished young lady of New York City." It noted that Ike, who at this point was running his own dry goods store in Lake Charles, Louisiana, and Mary would be stopping en route in Washington, DC—at that time called Washington City—to "take in the Knights of Pythias grand conclave," as Ike was a Knight.

Calling Blanche "young" may have been a slight stretch by the standards of the era, as she was likely at least twenty-nine or thirty. Henry was twenty-five. Perhaps owing to that, and to the fact that she was a divorcée, the evening nuptials were small and held in the home of her mother, Annette Lehman. Their brownstone-clad, neo-Grecian townhouse on East Sixty-Fourth Street in Manhattan was on a fashionable block and made for an elegant, if low-key, wedding venue. It was also to be the couple's new home. But before settling in, Blanche and Henry took to the rails for a roving honeymoon, a "Southern bridal tour" according to the *Daily Advertiser,* including a week in Lafayette, where Blanche and Henry could enjoy the congratulations of friends and family, some of whom Blanche was probably meeting for the first time. Henry was still Henry with a *y* at this time—it was spelled that way in three places on his marriage certificate, including in his own hand.

When he and Blanche returned to New York, he threw himself into work, taking full advantage not only of his old connections to the feathers and millinery findings market, but more

OPPOSITE: Carts, buggies, trolleys, and pedestrians jostle for space in lower Manhattan circa 1895.

BELOW: Back in Lafayette, a social squib was written in French about Henry and Blanche paying a visit.

LAFAYETTE OCT. 13. 1894.

NOUVELLES LOCALES.

Mr et Mmr. Henry Bendel de New York sont venus rendre visite à leur purents à Lafayette.

so exploiting his new status as member of Blanche's family, who had their own feathers import firm. In 1889 Blanche's brothers Mitchell and Albert had taken over Lehman Brothers, which their father had started, expanding operations to a six-story industrial building at 10 Bond Street in lower Manhattan, in an area known today as NoHo (north of Houston Street). (This business and these Lehmans should not be confused—though they have been, in several accounts of Bendel's life—with the famous Lehman banking brothers who hailed from Alabama and who founded what became Lehman Brothers investment firm.) According to Richard Eisner, his great-grandfather Mitchell handled business in America "while his brother Albert spent a great deal of time traveling to Paris and other European fashion centers looking for the latest fashion ideas to add to their line of feathers." The third brother, Charles—Charley, whom Henry had worked with in Morgan City—was coordinating the supply end of the business in New Orleans. Henry likely jumped into the mix as a buying or selling agent, or both. Where previously he had been a retail merchant with his dry goods store, now he was learning the ins and outs of selling wholesale, "to the trade," and at a greater volume than he had previously negotiated. This would've been a considerable step up and a move toward fulfilling his own ambitions.

Within the first few months of her marriage to Bendel, Blanche became pregnant. Sadly, the couple's joy wouldn't last. In general, specifics about their romance and brief married life have been shrouded by the passing of time, and details of her death at the age of thirty are scant. Yet it's easy to guess that whatever awful thing transpired, it came with shocking suddenness.

More than a few short histories of Henry's life, some taken from family accounts, some from passed-down lore, report that Blanche Lehman Bendel died in childbirth. This may be the case. But reading the pittance of evidence left behind, it's possible that that is an oversimplification. Her doctor-signed death certificate records that she died on July 12, 1895, of "acute edema of lungs (36 hours) and chronic endocarditis (4 years)"—so it seems that of the two ailments that killed her, the endocarditis, an inflammation of the heart, had plagued her for at least four years. And there's no mention of a baby on the death certificate. It's conceivable that Blanche lost the infant shortly before her own death, which may have contributed to her demise. The child's date of death was not recorded. In any case, Blanche was buried in the Lehman family plot in the Hebrew section of Salem Fields cemetery in Brooklyn; her marker was a small stone figure of a winged angel set atop an artfully stacked group of natural stones, with decorative flourishes and the face cut flat for the carved words, "To the memory of our dear Blanche née Lehman, beloved wife of Henry Bendel, died July 12, 1895, in her 30th year." Cemetery records list an unmarked grave of an infant in the family plot.

Blanche Bendel's grave monument today in the Lehman family plot in the Jewish section of Salem Fields cemetery, Brooklyn. The angel long ago fell off the base.

As he would throughout his life, Bendel sought solace and support from his family. In August his sister Louise, brother Sam, and brother-in-law Armand Levy (Henry's sister Lena's husband) all traveled up to New York to offer consolation. Louise stayed on for two months. By several accounts, in the following months Henry attempted to subdue his anguish with activity, working hard and trying not to dwell on Blanche and the family-to-be that was

snatched from his grasp before it had fully materialized. "Recovering from the shock of bereavement, he plunged into the advancement of his business with renewed vigor," according to Frances Anderson. "Like so many others, he sought forgetfulness through creative effort."

The year 1896 was a watershed. Though still new to the city and now a widower, Henry had no intention of going back to Louisiana. New York was the place for someone like him, and he had a foothold, thanks in part to his late wife's family. But seeking some independence, he partnered with an importer named Julius Saur to sell millinery findings and paraphernalia, including artificial flowers and feathers, to the trade, as well as offering finished hats, which he and hired artisans made by hand working out of their own space at 10 Bond Street.

Bendel & Saur, as the men called their enterprise, soon created their own showroom to highlight their wares, at 67 East Ninth Street. This was an ideal address, just one door east of the bustling avenue Broadway and close to many elegant residences, including those surrounding nearby Washington Square Park. Back then, much of commercial New York was centered in lower Manhattan, including the fashion industry, and Broadway above Fourteenth Street in the 1910s and '20s was dubbed the Ladies' Mile for the proliferation of dress shops and large department stores for women that peppered the thoroughfare. Wanamaker's, a dress and accessories store started by John Wanamaker in Philadelphia, had just opened a New York branch, an imposing five-story emporium around the corner from Bendel & Saur, at Fourth Avenue and Ninth Street. The original Macy's was a few blocks north, on Fourteenth Street at Sixth Avenue.

On November 26, 1896, a large ad in the *Nashville Banner* newspaper in Tennessee offered local merchants hats from a wholesaler named Mr. L. Jonas who had procured them from Bendel & Saur; the hats had originally been intended for the Great New York Horse Show but, not having arrived in time, were sold by B & S at one-fourth their original price. The ad reprinted Bendel & Saur's letter explaining the offer.

> *Dear Sir—We have decided to accept your very low offer of 25 cents on the dollar—cash—for all of our Imported Pattern Hats and Bonnets, and shall express them to your firm today. We are satisfied that these are perhaps the handsomest lot of Hats that ever left New York, and as the price is less than one-half the cost of production, you should have no trouble in disposing of them in one day.*
>
>

Yours truly,
BENDEL & SAUR

The letterhead reads

Bendel & Saur
Importers and Manufacturers of
Millinery, Novelties, Pattern Hats, Flowers and Feathers
67 E. 9th Street, one door west of Broadway
New York, Nov. 16, 1896

Most intriguing, in small type to the left of their name and address on the letterhead is a second address, 54 Rue des Petites Écuries, Paris. Henry and Julius apparently kept an office in the tenth *arrondissement* of the fashion capital of the world, but its scope and who might have run it remains a mystery.

Still, in the summer of 1896 Bendel sailed to Europe to assess millinery trends and procure hats. Perhaps also to broker feather sales. Despite his having that Paris address on his stationery, this was possibly his first visit to the City of Light and its devotion to aesthetic creativity—from fashion and cuisine to painting and architecture, everything—made an indelible impression. "Art in everyday things, that is the French," he later declared, "and art in their clothes is second nature."

Stateside, Bendel continued to run his business with Saur, but he kept his name alone on his Bond Street warehouse, and by 1897 the shop on Ninth Street had a new name out front, and Mr. Bendel had a new spelling. The sign said simply: Henri Bendel. Henri with an *i*. This seems to have been about the time that he added a retail component to his business, using window display to attract fashion-seeking women. Word spread among their set of the chic little hat shop in Greenwich Village. "Never before or since, except at one very fashionable wedding, has such a handsome assemblage of carriages and livery been seen in that part of the city," someone recalled years later.

An 1896 ad in the *Nashville Banner* in which Bendel & Saur offered overstocked hats to retailers at a big discount. The ad likely ran in other papers.

As if to prove he could wear almost as many hats as his customers, Henri about this time was hired as a junior buyer by the large, prominent women's department store B. Altman. Benjamin Altman had moved the store that his family had founded in the middle of the nineteenth century to its second location, up Sixth Avenue between Eighteenth and Nineteenth Streets, in the heart of the Ladies' Mile district. By one unsubstantiated account, Bendel's dealings with Altman's may have begun even earlier, perhaps shortly after he arrived in New York, though it's hard to imagine he could have juggled that job while also working with Blanche's family in feathers *and* while starting his own wholesale business. It's a bit mysterious, too, how he straddled both Altman's and the Henri Bendel showroom on Ninth Street, but apparently he did. Perhaps his role at Altman's was more along the lines of a consultant, someone hired for specific and limited assignments.

While working for Altman's Bendel soon made the acquaintance of their main foreign purchasing agent, John Dennison Blish. Blish was born and raised in Watertown, New York, and had moved to Brooklyn when he was nineteen, no doubt seeking work. "Handsome and debonair, Blish was 13 years older than Henri," according to Sally Robbins. And he appears to have awakened something in Bendel that had likely lain dormant since his boyhood—an attraction to men.

John Dennison Blish

In Paris "he was accorded the acceptance of a kindred soul, and world-famous designers outdid themselves to cater to his discriminating taste."
—*Frances Anderson*

Writes Robbins: "They quickly became close friends and would [go on to] have what Bendel himself [later] described as 'a lifelong intimate relationship.'" Did this thrill Henri? Did it scare him? Probably both. But the watchword was discretion. As Scott Bane points out in his book *A Union Like Ours*, about the relationship between painter Russell Cheney and literary scholar F. O. Matthiessen, "Gay socializing . . . could be dangerous [in that era] owing to fear of arrest by police or harassment from antigay vigilantes." Anything intimate between Henri and Mr. Blish would have been their deep secret.

At Altman's Blish may have been the one to suggest Henri follow in his footsteps as a foreign purchaser. Whatever arrangement he had, company brass apparently found the young man impressive. Though having only lived in New York for a few years, he had honed his millinery and ladies' dress expertise, and polished his comportment enough to be given a prized assignment: traveling to Paris to procure dresses and hats for the store. Without a doubt, his charm, wide-ranging knowledge, and ability to converse fluidly in French impressed the couturiers and eased his entrée. Most crucially, he understood his constituency back in the States. In time, according to Morris Crawford, Henri became "recognized in Paris as a keen judge of what American fashionables would accept."

Even with Bendel branching out, his partnership with Julius Saur was legally cemented in July of 1898, and their business continued to grow. The following year the *Fourteenth Annual Report of the Factory Inspector of the State of New York* listed the firm as having fourteen men employed in millinery, and thirty-two women and six men working in artificial flowers. In the latter half of 1899 Bendel & Saur ran help wanted ads in New York's *The World* newspaper for "experienced pasters," a "trimmer on ladies' hats," and "trimmed milliners." Another ad solicited artificial flower makers, pasters, and "violet makers," and noted that "learners [are] taken and paid while learning; good pay; long season."

Bendel & Saur placed a help wanted ad for crafters of artificial flowers.

ARTIFICIAL FLOWERS—Experienced hands on pasted roses, slipped up roses, also violet makers and learners wanted. Learners paid while learning. Steady work, long season. Apply all week at Bendel & Saur, 67 9th st., near Broadway.

In December of 1899 Henri returned to Lafayette to spend the holidays with his family, who must have been impressed with his business success. From there he journeyed on to San Francisco—presumably his first trip to the West Coast—where he likely visited the fine department stores and millinery establishments and rang in the new year and new century.

In a pattern that was becoming familiar to Henri, the year 1900 was marked by dramatic highs and lows. Various accounts vaguely report that his partner, Julius Saur, ran off with company profits and destroyed the business. The particulars are elusive but in recording a subsequent bankruptcy filing by Saur in 1902, the *New York Times* reported that the firm of Bendel & Saur was dissolved on March 10, 1900, "when Bendel withdrew and Sauer [*sic*] continued alone until December 15, 1900," when another man became Saur's partner.

A Bendel hat of lace and ostrich feathers was featured in national newspapers in 1903.

ARTISTIC SHAPE OF LACE.
This hat is made of narrow bands of lace with the underbrim of black velvet and white felt, and it is trimmed with two large white ostrich plumes on the crown, a cabochon of black velvet on the bandeau topped with a cabochon of black jet. This model is by Henri Bendel.

Whether any mismanagement or flagrant wrongdoing by Saur set Bendel back, it doesn't seem to have broken his stride. But 1901 brought a more personal blow, the sudden death in early November of his dear stepfather, Benjamin Falk, who was only forty-eight years old and in seemingly good health. Henri went down for the funeral; Falk's obituary in the *Lafayette Advertiser* called him "one of the wealthiest and most substantial men" of Lafayette who "used his wealth, not selfishly, but kindly and freely to aid the deserving." Falk's passing no doubt elevated Henri to a new paternalistic role in the family, reinforced by his success up north. While in town he visited the *Advertiser* who ran a short piece about him, noting that "he has succeeded in building up a paying manufactory of pattern hats, and neckwear, which now employs 125 ladies." (Presumably not all of them worked in the Ninth Street store, rather at another production facility, and some may have worked from home.)

Beyond juggling his retail and wholesale businesses, Bendel began expanding his reach in a powerful new way—via the press. In October of 1900, invited by the Minneapolis *Star Tribune*, Bendel wrote a long column on style trends he had seen abroad. "Henri Bendel sums up fashion features," read the headline. In the piece, Henri dives in with fearless authority, and reveals rhetorical postures and themes he would revisit in dictums and musings throughout his life. These include a slightly formal tone; a reverence for women; a distinguishing between American and European women and their contrasting sensibilities (with high praise for the industry and confidence of the former); and an almost fetishistic, poetical obsession with color.

"I have just returned from a long tour in Paris, Berlin and London, made for the especial purpose of gladdening the hearts of women by the creation of stunning patterns for the feminine wear," Henri

THREE-QUARTER LENGTH COAT ATTRACTIVELY PLAITED

The plaited style of garment is again going to be a feature this season and will make its appearance particularly in the three-quarter length style, of which the illustrated number is a good example. Made of lady's cloth in a cream shade the entire garment is plaited from the shoulder down, this being only relieved by a stiff gauntlet cuff and a large yoke-like collar adorned with lace. This portion of the garment is stiffened by feather-bone to give it sufficient body. The coat is a John Wanamaker importation, while the hat worn with it is by Henri Bendel.

In a 1903 newspaper fashion spread, a model sports an elaborate Bendel hat and a typical-for-the-era complicated frock (from John Wanamaker).

wrote. "The fact that impresses me most is that while continental ideas are very valuable, after all the American woman, with her picturesque and unique individuality, must have her own styles, her own colors and her own combinations. She accepts with grace the hints from abroad and then does just as she pleases."

He touted "the new shades and tints, which are almost numberless. I have compiled a list for my own use which I think will be found available by every woman who has the color sentiment strongly developed." To wit: "In the gentler yellows are the cream verging on the oyster shell white of last year, the Mais a little deeper and the color of thick cream, the Paille something of the old cornflower glinting," one that he said came "very close to the yellow violet [flower] of South Carolina and Georgia."

In the next few years Bendel took out first small and then larger ads in various New York papers and magazines. *Vogue* back then was not a magazine but a weekly newspaper for the fashion trade. It's March 6, 1902 issue includes a quarter-page vertical ad, placed near the back of the paper among local concert listings, touting "Bendel's—arbiter of fashion in millinery and neck dress"—an early example of the store being called Bendel's,

Trade-mark on all our Creations

Arbiter of Fashion in
Millinery & Neckwear
Autumn Styles

402
Alexander Sailor, chenille braid, with trim-
ming of velvet and taffeta forming a bow.
All colors

359
Large Dented Turban, chenille braid, with
combination of velvets with diamond feather.
All colors

Advance Models now on Exhibition

*Not all establishments sell our models;
only the best. Your dealer probably has
them, but if he hasn't write to us and
we will give you the name of one who
does carry them.*

HENRI BENDEL
67 East 9th Street, New York
Wholesale Only

not Henri Bendel. Those in the know would use this nickname for decades to come, like saying Bonwit's or Bergdorf's for Bonwit Teller and Bergdorf Goodman. The ad shows an illustration of a woman in a long gown with a swooping, over-the-shoes skirt, a big, feathered hat, and an ornate scarf nearly as long as the dress. The copy below reads, "If any smarter hats or neckwear could be made, we would make them. Not every house sells our styles— only the very finest in each city. You probably deal with these. However the name will be supplied if you wish." At the top of the ad is a royal-style crest featuring a crown, swords, and an eagle, with the words "trade mark" beneath it.

Beyond his own ads, Bendel's hats were now getting editorial coverage—not only in New York publications but across the country. In January and February of 1903 Henri's designs and imports were featured prominently in fashion spreads in the New Orleans *Times-Democrat* and likely ran in other papers at the same time. One hat made of lace and black velvet featured "two large white ostrich plumes on the crown [and] a chou of black velvet on the bandeau topped with cabochon of black jet." The typical-of-the-era hyped-up copy is more vivid than the somewhat grainy black and white newsprint photos. Of another hat: "The light blue shade is to be one of the most fashionable for the coming season, and this hat by Henri Bendel in ciel color [sky blue] is a particularly effective model. It is trimmed with maline and ostrich plumes." That winter, various spreads in multiple issues paired his hats with dresses and coats from such clothiers as Wanamaker and Julius Stein and Co. In late March a spread in the New York *Daily Tribune* touted "Latest novelties in Easter hats designed by Henry W. Bendel of Bendel's, importer, No. 67 East Ninth Street, New York." (Note Henry spelled with a *y*—was that careless typesetting, or was Henri still toggling between his two appellations?)

Upon returning from France in September of 1904 he was quoted in the *New York Times* about dress trends and the French knack for naming colors. "The French are the greatest people in the world to invent names for colors," he said. "A crisp orange shade will be the Cleopatré. Why? Well, the Egyptian Queen's eyes, like her favorite cats, glittered with gold lights—that's the reason."

An early Bendel's ad with its trademark crest at top

◆⊙◆⊙◆⊙◆

NAMING THE COLORS.

THE French are the greatest people in the world to invent names for colors, said Henri Bendel, art designer for the Four Hundred, who has just returned from Paris. " A crisp orange shade will be the Cleopatré. Why? Well, the Egyptian Queen's eyes, like her favorite cats, glittered with gold lights—that's the reason.

In the article Bendel was identified as "art designer" for the 400—"the 400" being a familiar if slightly tongue-in-cheek tag for the most socially prominent families of New York City (400 was reportedly the amount of people who could fit into Mrs. Caroline Webster Astor's Fifth Avenue ballroom). "Art designer" is an odd and imprecise term in this context, perhaps just a writer's flourish, and this early mention of Henri and the 400 may have been a way of saying simply that he was becoming an authority for that top-tier social set. But not too long after, the role was all but codified: for years Mrs. Catherine Donovan, a prominent New York dressmaker and importer, really was known as "the Dresser to the 400," whom the couture importer Max Meyer would later recall as "a great personality, a real force in fashion." When she died in 1906, according to Sally Robbins, "it appears that Bendel inherited the mantle. On his return from Paris, he would report . . . on colors and styles for the coming season." Perhaps this was on occasion done in person, in private consultations, but primarily it was by way of quotes and columns in various papers. Suddenly Henri was something beyond a top wholesale milliner in America's fashion capitol; he was a tastemaker, with an expanding audience. And that would come to be worth more than all the egret and ostrich feathers in the world.

With frequent trips to Paris–this was his passport picture–Henri (as he now more consistently spelled his name) brought back not just dresses but trend reports and insights into haute couture as in a *New York Times* squib of 1904 (ABOVE).

CHAPTER 5

PRIDE OF PLACE

$\mathcal{B}$Y 1905, A MERE ELEVEN YEARS SINCE HE ARRIVED IN NEW YORK, Bendel had conquered the wholesale millinery trade; become a frequent traveler to Paris, where he procured gowns and scanned fashion trends, which he reported on back in America; established a small but well-trafficked showroom; and gained a reputation for taste and enterprise within his industry. Still, that wasn't enough for Henri. He wanted to take his skills, his flair, his passion, and all that he'd learned abroad and merge them into something bigger, something that would reach a wider audience. He aimed to open a fine retail hat and accessories store. But not a mere shop—rather a luxuriously appointed salon, with a tantalizing array of high-style merchandise, which would raise the bar for fashion retailing.

Henri may have been nudged or at least enabled by an unusual opportunity. A woman he had befriended, whose name is lost to history, was a patron of the Episcopal Mission, on the East Side of Manhattan. According to a 1925 profile of Henri, she "induced him to go into the retail business and employ several young ladies in whom she had an interest. It speaks well for working conditions in the firm of Bendel, Inc. that fifty percent of these young women are still employed by him [nearly twenty years after the launch of the store]."

With or without these women, Bendel surely would've found his way to opening a bigger store. The question was where to put it. According to Frances Anderson, "he listened attentively to the 'little voice' known as instinct, which seemed to say that the chic type of shop should be uptown." In fact, this was more good business sense than instinct; Henri knew that the merchandising map of Manhattan was quickly shifting north. In 1904 his old employer, B. Altman, had announced plans to build a huge new store at Fifth Avenue and Thirty-Fourth Street, diagonally across from the grand Waldorf Astoria Hotel (in its original midtown location). Sally Robbins reports that this required Altman to do battle with some socialites who weren't keen to see their mostly residential area overrun with pedestrians and sullied by commercial signage.

OPPOSITE: Bendel's new location at 520 Fifth Avenue. Visible in the doorway is young James "Buster" Jarrett, the doorman who would have a very long career with the store.

45

ABOVE: Bendel's name on a flower box.
BELOW: Henri's business neighbors on the west side of Fifth Avenue (just north and south of Forty-Third Street) included Huyler's candies, Guaranty Trust, the tailor Edouard, dressmaker Madame Irene, and Sherry's restaurant.

In 1906, the year Altman's opened, Bendel made his move and planted his flag even higher, signing a long lease on a five-story townhouse at 520 Fifth Avenue between Forty-Third and Forty-Fourth Streets, flanked by the shop of Irene, the prestigious one-name dressmaker, and the elegant restaurant Sherry's, which, along with nearby Delmonico's, virtually invented the concept of fine restaurant dining in America. This stretch of Fifth was already a magnet for stylish and rich New Yorkers— where else would Henri want to be?

Beyond finding a location and transforming a residential building into a commercial space, Bendel needed a visual signature. He sketched out a pattern of alternating chocolate-brown and cream-colored stripes. This became the motif repeated on awnings, wrapping paper, ribbons, business correspondence, and, eventually, in advertising. It was both subtle and striking. Sophisticated. And it would prove to have remarkable staying power. Henri himself executed

the all-important window decoration for the store, and, according to Robbins, "his chic displays soon gained a reputation among fashionable women."

The store was heralded ahead of its opening with a full-page newspaper ad picturing the opera and popular singer Geraldine Farrar—"one of my distinguished clientele gowned for the season of Spring 1906." The word "importer" sat below Henri's name, and below that the new address. Farrar was a faithful client and friend of Henri's and would serve as a model in his ads for years to come, even as her own star ascended and she crossed over into silent films. She was a sensation in her day and Henri couldn't have bought better publicity—although considering she probably received dresses for free or at a great discount, he *was* in a sense buying it.

On-theme with Henri's reputation for importing fashions from Paris, his new store's serenely opulent decor was meant to mentally convey the customer not just to France but back in time: paneling, molding, mirrors, and furniture were in the style of Louis XVI, with most everything done in a "French grey" or other

Geraldine Farrar, one of my distinguished clientele gowned for the season of Spring, 1906

HENRI BENDEL

Importer

520 Fifth Avenue, New York

Telephone 7700 Bryant

Opera singer Geraldine Farrar modeled Bendel's finery in an ad circa 1906. Bendel would dress and costume her for years to come.

No Star Like Farrar

Having been an early promoter of Henri's business, opera sensation and silent film actress Geraldine Farrar continued in that role into the 1920s. The December 1915 issue of *Harper's Bazar* featured a page of four large illustrations of the diva in concert gowns by Bendel (BOTTOM LEFT). In 1918 she invited *Vogue* to photograph her at home (LEFT) wearing Bendel dresses and coats that were ostensibly part of her private wardrobe. "Though the stage makes many demands upon the prima donna, everyday life has its exigencies too," read the florid copy, "and in these Bendel costumes Geraldine Farrar meets them all." Farrar rated a private fitting room at Bendel's. When she signed with Goldwyn Pictures of Fort Lee, New Jersey, in the late nineteen-teens, she stipulated that Henri, who had gowned her concert performances, design her film costumes as well. "For all these screen stories," she later recounted, "[he] had created a luxurious wardrobe which intrigued the movie fans as much as it did my concert audiences."

neutral colors, down to the luxurious Axminster carpets. Chandeliers hung from bronze chains. A ladies' "retiring room" at the rear of the 125-foot deep main floor was made of mahogany with gold-colored fittings. Built-in cabinets reaching to the ceiling could accommodate nearly a thousand hats. French-style dressing tables and chairs were placed in niches with multiple mirrors to catch a woman's various angles, and a screen would be erected to give the customer privacy as she tried on one hat then another.

On the mezzanine, windowed offices that overlooked the main floor sported decorative flower boxes. According to the *Illustrated Milliner* magazine, which reported on the new store in April of 1907, there were mirrors galore and "natural plants in full bloom add to the charm and attractiveness and waft a sweet fragrance all over this unique shop." Lighting, they said, was of a soft amber hue, "which gives such pleasing effect to milady's complexion and her bonnets." Bendel was more than selling hats, he was creating an experience, which started from the minute a customer approached. Also from the *Illustrated Milliner*:

The store had the feel of a private salon and featured display cabinets and discreet bays for trying on hats.

Madame Purchaser finds it a pleasant task selecting her bonnet at this establishment. An attendant in tobacco brown livery assists her from her carriage and another attendant in the livery of the house opens the door, with its distinctive Bendel crest and splendid lace portieres. A well dressed and courteous saleslady conducts her quietly to a seat at a Louis XVI dressing table. A French screen with representations of antique prints of [Jean-Marc] Nattiers' paintings is adjusted just in front, and privacy is assured. The artistic atmosphere, the soft lights, the chic hats all combine to influence the sale, and Madame, smilingly, orders not one but possibly a half dozen dainty bonnets.

LACE MODEL
Imported by
HENRI BENDEL
FIFTH AVENUE, NEW YORK

Posed and Photographed
expressly for
THE
ILLUSTRATED MILLINER

Hat of Point de Esprit with handsome jet buckle and ostrich feathers. Velvet ribbon ties,one of which supports a large rose.

Working Directions on Page 65

A 1907 full-page Bendel's ad in the *Illustrated Milliner*

And adding to the rich ambience: live music. Taking a page from Wanamaker's, Henri installed a large Estey pipe organ to enhance the shopping experience. Among the musicians he hired to play was an Episcopal church organist of note named Abraham Beekman Bastedo, whose brother was the prominent opera singer Orrin Bastedo. It may have been around this time that Henri converted to Christianity, specifically to the Episcopal Church. Perhaps he was already a practicing Episcopalian when he befriended the woman connected to the Episcopal Mission. Sally Robbins suspects he had joined far earlier, shortly after he lost Blanche in 1896. It's not something Bendel commented on publicly in his lifetime. But such a conversion was not uncommon. As Robbins points out, "American Jewry had its own social elite—families that had come to America from Germany and prospered. The Guggenheims, the Lewisohns, and Warburgs, to name a few, were wealthy, intellectual and influential. Even so, at the end of the 19th century, anti-Semitism among the Anglo-Saxon Protestant upper classes was pronounced and overt. The socially 'in' religion among the very wealthy in New York, like the Astor family, was Episcopalian. And Henri aspired to be among the elite."

Abraham Beekman Bastedo, the church organist whom Bendel befriended, in a photo he sent to his sister Kate in 1922

One can't but imagine that Bendel's desire to fit in came from an even deeper place. As a southerner he would have endured a degree of subtle and maybe not-so-subtle condescension from snobbish New Yorkers. And he could well have had a bedrock fear of being found out as a homosexual. Perhaps playing down his Jewish roots would minimize another identity that he could be penalized for. And yes, it's plausible that he might have wished to blend in with his clientele. But it wouldn't be fair to rule out the possibility that his motive was foremost religious. After all, Henri has been exposed to the Catholic Church as a youth and attended catechism and Mass at school. That may have planted a seed with a long gestation. And seeing splendid religious art in France might have strengthened Christianity's allure.

Abraham Bastedo (LEFT) and his family, including his famous opera singer
brother, Orrin Bastedo (RIGHT), date unknown

Whatever the influences, and the timing, it's likely that Bendel's attraction
to Mr. Bastedo cemented the conversion. Bendel's great-niece, Elene Davis, for
one, heard family talk to that effect. Fair-haired, blue-eyed Abraham Beekman
Bastedo—Abe to family and friends—was quite fetching and ten years
younger than Henri. He came from a prosperous family in New Jersey. When
and where they met is unknown, though it was likely at church. In any case,
the relationship took off quickly because, in addition to periodically playing
the organ in the store, Bastedo was soon on the company payroll and making
business trips with Henri. More than a decade after losing his wife and child,
Henri, at thirty-four, had rediscovered companionship and perhaps reconciled
his true sexual nature, first through his relationship with John Blish, and now
with Abraham Bastedo. And, apparently, the latter did not displace the former as over time both Blish and Bastedo would come to hold high positions
in Bendel's firm and at various times cohabitate with him, the three of them
often traveling together. Although in contemporaneous newspaper accounts
and later recollections of their comings and goings the two men were variously
referred to as servants, colleagues, friends, or companions. Was that Henri's
spin, or was it the interpretation by later-generation chroniclers of his life who
were naive to what now looks obvious, or who were too timid or stymied by
propriety to utter the truth?

Over time, Henri's sexual orientation—or the presumption of it—became an open secret among members of his family. Decades later, his great-niece Marjorie Meyer Arsht, Elene Davis's sister who would go on to become a prominent Texas political activist and philanthropist, wrote about the once hush-hush topic in her memoir, *All the Way from Yoakum.* "Because the subject had never been mentioned, I became aware of Uncle Henri's homosexuality only when I reached adulthood. When I questioned my mother directly about this, she answered in a whisper that everyone had been so sad about it. I had never noticed any sadness, however. His companions were simply a part of our family."

Henri would later refer to dapper Mr. Bastedo as a "lifelong intimate friend."

In February of 1908 Bendel and Bastedo returned from a buying trip in France on the SS *La Lorraine*, which sailed from La Havre. Henri was averaging two trips to Europe a year, entrusting the running of the store to new executives he'd hired, including his nephew Leon Schmulen—called Buddy—the son of his sister Fanny. When Buddy was about eighteen, Henri brought him up to New York, where he apprenticed with dressmaker and importer Max Schwarcz, a friend of Henri's and a fellow Francophile, traveling to Paris and becoming steeped in the culture of couture fashion. "We were, all of us, trained in Paris," Schmulen recalled. "Uncle saw to that." According to Robbins, Leon would come to be thought of as a crucial business brain of the company. Many years later he would ascend to the role of head importer and eventually, after Henri's death, to that of the store's fashionable front man.

In mid-December of 1909 Bendel visited Lafayette. The *Advertiser* reported that he "left Wednesday for his home in New York, after a few days spent here with his mother, Mrs. Falk, and relatives and renewing friendships. Mr. Bendel is one of the leading milliner manufacturers in the United States and has a large and very prosperous [concern]. His many friends here are very proud of his great success. He has his nephew Leon Schmulen, son of Mr. and Mrs. Gus Schmulen, with him, and Leon's friends, we are sure, will be more than pleased to learn that Leon has 'made good' in the business, and his uncle has very rapidly advanced him until he is now holding one of the most responsible positions [there]."

Buddy Schmulen would not be the last nephew or niece to benefit from Henri's support. According to Robbins, "his many nieces and grandnieces could count upon Uncle Henri to design their baby dresses, wedding gowns and, of course, hats. During visits to Louisiana, his relatives catered to him, and babies' names were submitted for his approval." Marjorie Meyer Arsht's sister, for instance, was given the very French name Elene, although

Bendel's nephew Leon "Buddy" Schmulen

Henri's niece Myrtle Levy Meyer in the wedding dress he designed for her

throughout her life she, and everyone who knew her, pronounced it *Elaine*. In all family matters "if Uncle Henri said it then that was the way it was," she recalled late in her life. "He set the pace and the pattern."

Bendel's niece, Elyse Bendel, the daughter of his brother Sam, even got a fashion makeover from Uncle. According to John Goodman, her grandson, Henri "saved her from embarrassment when she wore a similar dress as another girl by pulling her aside and making simple alterations that made her look sensational."

He could also be helpful in matters of matchmaking. "It was important that all of the female members of the family be married," said Arsht. Whenever a niece seemed unable to find a husband, Uncle Henri generally made sure that eligible prospects learned that he usually gave his nieces a wedding present of five thousand dollars. That practice may not always have been followed, but there were no unwed nieces around."

His generosity was born of family fealty but could be practical too. Business was booming—the new store's sales in its first year were $200,000, or nearly six million in today's dollars—and Henri needed all the trustworthy employees, such as Buddy Schmulen, that he could get.

Back in 1907 Bendel had moved into an apartment in an eleven-story luxury building in midtown Manhattan called the Sonoma, at 1730 Broadway, on the northeast corner of Fifty-Fifth Street. By 1910 he had quite a full household there; the Census that year listed three men as "head": Henri, Abraham Bastedo, and a German-born man named Ludwig Ulman, twenty years Henri's senior and whose relationship to Bendel is unknown. Henri's nephew Buddy, now twenty, was also in the domestic mix, plus a house servant named Edward Coysh (whose age and nationality were not recorded).

On census forms and other official documents, such as passport applications, Bendel was sometimes identified as a merchant, sometimes a milliner, and indeed to many people the name Bendel was now synonymous with hats. In May of 1910 Bendel filed a patent for an innovation in hat construction involving inner and outer facings and particular stitching, which would keep material stretched taut and give a hat a more "finished appearance," as he wrote in his submission. Therein he outlined an elaborate description of the complex process and included precise illustrations. "Having thus described my invention," he said, "I claim as new and desire to secure by Letters Patent." This dedication to good construction, quality behind the veneer, became a hallmark of Bendel's brand. As Colin McDowell put it in his book *Hats: Status, Style and Glamour,* "A woman who patronized Bendel . . . did so because she knew that when she walked up Fifth Avenue everyone would recognize her hat as a Bendel hat—the 'Bendel bonnet,' which Cole Porter later decreed was 'the top.' The women who valued hats sufficiently to pay high prices for them were not just elegant—they were intelligent and sophisticated enough to appreciate the highest levels of creativity and workmanship."

But these same women also appreciated a bargain and Henri obliged. Bendel was committed to stocking fine merchandise, and he believed in the business mantra "keep it moving." One of his many innovations was the publicized clearance sale. A large ad in New York's *Sun* newspaper in early December of 1911 read:

> The remaining stock of rich furs consisting of seal, mole, ermine, baby lamb and caracul coats, also fur lined coats and the entire stock of model hats and gowns suitable for every occasion to be closed out regardless of cost.

Furs and hats and other accessories comprised a large portion of Henri's business, but his offerings in dresses, gowns, and coats were fast expanding—the premiere ones coming from Paris. Along with creations from the likes of Parisian designers Callot Soeurs and Louise Chéruit, Bendel was now importing designs by Drecoll, a Parisian couture house with old roots in Vienna, Austria, and the storied label Worth, founded in 1858 by Englishman Charles Frederick Worth. The Bendel firm was also starting to make its own dresses, as well as copy Paris originals, with the couturiers' permissions.

MILLINERY

New York.—Styles Often Really Not So Quickly Copied.—The incident reported in yesterday's WOMEN'S WEAR, where Henri Bendel had, six months ago, one of the advance styles in women's hats that are just now appearing here shows that the merchant or the importer with nerve to bring over these things or to make them here, is not so quickly copied as a great many imagine.

Last May, Bendel showed in one of his windows a hat which now has been duplicated and exhibited by one of the large department stores. Of course, from now on this style will undoubtedly be widely copied, but Bendel probably had it too far in advance for the popular trade, and perhaps even for his own following, because there is no gainsaying that styles are at times too extreme even for women, too far in advance for them to wear, and few merchants dare to put their money into such merchandise until the way has been paved to somewhat popularize or familiarize the idea, and then the pirating becomes at once widespread.

To the man who brings in new things, really the only benefit is prestige, just because of his courage in showing these things one season after another, his competitors being afraid to follow. From this point of view, it is not harmful to show styles publicly, because it takes six months or a year for the others to follow, and by the time they do follow, the originator is away on another tack, just as far ahead as he was in the instances that were copied. Yet undoubtedly those with courage enough to introduce new things promptly become completely discouraged at times, because few of their customers will buy the very new or radical things, and when they do get ready to make purchases of these, others stores have waked up to what the new mode is. The originator, however, has his reward in the prestige which always comes to the creative individual, who always does things in advance; and prestige is a tremendous asset in business today. The reputation that makes a customer go to one store instead of another makes the business very profitable.

A 1911 article in *Women's Wear* about a Bendel hat that had been copied by a large department store; Henri, it argued, tended to be ahead of the fashion curve.

822　PARIS. — La Rue de la Paix. — LL.

ABOVE: The Rue de la Paix in Paris, home to most of the great couture houses
BELOW: Illustration of the dining room of the ocean liner *Lusitania*

In February of 1911, US customs logs record Bendel returning from another semi-annual buying trip. Over the years he traversed the Atlantic on many of the prominent liners of the era including the *Majestic* and the *Oceanic*. This time he sailed back to the United States from Liverpool on the *Lusitania*—the Cunard liner that four years later would be torpedoed and sunk by a German U-boat, killing 1,198 passengers and crew, including 128 Americans, a horror that helped propel the United States into World War I.

These procurement trips to Paris were the soul of Bendel's business. So large were the orders he placed that French couturiers showed him great deference and allowed him to view dresses privately. He would disembark on the Hudson River from one liner or another not only with knowledge of the haute couture trends of the season but with crates of dresses in the cargo hold (or they would arrive later, on other boats, if they weren't ready to ship). And he carried home boxes of fashion sketches rendered in pastel, colored pencil, or

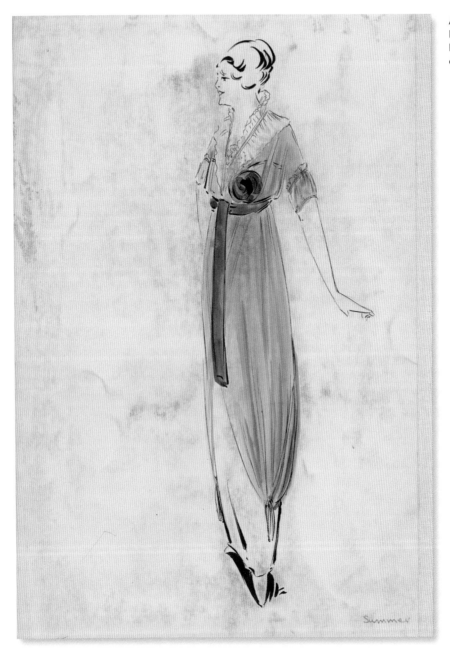

A sketch of a 1912 Parisian dress for Bendel to copy, designer unknown

watercolor, drawn by Parisian sketch artists or sometimes Bendel's own artists. These were used by his designers and seamstresses to recreate the gowns and dresses that he had permission to copy. A single designer's showing for a spring collection might consist of sixty different dresses—requiring one sketch for each. And Henri and his lieutenants could visit as many as fifteen or twenty couture houses in a three- or four-week period. In the 1950s, Henri's heirs bequeathed to the Brooklyn Museum a vast trove of more than

> "Mr. Bendel and Paris will always remain in the center of fashion and elegance, and in consequence Mr. Bendel is being favored everywhere."
> —*Women's Wear Daily*

seven thousand sketches, spanning the years 1912 to 1939, a vivid record of the work of the top Paris couturiers, particularly in the 1910s and '20s, like Chéruit and Callot Soeurs, plus many others including the Houses of Jenny (Jeanne Adele Bernard), Jeanne Paquin, Jacques Doucet, and Premet, among others.

As it had been for nearly two decades, France in all its rarefied glory—its fashion, of course, but also its art, architecture, food—was Henri's North Star. Even as he was beginning to create and sell dresses and accessories made in-house—made in America—Paris *style* was what he was selling, copying, and celebrating. As *Vogue*, *Harper's Bazar* (in the early years the magazine spelled "bazar" with two, not three, *a*'s) and other style bibles and newspapers of the era regularly showed French fashion imported by Bendel, they were also

A drawing of Bendel's store after an Estey pipe organ was installed in order to lend auditory ambience and encourage women to linger

interviewing Henri, and he hardly missed an opportunity to sing the praises of French style. But he had to be careful that in touting its virtues he didn't insult the American women who were his clients or prospective clients. His early public proclamations reveal a tightrope dance that Henri would do for much of his professional life, in one breath declaring French style supreme, in the next breath qualifying that notion, praising the more practical instincts and adaptations of the marvelous American woman.

An interview in the *New York Times* in the fall of 1912 captures this verbal highwire act, and Henri's flair for drama:

> When asked about the possibility of an American fashion independent of the Paris designer, M. Henri Bendel of Fifth Avenue sat down on a heap of new ratine and charmeuse and shook his head sadly.

Henri sat for a professional portrait (likely in the late 1900s or 1910s).

"Create? Never! We over here, we fix and change and copy a great deal, but we have not the environment [nor] the thousand things which are necessary to create the most beautiful in clothes. In Paris the designer must be an artist. And when he is to create a new gown, or a wrap, or a hat he goes for his inspiration to a work by the old masters or a beautiful bit of sculpture. Perhaps he copies off a wonderful piece of tapestry in pastel, and then he goes home and works it over, trying with every material to produce the effect which he has fixed in his mind.

"Here in America the poor designer has no place to go; it is all modern.

"And then, too, the dressmaker, the tailor, the manufacturer of beautiful materials—they all get more help from the women themselves. In this country women have something else to think about besides dress. They do not want to give up their lives to dress. . . .

"But the French women are content to devote all their energy to the art of wearing their clothes. . . .

"Above all, the American mentality is not creative. Americans adapt and modify and shape better than anyone else in the world. . . .

"They know what is fit. The American woman is, on the whole, from the time she gets up in the morning until she goes to bed at night, better dressed than the French woman, because she knows what suits every different occasion. But adapting and suiting, ah, that is not creation!

"And why should we be bothering our heads to create a new something when American women are perfectly content with the French styles? . . .

"American styles? Pouf!" and M. Bendel dismissed them with a wave of his hand.

By 1912 Henri was ensconced in a new home—he had moved to the still-emerging residential area of the Upper West Side, into a roomy apartment at 257 West Eighty-Sixth Street, between Broadway and West End Avenue. The recently completed seven-story, Italian Renaissance-style building featured a columned entrance, decorative balconies, and large windows, the latter a real luxury. In late summer of that year Henri hosted the distinguished French

ABOVE: No. 10 West Fifty-Seventh Street with signage announcing Bendel's impending occupancy and, to its right, the town house No. 12 (ALSO OPPOSITE), which would be replaced by a new building to be connected to No. 10, together forming Henri's new emporium

milliner Madame Georgette and her sixteen-year-old son for a monthlong visit; in addition to time in New York, they toured Boston; Newport, Rhode Island; and the White Mountains of New Hampshire.

Perhaps Bendel solicited Madame's advice about his exciting, as-yet-unveiled new venture. With the robust success of the store, growth was inevitable, and in late 1912 Henri announced another move, one that really got everyone's attention. He sold his unexpired lease on 520 Fifth Avenue for $22,500 to A. G. Spalding and Bros., the famous Chicago-based sporting goods outfit, and declared his intention to relocate to West Fifty-Seventh Street, a few doors west of Fifth Avenue. At that time that thoroughfare was almost strictly residential, lined with some of the grandest homes in New York City, including Harry Payne Whitney's house and, on the northwest corner of Fifth and Fifty-Seventh Streets, where the women's clothing store Bergdorf Goodman is today, the Cornelius Vanderbilt mansion. Some aghast residents saw Bendel's planned encampment as an invasion, a shadow-casting, traffic-exacerbating, there-goes-the-neighborhood catastrophe. Tongue-waggers and other merchants wondered if Henri—in this gambit to place his store so far beyond the established parameters of fashion retail—had lost his bearings. As the New York Tribune would write a few years after the fact, "competitors and friends alike sort of pitied him, saying he was going out of town with his business."

CHAPTER 6

THE OUTLIER

*A*T THE START OF THE SECOND DECADE of the twentieth century, New York City grew at a dizzying pace. Its population had jumped from 3.4 million in 1900 to 4.7 million a mere ten years later. On April 17, 1912, immigration at Ellis Island set a one-day record of 11,745 new arrivals. For a slender strip of land less than 22.8 square miles squeezed between the Hudson and East Rivers, Manhattan Island—the hub of the five-borough metropolis—seemed defiantly unbounded, with ever-taller buildings, teeming ship docks, and an expanding grid of housing and industrial buildings, bridges, roads, railways, streetcars, elevated trains, and the latest marvel: a subway. It could not be contained, neither physically nor in its vaulting ambition. Disparate groups—often defined by race, nationality, wealth level, and who got here first—challenged one another and themselves in a citadel of achievement. New York had become the American mecca of finance, trade, mercantilism, intellectual life, publishing, journalism, performing arts, fine arts—and fashion.

In 1913, as Bendel's new store was rising on Fifty-Seventh Street, just west of Fifth Avenue, a couple of miles to the south, near the tip of Manhattan, another tower went up, a 792-foot-tall marvel of vertigo-inducing engineering. When, at 7:30 p.m. on April 24, President Woodrow Wilson flipped a switch in Washington, DC, sending a signal 200 miles north that in an instant illuminated its sixty floors, the neo-Gothic Woolworth Building glowed like a vision from a fever dream. The tallest structure in the world, someone dubbed it the Cathedral of Commerce.

But by then fashion and other luxury businesses such as hotels, fine restaurants, opera houses, and theaters had moved uptown, many along upper Broadway and Fifth Avenue, and now were turning the corner way up at Fifty-Seventh Street. Henri's own cathedral of commerce was first announced as real estate news in 1912; jeweler and real estate investor Michael Dreicer would be building a nine-story loft at

OPPOSITE: Bendel's store at Nos. 10–14 West Fifty-Seventh Street, circa late 1910s. ABOVE: Years later, a sketch of the façade was used in marketing materials.

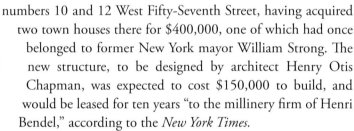

HENRI BENDEL

Importer of

Summer Hats

Evening Gowns

Afternoon Gowns

Novelties

10-12 West Fifty-Seventh Street

NEW YORK

Telephone 7700 Plaza

RIGHT: A simple but bespoke advertisement

BELOW: A "reception costume" by Callot Soeurs, imported by Bendel and featured in *Harper's* in 1914

numbers 10 and 12 West Fifty-Seventh Street, having acquired two town houses there for $400,000, one of which had once belonged to former New York mayor William Strong. The new structure, to be designed by architect Henry Otis Chapman, was expected to cost $150,000 to build, and would be leased for ten years "to the millinery firm of Henri Bendel," according to the *New York Times*.

Once it was completed and finished out to Bendel's specifications, his new emporium, which opened its doors late in 1913, felt like a hybrid of a boutique and a medium-sized department store. It had the elegant furnishings, soft lighting, decorative flourishes, and a muted color palette of serene grays and putty tones akin to the old Fifth Avenue shop, but there was much more space here, broken up by large square columns around which were positioned antique chairs where a shopper might relax as a salesperson brought around a dress for consideration or wrote up a sales order. Sweeping staircases whisked customers among three floors (an elevator stood at the ready too) to expanded departments for millinery, gowns, day dresses, coats, furs, bridal wear, and accessories, with ample dressing and fitting rooms, large display cases, and, as in the old store, mirrored nooks for trying on hats. Bendel was one of the first to send out live models around the floor to show off dresses. (Confusingly enough from a modern vantage, back then those

The New Bendel's

"KEEPING up with the times" is undeniably one of the secrets of business success. If proof were required, one need only contemplate the alacrity with which prosperous and long-established business houses adopt the latest in methods.

The establishment of Henri Bendel, Inc, at 10 West 57th Street is a conspicuous example of this. Recently enlarged by the addition of a new building—which, after the weather has had its way with it for a time will appear from the outside, as it is within, a continuation of the old structure—this house has also been reorganized throughout and fitted with the most up-to-date equipment in every particular. From the display rooms with their elegant fittings and carefully schemed lighting to the workrooms where the establishment's costume creations have their origin, everything is completely and scientifically modern and efficient.

Workroom conditions at Bendel's are as nearly ideal as possible. These long rooms, two or three on each floor of the buildings above the third story, are painted white, both walls and ceilings, and have large windows on the front for daylight and air.

Each workroom with its workers forms a complete unit in itself; in it a costume or garment is cut, fitted to a model, basted, stitched, pressed and given the finishing touches. This of course presupposes a complete work-

Photographie Bureau of The New York Edison Company

Bendel's Large Display and Fitting Rooms, with Their Neutral Tints and Artistic Lighting, Are Ideal for Showing Colors and Fabrics

ing equipment; and so each workroom has its complement of electric irons and electrically operated sewing machines.

The electric iron installation, taken all in all, is probably the largest and most varied in the city. The irons used in each workroom are generally connected to a central standard in the center of one large ironing table. Their cords are suspended from separate brackets extending out far enough for the workers to use the irons with freedom and convenience. To do away with the possibility of

In 1917 Con Ed's magazine for stockholders featured an article on Bendel's, focusing on its innovative electrical features and offering a glimpse of the store's look.

> "I'd give it to my mother-in-law if I didn't like her, but it's no gown—no style. Take it away!"
> —*Henri Bendel*

women were called mannequins, sometimes spelled manikin, and dresses were often referred to as "models.")

Above the third floor, out of sight to the public, were floors of stock rooms, executive offices, and several large, bright, and high-ceilinged work rooms where seamstresses and designers labored over both original designs and the recreation of Parisian dresses. The fact that within a year or so of opening Henri's employee ranks had swelled to a remarkable 1,100 speaks to the scale and ambition of the new store. Beyond the small army of salespeople was a behind-the-scenes battalion that included cutters, tailors, and fur and hide specialists, plus buyers, accountants, executives, sketchers, stock boys (as they were called), errand runners, and custodians.

Henri's niece Myrtle Levy modeled a dress and hat designed by her uncle.

As early evidence of the loyalty Henri engendered, some thirty employees had been with him since 1906, including James Jarrett, a Black man nicknamed "Buster" for the Buster Brown hat he wore along with his brown livery coat. Henri hired him when he was just fourteen years old to be the store's doorman and greet customers, and he served in that role at least until—believe it or not—1976, when he was eighty-four, a staggering seventy-year career. Upon that milestone *New York* magazine wrote a short piece on Jarrett, who recalled the heady days of the nineteen-teens after the store had moved to Fifty-Seventh Street amid "private homes, high-stooped houses. There was nothing but money on the street then." Buster remembered greeting Vanderbilts, Goulds, Astors, and DuPonts. "They'd drive up with their carriages and footman. That class of people didn't want to touch the knob."

Awaiting those coddled elite, as well as shoppers of lesser means, was the frisson of the new, as significant changes in women's fashion were afoot. The busty, S-shaped Gibson Girl look of the early part of the century was getting a makeover. Led by the bold Parisian iconoclast Paul Poiret and inspired by Grecian tunics and Asian robes, the silhouette of women's dresses was loosening up, taking on a somewhat more streamlined effect, often free of corsets and bustles and with reduced petticoats or no petticoats at all. This felt moderately liberating for women, and a good example of how fashion usually evolves—in part out of a designer's imagination, her or his vision, but equally in response to a shifting culture, with women in need of lighter, less constricting outfits that allowed for action, not just for sitting pretty.

Still, many fashionable dresses and suits looked and felt far from minimal; they remained long-skirted, layered, and voluminous. Some were heavy with brocade and other embellishments. Hats were dramatic and quite large, requiring strict posture and wide doorways. The new styles didn't augur the great liberation that would come in the 1920s, but they were a step in that direction. In November of 1913 *Harper's Bazar* showed a "parvenche blue" (a bright blue) chiffon and velvet "afternoon wrap" by Poiret, imported by Bendel. Other prominent French designers that Henri brought in such as Paquin and Worth were also starting to whittle away at the Gibson Girl who suddenly had come to seem matronly and out of step with the times.

Just as New York found itself at an inflection point wherein class lines were blurring and middle-class spending power was increasing, Bendel had the good sense to play to all constituencies. His brand had been built on what was known as the carriage trade (even as carriages were fast being replaced by motor cars)—the very wealthiest shoppers, the ones who didn't look at price tags. Purchasing original couture dresses and the most extravagant hats, they were Henri's ideal customer. But he realized that if he did it carefully, subtly, he could keep that clientele but expand his merchandise, and thereby expand his customer base and his sales. Hence, in this larger store he would offer something for everyone—or at least everyone at an upper-middle-class level or higher. A woman who might not be able to afford a Parisian original by, say, Worth, could buy a modified copy; or if not that, then a Bendel original executed by a designer who worked in-house, perhaps something in the general style of that Worth dress; or if

A 1913 dress and jacket by Callot Soeurs

not that, then something even less extravagant, but still in the *mode du jour*. Meanwhile, a shopper on an even tighter budget could nab a lower-priced hat or a pair of gloves. She would still be getting style, quality, and, not incidentally, the Bendel label and its cachet.

Bendel made no attempt to obscure the provenance of particular dresses. "One thing we do not permit is having our people represent domestic gowns as imported," he told *Women's Wear*, the influential garment industry trade paper. "If a gown is imported, we tell our girls to say so, and if domestic to say so. . . . We import a large number of gowns from Paris each season, but most of these are modified to meet the requirements of the conservative American woman, yet not so changed as to take away from their individuality or style points, for all of our styles are governed by the trend of the fashion. I do not mean to decry the art of the Paris designers, for I think they should be given the most consideration for what they have given to us in the promotion of styles; but I simply mean American gowns are better [when] adapted for American women."

A dramatically feathered, velvet cap-style hat from the 1910s, in the collection of the Metropolitan Museum of Art in New York

The fashion press regularly solicited Bendel not just for dresses and hats to show in their pages but for his opinions, which were bold and pithy. Recognizing his authority and his way with words, *Harper's Bazar* enlisted him to write periodic columns that would accompany fashion spreads. Their July 1913 issue featured an article titled simply "A Forecast—By Henri Bendel," in which he parsed current trends in hats. They will be larger, he proclaimed, but not too large, "and brims will roll slightly at the side . . . the trimmings are creeping toward the front. We shall have no shooting out at rakish angles in the back; that effect has passed out [of style] entirely." He declared that "almost without exception the hats will be dark in color, and the all-black hat will be very chic," explaining that "a dark hat is a necessity when the costume reflects brilliant colorings. If you top a freakish costume with a freakish hat, you are sure to get a garish result, but if you tone down the costume with a hat of a somber shade you will have a very up-to-date, smart effect." With his flair for conjuring colors, he wrote that "when black is not desired, there are Bordeaux colorings, the dregs of wine, [and] a rich deep blue, and [a] green bordering on the myrtle," in one phrase invoking libations of his beloved France and the flowering trees of his southern youth. Indeed, Henri's love of nature and gardening often seeped into his fashion prognostications. As he reported in the *Millinery Trade Review* in the winter of 1916, "Marine blue is a hue that Paris approves of this season, and is especially choice in ribbons because it combines admirably, if used with discretion, in the smart trimmings of flowers—the long-stemmed, thorny roses, the richly-hued passion flowers, variegated sweet peas, water lilies, and the languorous lotus, which rival Nature's loveliest blooms, and which the newest millinery has brought into vogue."

Henri's voice, resonating through magazines and papers, in effect was becoming its own product of Henri Bendel, Inc. And while in one breath he could wax poetic about fashion, in the next he could sound like the bottom-line businessman he was—with annual sales hitting a remarkable $1.5 million. "The growth of the Henri Bendel business has not been the overnight kind, but rather of the steady and sure character, each year showing a considerable increase over the preceding one," he told *Women's Wear* in a lengthy interview in the spring of 1914. He displayed no false modesty as he addressed the reporter's queries about his success. "We hear of other firms speaking of busy and dull seasons," he said. "With us there is no dull season. Every moment is a busy one. This is probably accomplished by our constant evolution of fashions.

In His Opinion

A Sampling of Bendel's Fashion Commentary

"Clothes should not reach their lowest ebb in the morning. They should receive as careful attention and be as becoming as those for evening. Begin the day right sartorially and you'll avoid much depression of spirit and save your disposition."

"The pajama is the ideal costume for the boudoir. It is more in keeping with the modern spirit than the very elaborate and lacey tea gowns beloved in the Victorian age."

"The scarf is a direct answer to that very harassing question—how can I stretch my too limited income? For it is almost miraculous what can be done with a simple frock and several scarves."

"Accessories do come and go, flourish and die."

"Don't wear a white hat unless you are so beautiful it doesn't matter what you wear . . . [and] don't wear your big hat with a self-conscious air. . . . Forget it entirely."

"What the petite blonde can wear, the exotic brunette of Juno-like dignity should never consider. The Titian blonde can scintillate in colors and cuts that the chestnut-haired girl must forego. The white-haired woman's beauty can be enhanced a hundred fold if she only knows how."

"It is always smarter to be informally dressed for formal occasion than to be formally dressed when everyone else is in afternoon or dinner attire."

"Outside of a musical comedy you cannot find a more captivating costume than [a bathing suit]. Many a woman has found she is infinitely more chic and appealing in her bathing togs than in her elaborate French frocks."

"Nothing that is essentially correct gives the appearance of over-decorativeness. It is ever in poor taste to have extraneous gee-gaws."

"Naturally when fabrics are so gorgeous lines must not be intricate, but flowing and ample. Like the lily, they need no gilding."

"Life can never become entirely dull to the woman who owns [even one fancy] frock and wears it at the right time. For its psychological value. It's a form of preparedness that should not be overlooked."

We have something new to give to the public every day. The woman who bought a hat or gown last week will find something new this week."

But, he said, being au courant didn't tell the whole story. "Giving the people values is really what counts in any kind of business. . . . All good houses put value first, and it is only the house of mushroom growth which attempts the old policy of 'fooling the public.' They do not last long, however."

In the article Bendel cleverly appealed to any reader who might be intimidated by the store's reputation. "Occasionally one hears the charge that Henri Bendel's is expensive," he said, unprompted. "Now, this impression is entirely erroneous. In our merchandise we give real value, not only style value. One of our hats, for example, cannot be duplicated elsewhere for less money. We believe in educating the public to know merchandise values. For instance, the velvet used on some of our hats costs as high as $8 a yard, while velvet that might at first look as well to the unsuspecting public will show the difference when it has been worn a bit. Our velvet, in fact, improves with age up to a certain point, while the other fabric lasts no time. Once a woman has worn a hat with real values, she cannot bring herself to buy a cheap one. She would rather have one $30 hat than three $10 hats."

The interview captures Bendel's fastidiousness, precision, and insistence on quality above all else. "Our hats are made entirely within our store," he told the reporter, "and we know to a penny how much each model costs to manufacture, for we keep complete records. We know how a certain model can be made for $35, and why it should cost that, and the same is true about our gowns."

There would be no subcontracting either. "With the exception of imports, nothing ever comes into this store except the raw material. We manufacture and assemble all parts. Once, when the demand was greater than the supply, we sent some work outside to be done, but . . . the work was of an inferior nature and the material used was not up to our standard."

In the same article, an unnamed executive—it may have been Mr. Blish or Mr. Bastedo—credited Henri for "his knowledge of merchandise and the fine organization he has built. . . . I have never seen a body of employees who work together so enthusiastically. . . . With Mr. Bendel, money is no consideration in hiring employees. If a man is worth it, he can secure more money for his services from Henri Bendel than he can any other place in the world. He has about him some of the highest salaried men in the business." The executive pointed out that beyond good compensation, Bendel offered his hires opportunity for mobility and demonstrated sensitivity to his staff's collective well-being. "No matter how busy he is, [any department head] with a proposition looking toward the bettering of the condition of his employees can manage to see him."

When a large New York syndicate tried to buy an interest in Bendel's, Henri turned the offer down, so as not to cede control. "Such an investment might take from Henri Bendel the final decision of what should be done at some time when his methods and policies might dictate a certain course," said *Women's Wear,* "and Henri Bendel apparently intends to remain his own master."

In a similar vein, a Chicago syndicate tried to entice Bendel into licensing his brand for a store in their city, offering to erect a new building and give him a "handsome interest for the use of his name" with no expectation for day-to-day involvement, perhaps just a few trips a year to guide it. "Again Mr. Bendel felt it wise to refuse. His New York store, he pointed out, was all that he could possibly take care of, and to watch him as he busies himself about the store is proof of what he says."

As he often did with the press, Bendel leveraged this *Women's Wear* piece to flatter his customer and wave the flag: "There is nothing too expensive, nothing too rare or too difficult to get, for me to bring to New York for the American woman to use to adorn her person, for the American woman is the most beautiful and the best of the world's women." And even as his store was becoming its own empire, with an astounding $3 million in sales in its first year, and needing constant attention, Henri entrusted it to his lieutenants for months at a time so that he could retain his role as chief procurer of the French finery on which his reputation rested. Mme. Gerber, the premier designer among the Callot sisters "always received him in a private room to view her collection," recalled Crawford of *Women's Wear.* This was not only a gesture of courtesy, Crawford concluded, but helped keep competitors' prying eyes at bay. Over the years Henri befriended many of the couturiers. Mme. Gerber entertained him in her rococo mansion, and, according to Crawford, Henri "was a warm personal friend of Mme. Lanvin and often visited her home. He had for her the deepest respect as an artist, but a far greater esteem [for her] as a woman."

Before international fame as a stage costumer and magazine illustrator, the Russian-born Parisian designer Erté sold dresses to Bendel, his first US buyer, who ordered thirty from his debut collection. This one, called "Splendeur," circa 1916, was the artist's own favorite.

In the summer of 1914, however, his time abroad proved to be an adventure far beyond dress salons and fancy suppers. As he had in summers past, Bendel had budgeted enough time in Europe to include pleasure as well as business. He left New York at the end of May and spent most of the first six weeks in or near Paris, attending to a buying office there and sizing up new fashions in the couture houses. In mid-July he left Paris on a driving tour through the Rhine Valley and the Alsace-Lorraine region, the latter perhaps of special interest to Henri as that's where his mother had grown up. He had just purchased a new car, driven by a chauffeur loaned to him by his banker in France. "From time to time he had heard of the Austria-Hungary and Serbia trouble, but no one had any idea that France and Germany would be drawn into it, he said," as *Women's Wear* recounted the tale. "When he heard [that] the German troops had started to mobilize, Mr. Bendel put back for the French line hoping to get into Luxemburg [*sic*] and so into France. Very near his destination he was stopped and informed that even though he was an American he could not go further without passports." Bendel then drove to Frankfurt and got in touch with the American ambassador in Berlin, who facilitated his getting necessary papers to leave the country. "On two occasions on his flight through Germany, Mr. Bendel saw the German emperor and his Imperial Guard." At some point German authorities detained Bendel's chauffeur because he was a Frenchman, but they assured Henri that the man would be treated properly, with room and board; Henri gave the chauffeur money and made arrangements to send more if needed, agreeing to keep him in his employ until March of the following year.

Heading on his own to Holland, Henri ran out of gas, could find none, and had to abandon the car. With friends and associates back home worrying, as they had lost communication with him, he eventually reached the Netherlands and then sailed to England. France was now at war with Germany, but instead of hastily scampering back to America, as so many other US citizens had, Henri headed back into Paris, where he managed to see couture collections on the last two days of August. As *Women's Wear* marveled: "While others were secure in the United Sates and were relating to their friends how they 'got out of Paris at the very last moment,' Henri Bendel was going into that French style center," and "while others waited in fear of the shelling of the city by the German army" he was "visiting the couturiers in search of models [dresses]."

"I landed in Paris on Aug. 30, [and] I found Paris listless as regards fashions," he told *Women's Wear* upon his return. "Some of the houses were open and offering models, and from them I secured my supply. I stayed over Aug. 31 and should have stayed longer, only the fear was expressed all over the city that the railroad tracks were to be torn up, and rather than risk an enforced stay, I left for London, taking with me all the models I could get through, and making arrangements for sending more to London. I had taken the precaution to take two couriers with me from London, and this greatly facilitated matters. All I had to bother with was to pick out what I wanted. The couriers arranged to get the models out in baskets."

Henri may have been the last foreigner to view that season's collections, and he found them splendid. "Had not the war been declared I feel sure from what I saw in Paris, that the fashion world would've seen gowns this season unequaled in history for their beautiful effects. Such gowns as we have been able to get denote this. When the trouble broke out two-thirds of the season's gowns had already been made, and Paris undoubtedly would have had a great season."

In the face of the escalating conflict, Bendel tried, perhaps naively, to be optimistic. "If the Germans are driven back, and Paris can again devote her attentions to fashions and if the material can be supplied, the war will have very little effect," he said. Failing that, the couture houses, he imagined, would need America's support after the war, "and when that time arrives I shall do all I can to help her get started again in furnishing the world with beautiful garments. If the war were over tomorrow and I could help the couturiers in any way, I should go right back."

The war, of course, was not "over tomorrow"—it would drag on until 1918, with the United States entering the fray in 1917. But even from the start, the effect on fashion in New York was immediate; Parisian houses reduced production, and most of their finery couldn't get out of the country, at least for a time. American buyers were reticent about traveling abroad. Beyond the volatility on the Continent, the sinking of the passenger liner *Lusitania* by the Germans was fresh in memory. Bendel's dear friend Max Schwarcz, the importer, in fact had perished onboard.

The implication stateside was that American dressmakers and department stores would have to step up and fill France's shoes, but this would be a tough sell to the style setters in New York who could hardly imagine such a surrender. For *Vogue* editor in chief Edna Woolman Chase this presented a daunting challenge. From her memoir, *Always in Vogue*:

> At the outbreak of the war, business in the fashion world was abruptly halted, and how to fill the pages of *Vogue* became my personal problem. Riding on top of a Fifth Avenue bus one early autumn day, racking my brains for a solution, in a flashback of memory I recalled the doll shows that *Vogue* had given in 1896, '97, and '98. Those miniature ladies had been dressed by New York houses, [so] I had an idea. Jumping down from the bus, I hastened to Mr. Henri Bendel. His shop was the smartest in New York and his clientele was a social register of fashion. Mr. Bendel had recently established himself in Fifty-seventh Street, at that time an exclusive residential district, which he was the first to invade commercially.

He had vision, taste, and courage and was greatly respected in the fashion world in both America and France. His heart was undoubtedly as sad as mine for our unfortunate friends in Paris, but he too had a business situation to meet and I felt that my idea might temporarily solve both our problems and benefit France at the same time. I said, "Mr. Bendel, if *Vogue* organizes an exhibition of original designs, created by the best New York houses and presented on living models, charges admission, and devotes the proceeds to a French charity, will you head the list of exhibitors?" I knew that if Bendel consented the other houses would fall into line. Armed with his agreement, I flew back to the office embroidering my plans as I went.

Thus began the first Fashion Fête, an elaborate three-day benefit in early November of 1914 at the Ritz-Carlton hotel, with food, drink, and music, in which more than a hundred garments—dresses, gowns, hats, even swimwear—were shown in various tableau, and then auctioned off,

Women's Wear article about the Fashion Fête of 1914, which promoted American designers

with the proceeds going to the Committee of Mercy, a fund set up to aid European women and children "left destitute" by the war. Many of capital-S Society's most prominent women lent patronage, and Chase tasked a seven-woman jury made up of some of the city's known style setters—including Mrs. William K. Vanderbilt, Mrs. Hamilton Fish Webster, and Mrs. Harry Payne Whitney (a.k.a. Gertrude Vanderbilt Whitney, who later founded the Whitney Museum of Art)—to vet which designs could be shown. The opening night gala garnered a crowd of some 700 swells. *Women's Wear* gave it front-page coverage and spelled out the event's implications beyond raising aid money: "The exclusive American society woman who hitherto has been dressed by Paris couturiers is at present in a receptive mood toward American styles . . . and the object of the organizers of the Fashion Fete has been to make the occasion a coming-out event for original American creators, by giving them an extraordinary opportunity to appear before the most exclusive clientele of the country: To bring together these two elements, the American fashion originator and the customer to be catered to, with charity as immediate object, and with a view to the development . . . of American fashions has been the double purpose of the Fete." The publication hoped the showing would assert that "American designers and dressmakers have original ideas which would develop under a favorable stimulus into a nucleus for American styles."

Some of Bendel's competitors who exhibited included Gimbel Brothers, Tappe, Thurn, John Wanamaker, Knox Hat Co., and Bergdorf Goodman. Henri, whose store was represented by several dresses including an "afternoon gown" in ecru velvet, didn't attend the Fashion Fête himself, but he followed it closely and praised it the morning after. "I think it a good move," he told *Women's Wear,* "and that it will show its influence in the spring. It will have the effect of establishing the confidence of the American women in the ability of the American dressmakers generally." As proof, he mentioned having received seven or eight calls about specific dresses, and it was not yet 10 a.m.

In a newspaper article about the operetta *Adele*, which featured gowns from Poiret, Callot, and Premet that Bendel had helped the producer procure in Paris the previous spring, Henri further indulged the idea of American designers stepping up. "Why is it," he asked, "that the American tailors have never been able to compete with the Frenchmen in developing these wonderful creations for feminine beauty? Is it that the American modiste is a coward? Does he lack the courage to originate and create his own ideas? There is an old saying that 'necessity is the mother of invention,' and perhaps now that gowns from foreign shores are becoming rare, [domestic designers] will recover their pluck and produce something that is worthy of America. At the present time it seems that they are striving to this end."

But Bendel's commitment to Paris fashion—and to the people who create it—wasn't in doubt. "I have ordered millions of dollars' worth of models and fabrics from France," he said. "The women over there have worked for me and with me . . . with ceaseless faithfulness. . . . Now they are suffering a horrible fate of desolation and destruction. Imagine me contriving how I could take away from them whatever they shall find themselves able to furnish; imagine me advising this American house or mill, and that enterprise, how to get a wedge in, to make a gain out of the losses abroad and a still greater handicap when the workers of France stagger back to their work, facing the disabling circumstances . . . [and] where familiar faces used to greet them! No! I am instead giving work for several years ahead to the fabric people, leaving an ample margin for [new designs]; so that they shall at least have my orders when they find themselves able and in need to begin."

Loyalty to the couturiers—and to France in general—was sacrosanct to Henri. "Anything it is in my power to do or to give, I am ready to do or give," he said. "I can't emphasize it enough: Nothing would make it seem right to me to abandon the source and means of my business success, now in the hour of [their] trouble, even though standing by them cost me great personal inconvenience."

And, really, what other position would he take? The Fashion Fête marked a minor milestone in the evolution of American fashion, but it was not a revolution—hardly even a warning shot fired in the direction of French couture. Many of the New York patronesses interviewed at the event made a point of saying, as *Women's Wear* put it, "that under no circumstances would they forsake Paris." Nevertheless, as the war dragged on, domestic-produced fashion did get a boost. As Caroline Seebohm writes in her book *The Man Who Was Vogue: The Life and Times of Condé Nast,* with the help of dress merchants such as Bergdorf Goodman and Henri Bendel, the period of 1914 to 1918 could be considered "the beginning of America's stylistic coming of age."

Around the time of the Fête the buzz about American design asserting itself had reached Parisian ears. If it caused *un peu* anxiety, the couturiers weren't letting on. As one slyly said, "Does Mr. Bendel say that New York will replace Paris?" But the question of course was rhetorical. "It's all nonsense to talk of 'American fashions for American women,'" Henri told *Women's Wear* in a burst of candor. "America is a great country for business enterprise. Our men and women have clever business heads. But as for creative genius in fashions—it hasn't come yet."

Henri's devotion not just to French fashion but to European culture and aesthetics in general found its reflection in his newest domicile, a sprawling and lavish apartment at 525 West End Avenue at Eighty-Fifth Street, on the Upper West Side, just around the corner from where he had been living. When the twelve-story apartment building was being constructed, Bendel had made

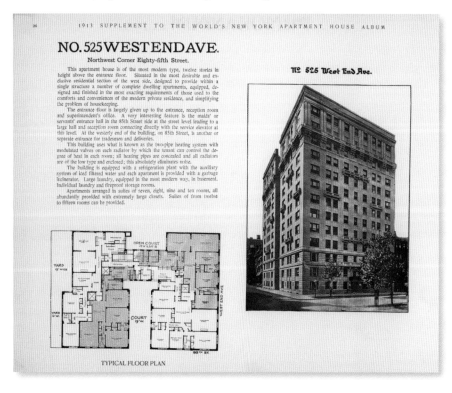

Bendel's deluxe apartment building on the Upper West Side of Manhattan

plans with the owner to lease the entire top floor and have it customized to his liking. This resulted in a fourteen-room, four-bath virtual mansion in the air, into which he moved in 1914. The owner even agreed to bump up part of the roofline to create a spacious studio with a mezzanine gallery. Henri filled his new home with treasures that he had been collecting for over a decade on his trips abroad. Walls of the main rooms were hung with seventeenth-century tapestries, including at least one manufactured by Gobelins and designed by Charles Le Brun, the decorator and painter of the court of King Louis XIV. Much of Bendel's furniture was of that French style, combined with a smattering of Tudor, Italian Renaissance, and Spanish pieces. Rare old Spanish velvet covered the walls of the main hallway. A music room accommodated a large pipe organ for Mr. Bastedo to play, and all about were marble statues. Henri had the antiques, including the tapestries, insured for more than $300,000 (nearly $9 million today).

But the crowning glory—literally—was an Italianate roof garden, installed in 1915, which, as the *New York Sun* reported in a feature from July of that year, "probably has not its counterpart anywhere in the world." It had been a dream of Henri's for some time and to realize it he first had to persuade his landlord to allow him the roof rights; accessible roof decks and even those with furniture and plantings were not unheard of in the city, but usually they were communal and not particularly fancy. Henri, of course, had something more fabulous in mind. Thinking of this undertaking as an experiment—and recognizing the logistical challenges—he decided to utilize only half the roof at first, with the ambition to expand later. The result: a 7,500-square-foot garden (actually two gardens, one square and one oblong, connected by a ten-foot pathway) filled with ornamental concrete planters, hedges and shrubs, trellises and lattice walls, antique statuary and other ornamentations, wrought iron tables and chairs, and stone benches.

The *Sun* relished giving its readers tantalizing details: "In a delightful little niche designed especially for it is a Venus done in France in the seventeenth century. Standing almost knee deep in a vast jardiniere filled with pink flowering geraniums she looks about shyly but quite composedly, for what could harm her classic beauty when guarded by a very fierce looking lion from the Borozzi Palace in Venice?" The newspaper spied marble cupids and two terra-cotta vases from Pompei, and a figure of St. Ignatius from a monastery in Dijon. Grapevines spread over wrought iron doors that also had been in the Borozzi Palace. Orange trees stood in handsome planters; hydrangeas exploded out of oversized vases; and border beds brimmed with nasturtiums, cornflowers, marigolds, Sweet William, and phlox—a kaleidoscope of summer color.

The roof deck afforded views in all directions, with the Hudson River and the high bluffs of the New Jersey Palisades sprawled out to the west, and, farther to the south, lower Manhattan and New York Harbor. The East River and Brooklyn could be seen in the distance. It proved ideal for entertaining,

The Sun, Sunday, July 25, 1915.

ITALIAN GARDEN TWELVE STORIES ABOVE NEW YORK STREET

Scene in the Italian garden atop a city roof.

Triumph of Landscape Gardening Effected Atop a Skyscraper Apartment Building

Where fancy carries one to Old World seclusion.

Novel Idea of Henri Bendel and How He Has Worked It Out---Superb View of the City

A few of Mr. Bendel's art treasures. Venus flanked by the Lion of the Borozzi Palace and an ancient balustrade.

and even when Henri served dinner in his dining room, he often began the evening with cocktails on the roof and would bring guests back up for after-dinner coffee. It was a magical place that invoked awe, in part for the extraordinary effort it had taken to hoist up such heavy and valuable objects, and for the transportive effect of the apartment and garden combined. As the *Sun's* reporter noted, "It is only when the visit is over and the elevator stops at the street entrance that one comes to and realizes that one is not in some French chateau or Italian villa but in much more commonplace New York."

As he didn't travel to France in the summer of 1915, owing to the war, Henri savored his own approximation of Continental living with mostly quiet evenings spent floating above the city, tending his plants and, as the *Sun* wrote, "enjoying the respite from business cares in the retreat he has designed for himself atop a city roof." Perhaps it was the fresh air, and being enveloped by greenery and flowers, that nurtured a new dream. This one, too, involved gardens and statuary, but on a far grander scale. From his elegant eagle's perch above West End Avenue, he could probably—on a clear day—even see the perfect spot to put it.

In 1915 the *New York Sun* regaled readers with details of Henri's unprecedented roof garden above his apartment on West End Avenue, the creation of which required herculean hoisting efforts.

Paris Forever

By

Henri W. Bendel

COPYRIGHTED BY
HENRI BENDEL

Paillettes seem always à la mode. Bendel uses them in bands on the tulle and lace skirt and as the bodice of this dancing gown. A tulle scarf forms the sleeves.

The exaggerated collar and huge pockets are the distinguishing features of the frock of white charmeuse at the left. A touch of vivid colouring is given by the girdle of Roman striped silk.

Black lace and tulle edged with jet are used by Henri Bendel for the skirt of this semi-evening dress in the centre sketch. The bodice is a lovely old blue taffeta under black lace and tulle.

The sash, crossing in front and fastening in the back, is the unusual feature of the sports coat of ashes of roses velvet worn over a white serge plaited skirt.

THE finer instincts for *les Modes* are inherent with the French alone. In acknowledging the preeminence of the Paris designer, the world pays tribute to a genius incomparable and unique—a genius flowering in the ambient traditions of beautiful women and brave cavaliers, drawing inspiration from the matchless treasures of art and priceless documents accumulated by generations of connoisseurs in this city beautiful.

When Napoleon plundered the galleries of Europe, revealing the measure of his conquests by the richness of his spoils, the foundation was laid for modern art. That which Napoleon brought to the Louvre not only stimulated an appreciation of painting and sculpture, but his encouragement of every art and craft was immediately productive of exquisite fabrics and charming designs for woman's apparel. The personality of the Emperor extended even into the shops of the modest couturier.

In succeeding years the French capital seemed in danger of losing prestige as the fountain source of fashion. The days of the restored monarchy were stormy. Revolution and riot followed in rapid suc-

cession as the nation struggled to find itself. Such turmoil was reflected in eccentricities of dress. But with the advent of the Second Empire, a change for the better became apparent. An effort was made to restore the brilliancy and elegance of the reign of the first Napoleon and Eugénie attempted to reestablish the French court as the dictator of fashion. But the Empress had a rival in England who exercised a powerful influence and withheld from Paris part of her sovereignty in fashion. Queen Victoria had her own ideas about the proper garb for women.

But the genius of France speedily overcame this influence and began to glow and flash until once again it drew to itself the eyes of the world. Before long admirers from every land were besieging the doors of Paris couturiers. Never before was there such a triumph for originality and art! Out of chaos the French designer, by the force of sheer merit and ability, created the modern school of dressmaking.

Perhaps the heritage of the past has contributed as much to the preeminence of this authority as individual ability and the influence of that beauty, which is Paris. For centuries the children have been trained in the art of making fine laces, embroideries and tapestries. This training is amplified by a culture inbred by contact with remarkable works of art and access to libraries from which ideas can be obtained and transmuted into new forms. Then there is the atmosphere and spirit of Paris from which emanates good taste in all things. And by no means least is a fine appreciation of the fitness of things.

As for the future of fashions, it will be as I said at the beginning, Paris forever! Her sovereignty is the gift of temperament and tradition. The supremacy she enjoys cannot successfully be assailed.

CHAPTER 7

VIVE LA FRANCE, VIVE LA BROADWAY

𝒜S THE UNITED STATES WARILY WATCHED the conflict in Europe and braced for the possibility of being drawn in, industry and innovation surged nationwide, and New York City set the pace. Bendel, too, went into high gear, supporting the war effort, expanding his product lines and customer base, and selling not just style but glamour by way of old and new entertainment mediums. He would expand privately as well, with a spectacular new house and new people to fill it.

Back in the winter of 1915, as the war's front moved far from Paris, Bendel and Bastedo had managed to make a buying trip. "The display this year was as splendid as in times of peace," Henri told the *New York Tribune* as he stepped off RMS *Adriatic* in Manhattan upon their return (along with fellow first-class passenger Gertrude Vanderbilt Whitney, whose disembarkation was also reported). "I never saw finer models, and every big dressmaking establishment in the city participated enthusiastically in the display." That year *Women's Wear* declared that Bendel was "the biggest buyer of high-class merchandise in Paris."

But the store had long positioned itself to offer a range of products and not just for New York women who could pay for Parisian gowns. As far back as the early aughts Bendel had offered, wholesale, some of his hats and dresses to other stores around the country which would sell them under the Bendel label. Throughout the 1910s and '20s, beyond larger markets such as Philadelphia, Boston, New Orleans, and Dallas (where he was carried by Neiman Marcus), women from the likes of Montgomery, Alabama; Kalamazoo, Michigan; Bellingham, Washington; and Macon, Georgia, could procure a genuine Bendel hat or garment. Local newspaper ads and fashion coverage played up the cachet. In January of 1915, the *Kansas City Star* reprinted a short piece from *Vogue* about new taffeta "dance frocks" for winter holidays in warm climes that declared, "Henri Bendel is ever in the van of the mode." The style-minded ladies of Kansas City and beyond could buy a Bendel garment locally and feel that they, too, were in the vanguard.

OPPOSITE: In a 1916 article in *Harper's* Bendel extolled the triumph of history-steeped Parisian designers and their "genius incomparable and unique."

Bendel was one
of the first dress
merchants to
extend his brand
with soaps and
perfumes, such as
these from a 1925
ad in *Vogue*.

Bendel was one of the first dress merchants to extend his brand with soaps and perfumes, such as these from a 1925 ad in *Vogue*.

That year Bendel launched his first perfume, Un Peu D'Elle, which was made in Paris. Eventually there would be about sixteen more scents, such as Ma Violette, Mon Jasmin, and No. 15, an homage to—or friendly capitalizing upon—Coco Chanel's distinctive No. 5. According to Sally Robbins, "Henri sketched exquisite designs for the perfume bottles, some of which were manufactured by Baccarat." He also created a house soap that became another Bendel signature. Such innovations extended his brand and offered merchandise at an attainable price point.

His influence even reached abroad as he offered wholesale millinery supply not only to shops in the United States but to some in Canada, Cuba, and South America.

Still, Bendel didn't take his eyes off his premier customers, women of means from the East Coast. In July of 1915 he contributed gowns to an elaborate fundraising fashion show held in Newport, Rhode Island, where the elite of New York and Boston and beyond lolled away summers on the terraces and lawns of seaside mansions coyly called cottages. In a season of endless croquet, picnics, and parties, this benefit for the French war effort at Rose Cliff, the Stanford White-designed mansion of Mrs. Hermann Oelrichs, set a new bar. Hundreds of guests wearing their summer finest, plus corsages of ribbons in the colors of the French flag, came up the long drive by motorcar or carriage to behold a festively decorated house and grounds with tented seating, a full orchestra on a bandstand, and an elaborate spread of fine pastries and an elegant tea service. Soon they were being treated to an hours-long show all around them, a series of *tableaux vivants* wherein both society women and models

enacted scenes invoking antiquity, mythology, and travel, while sporting outfits from prominent American dress and fashion houses. Akin to a play, it had
a title: "Fashion's Passing Show." Even *Vogue* wasn't sure what that meant exactly, but the magazine slavishly devoted fourteen pages to the fête and praised
Bendel's "remarkably beautiful afternoon toilettes," which included a dress of
black lace over blue chiffon; a gown of pink velvet; a tea gown with an over-
dress embroidered in pearls; and the standout: a white satin dress with rose and
white embroidery named "Tokio" for its Japanese-inspired stylings, worn by
"'the stately Josephine' as everyone calls Bendel's tall dark manikin, she of the
lacquered black tresses and the matte white skin." *Vogue* deemed the dress "a
wholly original and delightfully wearable creation."

In late summer, when the *Vogue* piece came out, Henri, alas, could
hardly savor the victory and the good press, as the spell of fashion and frivol-
ity was shattered by a call that he received on September 4, informing him
that his mother, Mary Falk, had died. It was a shock. At seventy-six, she was
still very active and had seemed strong and quite herself just the night before she passed away, as those in Lafayette who were near her attested. Mrs.
Falk's obituary credited her with having built up "one of the largest and most
successful businesses" in town and wrote that "she was indeed a 'mother of
Israel' and her exemplary life and noble acts will long be cherished by her
children as well as the community." It praised her "genial disposition" and
"generous nature."

Bendel gowns
featured
prominently in
an elaborate
fundraiser at a
private home in
Newport, Rhode
Island, in 1915
in which society
ladies modeled
the clothes.

Four generations of Plonsky women: Henri's mother, Mary Plonsky Bendel Falk (RIGHT), her daughter, Lena Bendel Levy (LEFT), Lena's daughter, Myrtle Levy Meyer (TOP), and Myrtle's infant daughter, Marjorie Meyer, circa 1915

Mary Falk had given Henri love, security, family, confidence, and know-how—she had been his best role model in how to run a mercantile business. In every sense she had made him, and her passing must have been devastating. The weight of his grief and the depth of his devotion were made three-dimensional a few years later, in 1918, when Henri paid homage to his mother, father, and his beloved stepfather Benjamin Falk by commissioning for their mausoleum a dramatic monument set on massive granite steps that featured larger-than-life-size bronze figures—a woman throwing herself on the steps in sorrow, and, above her, a towering angel. Under the hands of the weeping lady are two wreathes intertwined with a banner that reads "mother" and "father." Designed by a French artist named Charles Lemarquier and fabricated in Italy, *Angel and Mourner* was shipped to New Orleans before traveling by train to Lafayette, where it was installed by the A. Weiblen Marble & Granite Company of New Orleans. To this day it dominates the Hebrew Rest cemetery. Visible past a high fence and shrubberies, it stands out not

Several years after Henri's mother died, he commissioned a monument, *Angel and Mourner*, for her grave in Lafayette, which ultimately would commemorate both of his parents and his stepfather.

only for its height and artfulness but also because angels are not a common motif in Jewish cemeteries. In 1926, Henri and his brother Ike donated money for improvements to the small cemetery, and at about that time he had an inscription added to the monument: "To the glory of God and in sacred memory of our beloved mother Mary Bendel Falk, 1839–1915." In an earlier gesture of tribute to his mother shortly after she died, Henri, who had been giving money and supporting the French in their war efforts, donated an ambulance to France in Mary Bendel Falk's name.

In January 1916, Bendel made his commitment to that country vividly clear when *Harper's Bazar* ran a two-page fashion spread and attendant column entitled "Vive la France" with his byline ("*par* Henri Bendel"). The captions under the six dresses shown were written in English, but his impassioned essay was entirely in French. "France will always be the arbiter of fashion," he wrote.

> I am not one of those who has sought to take away her supremacy . . . and I think the greatest genius of her designs is not just what they are unto themselves, but what they inspire in other designers [abroad]. . . . When I think of this beautiful, ravaged country, think of her heroic calm and her absence of complaints, I realize that she who now endures all her sufferings with Spartan courage was once the spoiled child, flattered, encouraged to live only to spread beauty and joy in the universe. In the whirlwind that is business and commerce, France continues to preserve the ideals of elegant living, and until the end of time we will hear the echo 'Vive la France.'

A month later he penned another essay in *Harper's*, this one in English, called "Paris Is Forever," in which he looked at France's history and art and argued that "the finer instincts for les Modes are French alone." He called the French designer "a genius flowering in the traditions of beautiful women and brave cavaliers, drawing inspiration from the matchless treasures of art and priceless documents accumulated by generations of connoisseurs in this city beautiful." He praised the "heritage of the past" and training "in contact with remarkable works of art and access to libraries from which ideas can be obtained and transmuted into new forms. Then [too] there is the atmosphere and spirit of Paris from which emanates good taste in all things."

And he drew a direct arrow from that aesthetic culture to the clothes he was seeing now in the couture ateliers. "Paris has transcended expectations this spring," he had told the *Millinery Trade Review* that January, "for her artists and designers—most of them women, of course—have applied their genius to production, even under the handicap of a devastating war, and have given

A feathery dress and matching coat from Chanel's fall collection of 1920

us such styles, such flowers, such chapeaux, as have never been seen before." One of those women was Gabrielle "Coco" Chanel, who was just starting out as a dressmaker in Paris; her startlingly original marrying of fitted jackets, sailor-and-fisherman outfit flourishes, pared-down silhouettes, and innovative, stretchable cotton jersey would soon revolutionize women's fashion. By a number of accounts Bendel was the first to show her creations in the United States, probably starting in 1915, about four years before she officially registered as a couturier in Paris. By 1917 Bendel's was promoting her in ads and fashion editorials, and in the early '20s he was selling and copying (with permission) her dresses regularly, as evidenced by dated sketches of Chanel garments in the Bendel collection (now held by the Brooklyn Museum).

Bendel too was transcending expectations. In 1913, its first year, the Fifty-Seventh Street store brought in sales of $3 million, double what it had done in its Fifth Avenue location, and by 1916 that number would rise to $5 million. Henri was widening his footprint as well. Newly a member of the Fifth Avenue Association, a business booster group, along with Bonwit Teller and B. Altman, he spent $250,000 to purchase an existing building at 14 West Fifty-Seventh Street, next door to his current store, to tear it down and build a ten-story addition. With such ambitions his attention was now being tugged in dozens of directions. Asked by the *Millinery Trade Review* whether he planned to go to market in Paris in the spring, he replied, "I hope to do so, but I cannot tell just yet how my building activities, or the war, may interfere with that plan. Mr. Blish, our personal representative, now over there, is expected to reach these shores on the first of March—returning to familiarize himself with affairs over here, and I may go back in his place. . . . Mr. Miller and Mr. Bastido [*sic*] look after our millinery department, and except for my building intentions, I have no reason not to be deterred from going."

He explained to the publication why he needed to grow the physical store. "We are much too crowded here," he said, "and the additional floor space will enable us to carry on our enlarged business with dignity and circumspection. . . . We need more elevators and more width. At present our wholesale activities are conducted at the rear of this main floor, and buyers

Forecasting

By HENRI BENDEL

A—Bendel faces a modish white straw hat with black straw and makes the crown of white feathers.

B—Le dernier cri is a green taffeta parasol edged with fringe and laced with taffeta ribbon.

C—Carry a rose chiffon crêpe parasol with black velvet bands and white bamboo handle and be completely fetching.

D—"A transparent hat?" Nothing better—appliqué Leghorn straw on black malines and add a single wax rose.

E—Embroider dark blue chiffon voile in old silver, use flesh-coloured muslin for the vest, undersleeves and underskirt and add a taffeta collar. Black straw hat faced with white and trimmed with bird of paradise.

F—Shimmery blue faille is embroidered with gold threads and beads; the inside collar is of flesh muslin, the facing of gold braid. Hat edged with velvet and trimmed with uncurled ostrich.

G—With a pale grey chiffon frock, embroidered in the same colour, is worn a flesh-coloured chiffon underwaist trimmed with two narrow bands of gold braid. African brown straw hat with brown velvet bow and sours.

H—A black and white striped chiffon has a half-length panel of black chiffon in front and back, double satin collar, and jade girdle set in old metal. Black chiffon hat faced with horsehair; crown and bow of black silk.

Drawings by Natalie and Marguerite Gaubert

THE mention of velvets and woolens in July is] usually avoided as if it were an indelicacy, yet at this season we have to begin thinking about heavy fabrics and planning a fall wardrobe.

Even in America there is less racing, less public life, and more and more of festivity screened behind the sheltering walls of villas, as in Italy. The echoes that reach the outside world bring little news of change and no inspiration, hardly even the old demand for something new.

Lines are second in importance to fabrics. If I could have taken you with me through three of the greatest fabric houses in the world you would

Copyright, 1916, Harper's Bazar for July

realise that the die has already been cast and that the wonderful silks, velvets, brocades and cloth of gold shot with silver and iridescent colours, manufactured by these houses, mean a return, at least in materials, to the days of the Second Empire; there are vivid reds and robin's egg blues brocaded with huge silver roses; there are stiff plain velvets and satins brocaded in velvet. The mixed or Persian brocades are *passé*, and the rage is for the single flower or motif.

Most beautiful of all are the ribbons with velvet flowers on satin foundations; they are intended for entire gowns. There are also superb braids that are almost like lace, with designs in rose patterns.

Still and rich as are the materials for evening wear, the new fabrics for the street are mostly of clinging weaves. Woolens are soft, often ribbed; the variety is not great, but they meet the American woman's demand for supple weaves for street wear.

There is a marked tendency toward extreme simplicity in the gowns ordered by fashionable women. I note, among my patrons, the same moderation that characterizes the taste of the Frenchwoman of to-day, but here in America it is less the art that creates an impression of beauty out of almost nothing than the simplicity that spells extravagance—elaborate eyelet embroidery, filet and embroidered nets, and a wealth of lace that must be unadorned.

A *Harper's* column by Bendel in September 1916 touting richly hued velvets, satins, and brocades he had seen in Paris

from all over the United States avail themselves of the unusual opportunities we offer, to procure not only well-selected French models, but also originals devised in our workrooms, where exclusive styles are developed by eight designers—four of them French— and a competent corps of copyists." Demolition of the existing house was to begin in April. The new building was designed to be "an exact counterpart of this one," said Henri, with a ten-and-a-half-story elevation and "possibly some requisite changes of façade, in order to obtain conformity and harmony."

Remarkably, this expansion was not the biggest construction project Henri had going. His enthusiasm for beautiful gardens and gracious open-air living, which he had nurtured on his rooftop on West End Avenue the previous summer, had led him to an ambitious plan—building his own country estate—which he effectively announced in that same interview with the *Millinery Trade Review.* "Yes," he confirmed, "I have bought a place down at Great Neck, Long Island . . . right on the Sound, just 45 minutes from Broadway by motor, and shall begin the work of tearing down [the existing house] immediately."

Great Neck and neighboring communities along the Long Island Sound were where some of America's most prominent old money families and new money titans of industry owned, or were building, grand estates—names such as Gould, Guggenheim, Whitney, and Woolworth. Former President Teddy Roosevelt's home, Sagamore Hill, was less than twenty miles down the road, near Oyster Bay. This area of rolling meadows and meticulously trimmed lawns would come to be called the Gold Coast. It was *Great Gatsby* territory, and in fact F. Scott and Zelda Fitzgerald lived in Great Neck from 1922 to 1924. Henri's announcement of plans to build a house in the township of Kings Point was not only evidence of his wealth but also a declaration of his arrival at the top of the New York heap. Which essentially meant the top of the American heap.

Asked by the *Millinery Trade Review* what style of architecture he was planning, Henri volunteered, "My ideal of a country residence is the Italian villa, and a very attractive plan—to be developed in white stone with arched colonnades extending out in wings on each side—has been submitted to me and approved." The architect Bendel chose was Henry Otis Chapman,

Henri's crowning glory, a beaux arts mansion beside the Long Island Sound

Henri walking his property on a winter day

who had built Henri's Fifty-Seventh Street store and who worked in a range of styles; he designed several prominent office buildings, banks, and churches in Manhattan. But whatever Italianate model Bendel was envisioning, in the end his love of French style won out. Ultimately the house that Chapman designed was of the fashionable beaux arts variety, based on French neoclassicism along with baroque and Renaissance influences.

Bendel had acquired the property late in 1915: twelve lush acres with 400 feet of water frontage on a promontory called Elm Point. The previous owner's far smaller house was knocked down so that R.H. Howes Construction Co., Bendel's builder, could spend nearly two years creating what would be Henri's waterfront Xanadu—which by one news account he dubbed Henriour, and by another, Fair Lodge. The white stucco house, with a footprint of 85 by 150 feet, sat commandingly atop a hill with views of the Sound and New York City in the distance. With arched first-floor windows and an arcaded loggia, it was designed around a large and wide two-story central hall with a wrap-around mezzanine, from which the main rooms radiated out. "Vistas leading out to the water, as well as to the formal entrance and gardens, serve as an extension of the central axis," according to *Beaux-Arts Estates, A Guide to the Architecture of Long Island* by Liisa and Donald Sclare.

The house, photographed after Henri's era, when Walter Chrysler had added an in-ground pool

Long Island Luxury Writ Large

Bendel's rapid accumulation of wealth manifested itself unshyly in his beaux arts mansion at Kings Point, New York, completed in 1917. Big, blinding white, and tailored with an arcaded loggia, Palladian doorway, quoined corners, and second-story balustrades, the stately house, perched above the Long Island Sound, epitomized gracious living: thoroughly modern in its comforts, resolutely Old Europe in its affect. Henri's around-the-cove or down-the-road neighbors bore names synonymous with American money and might, such as mining scion Daniel Guggenheim; paleontologist and steel heir Childs Frick; and Gertrude Vanderbilt (who would found the Whitney Museum of Art) and her businessman husband, Harry Payne Whitney, whose elegant stables in nearby Old Westbury nurtured champion racehorses. Whether he called it Henriour or Fair Lodge or just "my country place," Bendel's house helped mint what came to be known as the Gold Coast.

The Gatsby-worthy terrace facing the Sound

The imposing main gates were created by acclaimed Samuel Yellin Ironworks, which executed lots of decorative metalwork installed in and around the house.

The twelve apostles of Christ appear in an iron window grille outside the music room.

The great central hall was both an entrance and an entertaining space.

Architect Henry Otis Chapman, who had worked on Bendel's Fifty-Seventh Street store, designed the house in a near-symmetrical configuration with a two-story central hall featuring a wrap-around interior balcony and extra-large common spaces, including a double height, Gothic-ceilinged music room conceived for a built-in pipe organ. Terraces, patios, and the loggia afforded maximum appreciation of nature and views of the Sound. Upstairs held six bedrooms for family and guests plus several more for servants, as well as a library. In the basement one found a swimming pool, massage room, and billiards parlor. Out buildings included green houses, an eight-car garage, and extra staff lodging. There's no evidence that Henri had any big enthusiasm for boating, but a boathouse and 150-foot-long pier were almost de rigueur for such a lavish property.

The view of the music room from an upstairs interior balcony

All common rooms had fireplaces,
including the dining room.

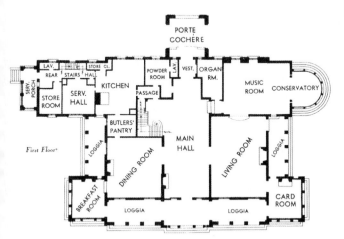

PORTE COCHÈRE

First Floor

The living room was positioned
two steps down from the central hall.

The wood-paneled library

Second Floor

Guest bedrooms weren't particularly large,
but they were ornate.

The home featured such built-in artistry as an elegant marble gallery, an imported carved marble fireplace surround, and paintings set into highly decorative paneling, or *boiserie*.

On the first floor, the main hall opened onto a living room, a large dining room, a card room, a conservatory, and a Gothic music room that included a large built-in Estey organ that would have been, to Henri and Abraham, the soul of the house. In a pre-electronics age, the organ was specially engineered to direct the music throughout the home presumably via echo ducts.

Fourteen bedrooms, including several for servants, and ten bathrooms spread out over the three residential floors. Each public room featured a huge fireplace, with some of the mantle work brought over from Europe. A powder room and coat room flanked the foyer. Upstairs held two sitting rooms and a library. In the basement were a laundry room, a billiards room, a swimming pool with dressing rooms for male and female guests, a massage room, and a "steam cabinet." Formal gardens framed the house and down the hill, on a natural plateau, was a terrace with steps leading down to the swimmable Sound. Adjacent to the house was an eight-car garage. Elegant and capacious greenhouses by Lord & Burnham, probably the foremost plant conservatory designer/manufacturer in America, blended seamlessly with the house and grounds.

For Americas' leading importer of foreign fashion, Bendel's new home was the ultimate import: a full-scale homage to the great houses (and palaces and castles) that Henri had fallen in love with on his many trips to Europe. And a proper setting to display the furniture, silver, art, and rare tapestries that he had hauled back to America. But building a pile in the country was not just an exercise in vanity or might; it was a way to offer space and luxury to a family—Henri's new, and some might say unorthodox, family.

In April of 1915 William Levy, the husband of Bendel's half sister Emma Falk, committed suicide, leaving her, at thirty-six, widowed with two children—daughter Florye, eleven, and son Benjamin, seven. Henri always had a fondness for Emma and now he had a chance to help her out by inviting her and the children to move to New York from their home in Lafayette and live with him. This was possibly not altogether selfless. By the time they

arrived—likely in early 1916—and moved into the
apartment on West End Avenue, Henri's construction
of his Kings Point house was well underway. Family lore
posits that even as he wanted to give Emma a boost, he
may have desired having a woman to help run the huge
house. Yet in a nobler vein, Henri clearly craved a family, considering that he eventually took guardianship of
the children. Benjamin was renamed Henri Bendel II,
whom everyone took to calling Little Henri.

In taking legal and practical responsibility for the
youngsters, Bendel not only provided them with top-
flight educations and secured futures—eventually he enrolled Florye in the Ossining School, a boarding school in
Westchester County, New York, and Little Henri went off
to the Peddie School, a well-regarded boarding school in
Hightstown, New Jersey—but he was giving himself heirs,
and perhaps a veneer of conventionality. He might once
again be seen to the world as a family man, as he had been
when he married Blanche all those years ago. Henri, now
forty-eight, had likely given up on acquiring a conven-
tional family with children and wouldn't have expected to
gain one this deep into middle age. His new household, a
blending of blood family and chosen, must have felt like a
miraculous second chance. This change of affairs did not,
however, push Mr. Blish nor Mr. Bastedo out of the picture.
After all, there was plenty of space to go around. The 1920
Census lists both Bastedo and Blish as "boarders," along
with Henri, Florye, fifteen, Little Henri, eleven, plus about
ten live-in servants. (In 1917 one of those servants, a butler named Walter Priess, took advantage of Henri's being
in Europe and stole $15,000 worth of valuables, including
bed linen, twenty suits of clothing, some very pricey un-
derwear, two Panama hats, and an antique lace tablecloth
valued at $5,000. Priess was duly prosecuted but only some
of the possessions were recovered.)

Who back then might have known of the unusual
dynamics at play in that great edifice of a house, behind
imposing gates and tall hedges? And what would they
have made of it? Perhaps in certain theatrical or literary circles in New York—a club that Henri held at least
guest privileges in—homosexuality was acknowledged
and nervously accepted. But it would've been spoken of

Benjamin Levy, not too long after he moved
with his mother, Emma, and sister, Florye, to
New York from Lafayette and was renamed
Henri Bendel II

"Little Henri" and his sister Florye Levy,
whose name was changed to Florye Bendel

sotto voce, if at all. In an era in which widowers (such as Henri), bachelors, and "spinsters" often shared a home and a life with "companions," the arrangement would not automatically be presumed to be of an amorous nature. And no letters or diaries have emerged to reveal exactly how Henri's relationship with both men manifested itself. Whatever the interpersonal dynamics and however they may have evolved over time, the arrangement was discreet. And Bendel's public stature, great wealth, and natural mien of deep propriety would've silenced idle speculation. He could, to a high degree, live as he liked with impunity. Membership in such organizations as the National Association of Gardeners, the Merchants' Association of New York, Trustees of the Aged and Infirm Hebrews, and later his Masonic order (Union Lodge No. 5 of the A.F & A. M. in Stamford, Connecticut), as well as his attending All Saints church, put his reputation above reproach.

His own extended family, it turns out, knew the truth and accepted it without much fuss, and members of his clan were more than happy to take advantage of his open arms and plentiful guest rooms, with various ones coming up for extended stays at Kings Point. A photo from the era shows Henri in swim attire with his sister Emma, Emma's daughter Florye, and his niece Josie Kahn. Several relatives even moved to New York. At some point Henri's nephew Edward Schmulen had come up to work at the store

Henri with (FROM LEFT) niece Josie Kahn (daughter of his sister Rose), sister Emma, and Emma's daughter Florye in swimming attire, down by the Sound

alongside his older brother, Leon, and by 1917 their parents, Fanny and Gus Schmulen, moved to Long Island, not far from Henri's place. (Before leaving Louisiana, they sold their successful clothing store to merchant Maurice Heymann, who would become Lafayette's most prominent clothing retailer as well as a commercial properties developer and philanthropist.)

Back in Manhattan, Bendel was busier than ever, not only with the store itself and the work of importing, manufacturing, and selling wholesale, but in another aspect of his business that had taken off: costuming for the theater. The world of the stage opened a new avenue for Henri's creativity and another route to expand sales and his reputation. Theater in America in the 1910s came in all styles and sizes ranging from classical drama to low comedies, from light opera to musicals (which hardly resembled today's integrated-story "book" musicals), and to large-chorus extravaganzas like the *Ziegfeld Follies*. Melodramas and drawing room comedies were popular, with upper-crust characters conversing in elegant salons while draped in stylish outfits. Producers would solicit the city's top stores and dressmakers for the leading actresses' wardrobe in exchange for program credit, adding luster to their productions and a bonus for ladies in the audience with a yen for style. As *Harper's Bazar* observed: "The feminine playgoer takes an added interest in a modern play when the actresses are wearing the modes of tomorrow rather than today." Both theater and fashion publications wrote about the "costumes" as they might cover fashion shows in later years, sometimes with comic flair. As a reviewer of 1916's *Our Little Wife* put it: "[Actress] Margaret Illington has placed herself in the hands of Henri Bendel, who has furnished her with two evening gowns, a wrap, a negligee, a street costume and a motor coat to torment mankind in general and her husband in particular."

Henri, like those in his social orbit, may have attended the theater once or twice a week in season, and he would've eagerly seized the opportunity to

Mrs. Parker's Playgoer's Peeve

Even some classic plays and period dramas got the high-fashion treatment in costuming, which could make for a schism between the subject of the play and the anachronistic way in which the actors were garbed. The writer Dorothy Parker, who contributed theater criticism to the popular magazine *Ainslee's* in the early 1920s, took her fabled razor wit to this phenomenon in her review of *Mary Stuart*, invoking Bendel.

❝About the most helpful thing that an actress can do for her audience is to look the part. An audience has a hard enough time in the world, straining pathetically to keep a hold on what few illusions it may. And it seems unnecessarily rough on the poor souls when the star impersonating Jeanne, the French peasant lass who has worked in the fields up to the time that the Americans came, insists upon wearing a Bendel gown, had a Marcel wave half an hour old in her hair, and gesticulates with white enameled hands ending in fingernails polished to a blinding point."

Parker's comical grousing didn't change anything; audiences loved the fantasy, and the style preview.

Star Ina Claire, costumed by Bendel in *The Golddiggers* on Broadway in 1919

make his own contributions to this exciting art. Fittingly enough, one of the first shows in which his name appears in the playbill was a revival of a popular play called *Mlle. Modiste*, back in 1913—modiste being a now-obsolete word for a fashionable milliner or dressmaker. The comic operetta centered on Fifi, a "beautiful hat shop heroine," as one magazine referred to her. That same year, renowned producer David Belasco, a friend of Henri's, commissioned gowns from him suitable for the middle-aged stars of the play *Years of Discretion*. Reported the *Washington Herald*: "During the months that Mr. Belasco was rehearsing his players, Bendel was laboring over the designing and executing of the most sumptuous wardrobe ever worn in a 'society drama.'"

Deep into the 1920s, Bendel himself or Bendel's the store was credited with contributing designs to at least two dozen plays or musicals, including the opera *Adele* (1914) and many comic plays such as *The Great Pursuit* ('16), *A Successful Calamity* ('17), *Lightnin'* ('18), *The Little Blue Devil* ('19), *Go Easy, Mabel* ('22), and *Mary, Mary, Quite Contrary* ('23), and *Kid Boots* ('24), produced by impresario Florenz Ziegfeld and starring Eddie Cantor. In a 1920 show called *Honey Girl*, the actress Cissie Sewall sported a blue and green voile skirt with a silver lace underskirt and, reported one review, "to complete this dream of a dancing frock Henri Bendel has added a corsage of silver cloth, studding it in jewels, and has girdled the waistline in feathers."

There were perhaps dozens more shows, unrecorded, or for whom Bendel provided the dresses without credit. None of the productions Bendel costumed made a lasting contribution to the theatrical canon, but they proved satisfying diversions to their audiences. *The Golddiggers,* a racy 1919 comedy produced by Belasco and featuring Ina Claire, a big star, stood out from the pack; it had a long run then toured for years and was made into a string of movies. Yet each play, no matter how short a run it had, proved to be a branding asset for Bendel who must have lapped it up when *Harper's Bazar,* writing about 1915's *Unchastened Woman,* asked naughtily, "What woman, wearing the gown designed for Emily Stevens by Henri Bendel, could ever become chastened?"

"The stage is the greatest factor in the world of fashion," Henri would tell a reporter in the 1920s. "The well-dressed woman on the stage is the mirror for fashion-seeking women everywhere."

Designed for **Billie Burke** *by* **Henri Bendel**

For her moving-picture play. These gowns are shown exclusively in Harper's Bazar.

Costumes by Bendel for Billie Burke's film *Gloria's Romance*, shown exclusively in *Harper's* in 1915

The new medium of moving pictures was snatching actresses from the New York theater and turning them into stars, so naturally Bendel was recruited to help costume films, too. He's only credited on a handful, including a silent melodrama with Norma Talmadge, but several made a splash. For her 1916 hit feature *Gloria's Romance,* Billie Burke—the wife of Florenz Ziegfeld and who was later immortalized as Glinda the Good Witch in *The Wizard of Oz*—sported gowns by Bendel as well as by Balcon and Lucile, together valued at more than $40,000, or about a million dollars today. Burke also wore Bendel dresses in editorial fashion spreads and in Bendel's ads. As did the actress Elsie Janis, who modeled a Bendel dress in an ad promoting Yo San fabric. In D. W. Griffith's 1920 silent classic *Way Down East*, before Lillian Gish famously struggles atop treacherous ice floes, she dazzles in finery from Bendel.

Happily complicit in this symbiotic relationship between the performing arts, the fashion business, and magazines and newspapers, Henri—beyond costuming shows—loaned dresses to

The great Lillian Gish wore a morning gown designed by Bendel in the 1920 film *Way Down East.*

A sketch for a 1921 stage costume for Billie Burke

stars and starlets for photo shoots, and deployed actresses in his own ads. Many of the names are now forgotten but some were quite big in their day, such as Jane Cowl, Hazel Dawn, and Emmy Whelan. In the *Evening Star* newspaper in Washington, DC, actress Alice Brady modeled a velvet brocade wedding gown from 1885, loaned by Bendel—apparently, he not only collected antique furniture, but he also kept a cache of vintage clothing. Over the years, and long after Henri died, Bendel's would use celebrities in its advertising, and stars would wear clothing from Henri Bendel in fashion layouts—everyone from Tallulah Bankhead and Estelle Winwood to—in more modern times—Lauren Hutton and Naomi Campbell.

In April of 1917, as the country's entry into the war triggered rationing and shortages of goods and some women reined in their extravagant dressing, Henri was asked by *Women's Wear* whether a new austerity might

FROM ENGLAND, PERSIA, AMERICA AND FRANCE

MISS ESTELLE WINWOOD

Who plays the progressive and romantic heroine of "Why Marry" at the Astor Theater, posing in models from Henri Bendel. Miss Winwood is English, the vases in the upper photograph are Persian antiques, the frocks are French and American. Hence the applicability of the large type description over the pictures. As to the clothes: The dance frock is nile green and white chiffon; the organdie is also nile green, with wide bias tucks and blue embroidered bandings. The sports effect is a Premet import of yellow and white hand-knit wool

38

In 1918 the stage and film actress Estelle Winwood posed in Bendel frocks for a fashion spread in *Town & Country* magazine.

affect his sales. He first responded with a playfully epigrammatic (if typical-for-the-era chauvinistic) answer. "Newport will be as gay as ever this summer," he declared, "for the women of society know that if they do not wear handsome clothes there, women in other places will, and the men will go to the other places to see them, instead of going to Newport." But then he went further, revealing his logical—mathematical, really—approach to business. "I cannot see how the incomes of people of the class catered to by houses of our character will be lessened by the war. In fact, I believe a large number of new millionaires will be created by the war conditions. This house has never yet, in its entire history, been able to satisfy the demand for its wares. If, therefore, the women who formerly bought 30 evening gowns should for any reason decide to buy only 12, there will be plenty of other women we have formerly been unable to supply who will thus have a chance to buy our garments."

RIGHT AND
OPPOSITE: Henri's
Harper's article
on "Gowns for the
Newport Season"
in the summer of
1917

Gowns for the
Newport Season

By

Henri W. Bendel

Again the printed chiffon and the Chinese influence! This gown is strikingly effective, thanks to the sleeves and flounce of black embroidered chiffon. The background of the tunic is absinthe, masking the chiffon underslip. There is a great diversity in necks, but the straight line continues popular.

Blue and yellow are the predominating colours in a printed chiffon that shews the Chinese influence most emphatically. With its graceful tunic arranged over a robe of golden yellow lace, this costume was designed for a Newport matron.

THE feminine note will predominate in the summer fashions, although to be sure the sports hour will still call for the regulation plain skirt, blouse and sweater that have been with us for so long. It is safe to say that dresses of white batiste, handkerchief linen and dimity will be de rigueur on all those mornings when something other than a sports suit is necessary.

For the Newport season, for example, morning dresses of sheer batiste, beautified by delicate hand embroidery and Valenciennes lace, will be seen on the Casino lawns, Bailey's Beach and the golf-links. Such dresses will have skirts measuring from two and a half to three yards at the hem, and will be, of course, hand-made. Tiny hand-run tucks, which have quite replaced smocking, are very much in evidence on all lingerie gowns. Tucks, graduating from three inches to one-quarter inch in depth, frequently form the only trimming on the skirts,

Cherries are ripe and red too on this little dance frock of peach chiffon and satin, which is included in a trousseau made for a bride who will spend July in Newport. Draped effects are still the height of the fashion for formal and informal evening gowns when chiffon is the favoured fabric.

Bendel's invoking Newport was more than just his giving an example of a place where stylish women spent time; it was a plug for his latest exploit—a few weeks later, he announced plans to open a satellite store in Newport in the coming July. His wasn't the first prestigious clothing outfit to set up a seasonal-only shop (think pop-up) in a posh vacation resort, but he was quick to recognize the potential for enhanced sales and branding. Always with an eye for the prime location, he situated it in Casino Court, at the corner of tony Bellevue Avenue, the fine shopping street. Then he used his platform

"You go into the home of an American millionaire and it smells of money, but in the home of a French marquis you breathe!"

—*Henri Bendel*

with magazines to reel in the customers. "In casting my mind's eye over the summer," Henri told *Women's Wear,* "I can conceive of no lovelier sight than the Newport Casino on a bright sunny morning with the vivacious younger element playing strenuous tennis before a gathering of those beautifully dressed women who summer in Newport, war or no war."

Yet Henri himself wasn't lounging around Newport or anywhere else for that matter. Even with the war on, summer for him meant buying trips abroad, usually departing in mid-July and returning in September. This ritual was repeated every winter. Ship logs and passport records show Henri, often with Abraham, making the crossing on such liners as the *Adriatic,* the *New York,* and the *Philadelphia.* In April of 1917 he sailed back to New York from Vigo, Spain, on the *Alfonso XII.* A trip to Spain was likely a mostly-pleasure excursion, and an opportunity to shop for antiques and fabrics and gifts for his family.

In September 1917 *Harper's Bazar* announced that it would be showing Bendel garments exclusive to the magazine, along with those of designers Tappé and Lucile (other Bendel fashions naturally continued to appear in *Harper's* chief rival, *Vogue*) and in that same issue Henri wrote a fashion feature about trends he'd seen in Paris, including Chinese, Japanese, and Spanish influences, and the ascendancy of less formal clothing. "American women may look forward . . . to a prolonged season of 'day dresses', 'chemise dresses', 'little dresses'—call them what you will."

When Bendel expanded his store that year (now with the address 10-12-14 West Fifty-Seventh Street) he modernized it for efficiency, and with concern for workers' needs and comfort. A feature in the *Edison Monthly,* a publication of New York's electricity provider, looked behind the scenes, applauding the "subdued illumination" from the brass fixtures with beaded glass bowls, and, in the fitting rooms, tubular bulbs with reflectors "for flattering light." It praised the long workrooms, of which there were three or four on most floors starting on the fourth floor, with large street-facing windows for light and air. "Each workroom with its workers forms a complete unit in itself; in it a costume or garment is cut, fitted to a model, basted, stitched, pressed and given the finishing touches." An elaborate system of irons radiated out from a central electrical trunk, with red lights to remind workers when an iron was still turned on, and cords were held on individual hooks for minimum intrusion. Wide shade and inverted bowl fixtures worked to "brighten corners and throw no shadows" and eliminate the need for drop lights, which "contributes to a certain restfulness that these rooms, despite their busy character, undoubtedly possess, which must have its beneficial effect on both workers and on product." The fur storage unit, lined with cooling pipes and set at a frigid eighteen degrees Fahrenheit, was "powered by its own mini electric plant."

A Henri-penned article on dress and hat trends for winter of 1917 in *Harper's*

A dramatic black silk hat from Bendel's circa 1916–17, now in the collection of the Metropolitan Museum of Art in New York

Airy workrooms with agreeable lighting weren't the only accommodations Bendel was making for his team. The war had compromised many aspects of business, including sales and materials; costs had gone up. A lot of companies had felt pressure to reduce staff rolls. Henri took a different tack by instituting a six-and-a-half-hour workday in the spring of 1917, trimming the normal workday by two hours. That brought workers' pay down a bit (most were paid by the hour), but it meant not having to lay off anyone. Albert Frank, Bendel's manager at the time, told *Women's Wear,* "We employ over 1,200 people, and not one will suffer because of any decline in business. The law permits [a] nine-hour day, but we have never worked our operatives more than 8 and a half hours, and Mr. Bendel now considers it the duty of every merchant to create the impression of industry and not bring about misery by any wholesale cutting of payrolls." A year later Henri himself would reiterate the point, to *Women's Wear*: "I have not dismissed a single employee because of the war."

In mid-October 1918 World War I was just weeks away from its conclusion, but America was still actively confronting the epic conflict's literal costs, so Henri's friend Geraldine Farrar took over Sherry's restaurant (next door to Bendel's old shop on Fifth Avenue) and held a fundraiser for the Liberty Loan war bonds. The Russian ambassador to the United States attended, and President Woodrow Wilson sent a message of support. Financier J. P. Morgan initiated the bidding at $100,000. Henri pledged next, offering $50,000 (he eventually bought $200,000 worth of bonds that night). Farrar sang "My Country 'Tis of Thee" and a total of $4 million in bonds were sold in one evening.

On November 11, 1918, when Germany signed an armistice with the Allies, bringing the war to its conclusion and the world breathed a collective sigh, repercussions in the American fashion business were immediate and up-tempo. "In the language of the small boy," Bendel told *Women's Wear* that month,

Two sketches from 1917: a Callot ensemble (TOP) and a Pierre Bulloz outfit (BOTTOM)

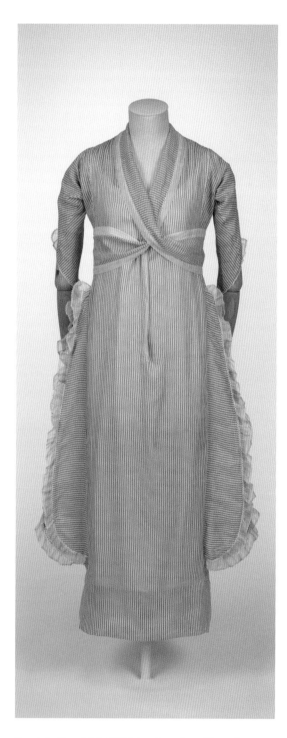

Bendel offered this 1919 day dress from Mme. Jeanne Paquin, currently in the collection of the Metropolitan Museum of Art.

"the women are on a clothes jag. It is not only that they are acquiring a few evening frocks, with which they must be equipped after the years of semi-dress styles, but they are buying everything. We have sold more clothes in November of this year than we sold in September, October and November of last year. . . . One woman came in and ordered 14 frocks at once, which is more than she has ordered in the last three years."

The war era, awful as it was, had been a time of tremendous growth and prosperity for the store. Throughout 1919 business kept booming. Henri continued to be quoted in magazines and newspapers. (From a Neiman Marcus ad in the *Dallas Morning News* that September: "'For fall we don hats all wreathed with feathers,' so says Henri Bendel—and he should know.") And he and Abraham continued making regular trips to France and beyond.

Late that year Henri's half sister Emma, who was now forty, had become engaged to a wholesale furniture salesman from Indiana named Adolph Mayer. Henry insisted the wedding be held at Kings Point. The nuptials took place on December 27, so the house glowed and sparkled with holiday decor. The following day's *New York Herald* account got prominent billing at the top of the society page, adjacent to the wedding announcement for a great-niece of President Ulysses S. Grant. "Amid a bower of roses, chrysanthemums and greenery," it reported, "Mrs. Emma Falk, sister of Mr. Henri Bendel, of New York and Great Neck, was married to Mr. Adolph Nathaniel Mayer at the house of her brother in Grenwolde Drive by the Rev. Dr. J. B. Kress." Henri gave his sister away. Florye was a bridesmaid; her brother "Master Henri Bendel 2d" was listed as "page." Abraham's young niece, "little Dolce Bastedo," served as flower girl and trainbearer. After the ceremony,

Bendel's executed a unique 1919 costume by the Russian-French designer Léon Bakst using a textile designed by the famous French Fauvist painter Raoul Dufy. The dress was donated to the Metropolitan Museum of Art by Flora Miller Biddle, former president of the Whitney Museum of Art and the granddaughter of Gertrude Vanderbilt Whitney.

- MRS. ADOLPH N. MAYER
PHOTO. by DAVIS & SANFORD -

Bendel's half sister, Emma, at the time of her marriage, when she moved out of Henri's house

some two hundred guests—including Henry Otis Chapman, the architect who designed both the house and Henri's store expansion in Manhattan, and Geraldine Farrar—stayed for dinner and dancing.

The New Year of 1920 rang in with more business growth and good PR. In January Bendel bought the properties at 13–15 West Fifty-Sixth Street, directly behind his Fifty-Seventh Street store, with the intent to tear them down and build a rear annex, giving Bendel's still more space. The fur storage and cleaning departments alone would double in size and there would be more room for merchandise. Fur coats and stoles had long been a foundational aspect of Henri's style offerings, and, according to Crawford, "whenever a lady bought a fur coat [he] always supervised the final fitting to make sure that everything was right and then pinned a pink rose to the lapel. This became almost a ritual of fashion, a decoration of honor, the artist's signature on the finished work." In February of 1920 the Couture Division of the National Garment Retailers' Association held a Spring Review at the Hotel Commodore and Bendel featured prominently, along with Bergdorf Goodman and other top dressmakers. Franklin Simon, president of the association, regarded it as an overdue assertion of US fashion emergence. It would, he assured the *New York Times,* "open the eyes of many persons who are unaware of the excellent creative work being done in this country. . . . The coming review is the first of its kind . . . in as much as it represents the first appearance of the leading houses in a group exhibition." Although Simon added by way of disclaimer, "It is foolish to think the French will be put in the background when it comes to things artistic."

Henri agreed, of course, and he and Abraham returned from France that March on the RMS *Adriatic* bearing loads of couture dresses and toting piles of sketches to aid in copying. In a *Women's Wear* article that month on longer lines in skirts, Bendel singled out his premier French artists: Lanvin, Chéruit, Callot, Worth, Doucet, and Chanel. In December of 1920, the *San Diego Evening Tribune* reported that "Henri Bendel and Lucile, the greatest importers, are now in Paris, and their following are anxiously awaiting the first display of Paris creations." In the eight years since Bendel arrived on Fifty-Seventh Street, other fashionable merchants had followed, including Herman Bergdorf and Edwin Goodman, who opened their prominent store at Fifth Avenue in 1914. Who knows who first gave the wide, previously all-residential thoroughfare the moniker "the Rue de la Paix of New York" or "the Rue de la Paix of America"—invoking Paris's "street of peace," home to the top dress shops and couturiers' ateliers. But this much was agreed on: Henri had paved it.

Fall 1920

A dress from the house of Worth's fall 1920 collection
typified the streamlined look of the decade ahead.

Fall 1921

CHAPTER 8

A MAN IN MOTION

Throngs Storm Bendel's at Clearance Sale" blared the *Women's Wear* front-page headline atop an article that chronicled a near melee. On the first day of the three-day sale just before Thanksgiving 1920 there were some three hundred people lined up at seven in the morning, even though the doors weren't supposed to open until 8 a.m. Eventually, the paper estimated, there were as many as 1,200 hungry bargain hunters inside; Henri had brought in fifty extra salesclerks to accommodate them. "It took three mounted police-men to keep the crowd in order on the sidewalk," according to the paper, and the cars "from the carriage trade" created a traffic jam on Fifty-Seventh Street. On the main floors, cleared for millinery, 250 trimmed hats priced at $5 each "were snatched up before 10 o'clock in the morning." Gowns, wraps, and furs were arrayed on higher floors and by the afternoon only a handful of those remained. Henri himself bragged that the sale had not been advertised beyond letters to favored customers; word-of-mouth had done the promoting.

Bendel and Bendel's were indeed roaring as the 1920s began, and—that chaotic scene aside—Henri held the rudder with a firm grip as, over the next few years, he sailed into new adventures and opportunities that included opening another satellite branch of the business, sharing profits with employees, investing in more real estate, and taking his nephew "Little Henri" on a five-star tour of Europe. His voice would travel too, by way of newspapers across America.

Soon after that frantic and profitable November clearance sale, as the December holidays approached, Bendel expanded on an idea he had tested out a couple of years prior—selling antique furniture, tapestries, paintings, and *objets d'art* during that season. He had long decorated his store with art and tapestries; now he wanted to offer decorative furnishings for sale in order to bolster business at a sluggish time of year—traditionally, women didn't shop for clothing for themselves much between Thanksgiving and Christmas. By December most of the first floor, usually devoted primarily to millinery, had been rearranged for chairs, tables, tapestries, and "fine cloths of the old periods

Opposite: A ruby-red evening dress from Lanvin for its fall 1921 collection

111

ANTIQUES
AUTHENTIC AS
HIS STYLES

PERSONALLY SELECTED
AS A BACKGROUND
FOR MADAME
BY
FASHION'S FOREMOST ARBITER
Henri Bendel

NEEDLEPOINT AND
ARTISTIC CHAIRS
16ᵀᴴ TO 18ᵀᴴ CENTURY
TAPESTRIES
RARE OLD VELVETS
AND BROCADES
AN UNUSUAL COLLECTION
OF OTHER GIFTS

Henri Bendel Inc
GOWNS   HATS   FURS
WEST FIFTY-SEVENTH STREET
NEWPORT   NEW YORK   PALM BEACH

A 1925 ad in *Town & Country* for
Bendel's antique furniture and tapestries,
"personally selected for madame by
fashion's foremost arbiter"

with their hand weaving and decoration [and] pillows made with old tapestries," according to *Women's Wear.* "Mr. Bendel [has] long been a connoisseur of antiques and [has] a large knowledge of them as a collector. . . . The presence of these antique gifts is not advertised generally, but patrons of Henri Bendel receive letters telling them of what the house has to offer and suggesting the antiques as possible gifts of real worth and permanent value." As with his clearance sale, this proved a hit, and most of the furnishings, which were priced below antique store levels, sold out.

Between Bendel's importing of fashion and now antiques and tapestries, Henri found it necessary to deputize a Frenchman, one Edouard Ziegler, to handle business on the Paris end. In late autumn of 1920, he formed a new corporation for export and import under Ziegler's name, with himself and John Blish listed as co-directors. *Women's Wear* reported the incorporation and explained that "the large business of antiques and tapestries, as well as imports in fashion merchandise, have increased foreign business to such an extent that they required a personal representative in Paris, rather than having their business done through a commissionaire." Fittingly enough, the office address was 10 Place Edouard VII, in the centrally located ninth *arrondissement* not far from the Palais Garnier opera house and the Hotel Ritz.

Even with Ziegler ensconced in Paris to expedite affairs there, Bendel naturally continued to make trips for dress selecting and trend reporting. Arriving stateside on the RMS *Olympic* after a months-long visit to both Paris and Cannes, the French resort town on the Mediterranean, in the late winter of 1921, Henri, speaking to *Women's Wear,* marveled at the brighter clothes French women were wearing. He refuted the notion that in the early post-war years they had all been wearing black "for sentimental reasons. . . . The principal reason was economy," he argued, "[and now they] have found that in order to share in prosperity they must look the part and for patriotism's sake they are gradually returning in dress to what France was before the war." He touted the cheerful "sur-la-plage" (beachy)

Abraham and Henri relaxing in nature, but the when and the where are unknown—possibly in Florida, judging by the flora and what looks like a fan in Henri's hand.

tones he saw in Cannes both by day and at the casino at night. "The couturiers are making a real effort to get away from the somber veil that has hung over them for six years," he told *Harper's Bazar* that spring. "Even the woman who looks her best in hats of black or dark blue is now favoring the brighter colors."

Bastedo had been on the trip with Henri and the *Women's Wear* article identified him as a milliner with Bendel's and quoted him on the trend of bright colors in hats. By now Bastedo was considered a full-fledged fixture of the store, no longer recognized as the acclaimed Episcopal organist he had been. Nor, of course, as Henri's boyfriend.

In May of 1921 Bendel's three-day spring clearance sale proved to be at least as robust as the fall one had been. "Bendel Sale Draws Swarms of Shoppers," announced *Women's Wear*. For the markdowns on an estimated $250,000 worth of merchandise "a large number of customers swept up like a whirlwind the millinery displayed on the main floor." By 9 a.m. more than six hundred hats were gone. One woman took nineteen and had them sent to her home. "One had to elbow her way through the crowds," said the reporter. Henri even recruited his workroom force to sell. "Everything in the store, except the fixtures, will be disposed of." Merchandise had already been marked down the week prior, and Henri estimated that two thousand people visited the store each day that week. He told *Women's Wear* that this year's clearance sale set a record for the store, "and it is his opinion that the 'moneyed classes' are waiting for sales as they never did before." It's no mystery where Florine Stettheimer got the idea for painting *Spring Sale at Bendel's,* with its fanciful depiction of frantic shoppers diving for frocks—it had leapt out at her from her newspaper.

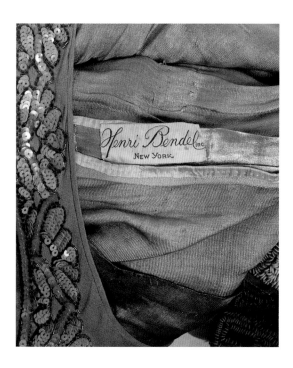

How many hours must have gone into making this lively 1920s
floral-themed flapper dress with its hundreds of hand-sewn beads and sequins?

One Paquin (LEFT) and two Chanel dresses shown in *Vogue* in 1922

A plethora of Bendel-imported dresses from
Callot's spring 1922 collection featured in *Harper's Bazar*

Bendel's in this period and throughout the 1920s continued to garner heavy coverage not only in the trade bible *Women's Wear* but also in the top fashion magazines. Between style spreads and shorter news items, and in its own ads, hardly two months went by without the Bendel name popping up in one major publication or another, sometimes in multiple places in the same issue. *Vogue*, in September of 1921, dedicated seven pages to hats by top European milliners including Reboux, Molyneux, Camille Roger, and Maria Guy, with Bendel prominently identified as the importer. A March 1922 *Harper's Bazar* showed illustrations of French day dresses paired with coats from the designers Elaine, Jenny, and Poiret, all "imported by Bendel's." In May the same magazine filled a spread with "a series of costumes in Callot's best manner shown in the spring collection of Bendel." The phrase "best manner" likely speaks to the fact that these were designs by Callot that Bendel had, with permission, copied and perhaps adapted for his American clients' taste. That same month *Vogue* ran a spread of dresses by Lanvin, Jenny, Worth, Paquin, and Chanel, all sold exclusively at Bendel's. Discussing what he saw as a marked individuality in each of the different French houses that spring, Henri concluded that dressmaking "like all art is autobiographical."

LAVISH FROCKS THAT BESTOW
A CONSCIOUS GRACE
Models from

More and more stars of stage and screen turned up in these publications dressed by—and therein promoting—Bendel's. In 1921 thespian Margaret Lawrence posed for *Harper's Bazar* wearing both a floral-patterned coat over a blue crepe skirt with accordion pleats and a brown corded silk coat over a henna-colored crepe skirt. In 1923 *Harper's* offered up a set of illustrations of the popular southern-born stage actress Tallulah Bankhead, looking glamorously nonchalant in dresses and gowns from Lanvin, Drecoll, and Vionnet, including a "restaurant dance frock of white crepe de Chine with embroidery of crystal tubes," all carried by Bendel's.

TOP: "Lavish frocks" featured in *Harper's* in 1920, including two by Chanel, one by Jenny, and a fourth (AT RIGHT IN THE GROUPING) apparently of Bendel's own devising. RIGHT: From the same article, a Lanvin dress with embroidered *pantalettes*.

Payment Overdue

Many actresses bought clothes outright from Bendel's, and Henri was not blinded by stardust when it came to collecting debts. He was forced to come after more than a couple of fair thespians for running off with the goods, such as Fritzi Scheff (the star of the original 1905 production of *Mlle. Modiste*, ironically) whom Bendel sued in 1914 to recover the $682 he said she owed. Or an actress of some fame named Gail Kane, who surely never intended to get her picture in the *Washington Times* this way, under the July 11, 1921, headline "Stage Star Must Pay Modiste $1,000 for 'Pretties.'" And it wasn't only actresses whom Bendel had to periodically sic his lawyers on. In 1926, a collector on his behalf sued a Miss Claire Cornell, seeking compensation for $18,000 worth of gowns, which was quite a lot of "pretties" back then.

Actress Claiborne Foster modeling Bendel outfits in *Town & Country*, summer of 1926

SUED BY COSTUMER

FRITZI SCHEFF,
Musical comedy star, for whose wardrobe Henry Bendel, a New York merchant, claims $682 in a suit filed in New York city.

Dorothy Burgess modeled Bendel's "picture hat of soft Milan straw in coral pink" in *Town & Country* in 1925. In the same magazine in 1926, Alden Gay sported two dresses of Bendel's—a canary yellow chiffon "costume for the South" and a black chiffon dress with elaborate cream lacework in the skirts and on the long sleeves—and Claiborne Foster, a film star (from Louisiana, as it happens), wore two summer hats and a scarf, all from Henri.

Remarkably, Bendel found himself in the spotlight about as often as the actresses he dressed. In a testament to his growing renown, he even appeared in caricature. To tout the contributors to their September issue of 1922, *Harper's Bazar* commissioned satiric cartoonist Ralph Barton to illustrate an overcrowded elevator stuffed with some thirty influential creative scene-makers of the Roaring Twenties. Looking wide-eyed and confident and sporting his fashionable flat-line mustache and wide-knot tie, Henri's pen-and-ink avatar seems

IN THE ELEVATOR

A supposititious arrangement of contributors to Harper's Bazar by Ralph Barton

THIS is the height of editorial meanness. Here are thirty-one of the sixty-four amiable and versatile writers, artists and couturial advisers who have given the fine fruits of their toil to the development of *Harper's Bazar* during the past three years; yes, and what is their reward? They are thrown to the cruel and cynical Barton. Dastardly! "And that isn't the half of it, dearie!" Next month another elevator load is coming up (of course, precluding the possibilities of murder or arson), including for contrast and good luck G. B. S. and Herman Patrick Tappé!

1. Erté
2. Margery Williams Bianco
3. Pamela Bianco
4. Katherine Sturges
5. Mildred Cram
6. Lady Duff Gordon
7. Henri Bendel
8. Mrs. Fred'k. Y. Dalziel
9. W. L. George
10. Stephen Vincent Benét
11. Gilbert K. Chesterton
12. Etienne Drian
13. George Bellows
14. Dean Cornwell
15. E. F. Benson
16. Arnold Bennett
17. Maurice Bower
18. Rachel Crothers
19. Gertrude Atherton
20. Lord Dunsany
21. Mrs. Larz Anderson
22. Laurids Bruun
23. Acquisitive Connoisseur
24. Lucian Cary
25. Josephine Daskam Bacon
26. Jean Gabriel Domergue
27. Charles Collins
28. Grace Corson
29. George Agnew Chamberlain
30. C. Le Roy Baldridge
31. Ralph (Himself) Barton

In a 1922 *Harper's* illustration of its contributors, Henri shared a tightly packed elevator with prominent names of the era (he's near the lower left, number 7 in the illustration's legend).

quite in his element squeezed in among the likes of fellow fashion purveyor Lady Duff-Gordon (a British designer—and survivor of the *Titanic* sinking—who sold under the name Lucile); the humorous British novelist E. F. Benson; novelist and essayist G. K. Chesterton; playwright Rachel Crothers; the poet and short story writer Stephen Vincent Benét; the painter George Bellows; style-setter Mrs. Frederick Y. Dalziel (mother of legendary fashion editor Diana Vreeland); and Erté, the one-named stage and film costume designer whom Bendel had helped to launch in the early nineteen-teens when he designed dresses for Henri. Fine company by any measure.

The wedding dress Henri designed for his niece and ward Florye
was soon after rendered for *Vogue* as an example of the ideal modern bridal gown.

The end of 1922 and the arrival of
1923 brought milestones and transitions
for Bendel and his family. On December
27, the same date as her mother's wedding
four years prior, seventeen-year-old Florye
Bendel married Jacob Loewenstein, a furniture manufacturer from Peoria, Illinois.
Instead of having the service and reception
at the Kings Point house, an evening ceremony took place in the marble ballroom
of the St. Regis hotel in Manhattan.

Although Henri had converted to
the Episcopal Church, most of his family
members had held fast to their Hebrew
faith, so he gladly acquiesced to a traditional Jewish ceremony, presided over by
the head rabbi of the Temple Emanu-El
on New York City's Upper East Side.
Garlands of smilax and roses festooned
the aisles. Little Henri served as a grooms-
man. Big Henri himself designed Florye's
dress, no doubt with help from his best

A formal portrait of
Florye Loewenstein
wearing the gown
designed by Uncle
Henri

in-house designers at the store: a dazzling gown of white crepe de Chine embroidered in pearls and crystals, with a voluminous floor-length veil anchored
by a crown-shaped headpiece. *Vogue* found it so spectacular that the magazine
ran a full-page illustration, holding it up as model of the new-style wedding
gown. "Young in line, in silhouette slim, straight-lined and draped—that is the
creed of bridal gowns, since fashion has supplanted custom and individuality
has supplanted both."

Likely the reason that Florye's wedding wasn't held at Kings Point is because, in another big move for Bendel, the house there was moments away
from being sold, or swapped to be more precise, which is what transpired in
late January of '23, just a month after the wedding. Although he had lived in
the mansion for little more than five years, an opportunity presented itself that
Henri couldn't resist: a complex, three-parties real estate deal in which automobile baron Walter Chrysler would take possession of Kings Point and Henri
would get a massive, state-of-the-art apartment complex in New York City—
the Astor Court—which ran along the entire western side of Broadway between
Eighty-Ninth and Ninetieth Streets, on Manhattan's newly fashionable Upper
West Side. The brick-and-stone colossus had been designed by renowned architect Charles Platt and commissioned and funded by a young Vincent Astor
(he went on to marry fabled society doyenne Brooke Astor), who came into his

The Astor Court lobby and (BELOW) the exterior of the block-long apartment building on the Upper West Side

fortune prematurely in 1912, while at Harvard, when his father, John Jacob Astor, perished on the *Titanic*. (Henri would have been well acquainted with at least three *Titanic* victims—Astor, as well as Isidor Straus, co-owner of R. H. Macy and Sons department store, and his wife, Ida.) Construction of the ornate twelve-story brick-and-stone landmark—still standing today—had begun in 1914, and it opened in 1916. Its many luxurious features included an elaborate interior-courtyard garden, a first for an apartment building of its size. Bendel put down $1.5 million on the $3.5 million total. He considered the acquisition of Astor Court an investment foremost, but he also moved in, bringing along John, Abraham, and Little Henri.

Additionally that January, *Vogue* marked its thirtieth anniversary and it reprinted letters of congratulations from many prominent admirers, including famed interior designer Elsie de Wolfe, the stores B. Altman and Bonwit Teller, and Mr. Bendel.

I consider *Vogue* not only the best fashion magazine in America, but one of the leading and finest magazines in the world and a book every American should read. With very best wishes for your continued success, I am . . .
Very truly yours,
Henri Bendel

This had become a mutual admiration society. In the same issue, *Vogue* ran a story on the long and illustrious history of New York's relationship with French couture called "Who's Who in the Mode: A Tale of Two Cities," wherein it explained that "the great New York houses probably reproduce greater numbers of many of their models than are made by the houses which created them," and it reminded its readers that "the great New York House of Bendel, now probably the largest importer of Paris frocks in the world, was then [back in the late 1890s] a little hat shop in East Ninth Street." The piece shed light on US fashion's complex French connection. "Without first-hand knowledge of life in America, without more than the most limited experience with American taste, the Grande Maisons of Paris continue to create year after year increasing quantities of models which are eagerly accepted by the great majority of smartly gowned American women. It is, nevertheless, true that most of the notable New York houses do create every season a certain number of models of their own, though these are seldom radical departures from the prevailing mode in Paris." Bendel's own ad in *Town & Country* in 1925 kept the messaging simple: "Original French models and Henri Bendel creations of exclusive costumes for the smart New York season."

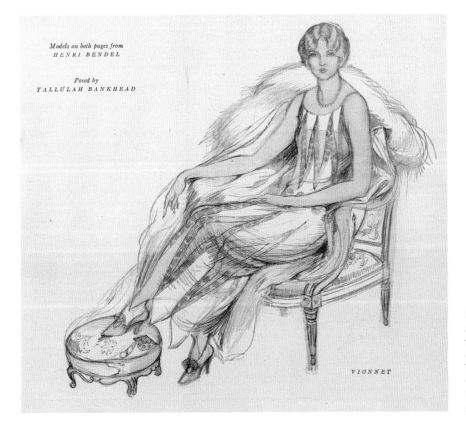

In January 1923 *Harper's Bazar* featured sketches of stage star Tallulah Bankhead wearing dresses by Vionnet and sold by Bendel's.

About the same time that the Astor Court deal transpired at the hands of real estate agents and lawyers in the winter of 1923, Henri, with Abraham, headed down south for his nearly annual pilgrimage to Louisiana to see his siblings, nieces, and nephews. But this year they added a new stop, Palm Beach, Florida, the Atlantic Ocean winter getaway favored by Americans of means, especially socially connected New Yorkers and Bostonians. Bendel's name had arrived there before he had, a year prior, when he conscripted an established Palm Beach dress shop proprietress named Mme. Jeanette, serving as his proxy, to set up a small seasonal shop adjacent to hers. This winter, coming to inspect it himself, he became immediately besotted by the picturesque and posh town. Reported the *New York Times*: "Henry [*sic*] Bendel of New York, after seeing Palm Beach for the first time, has cancelled a Mediterranean trip and leased an apartment on Sunset Avenue for the season." Beyond the community's charm and liveliness Bendel saw something more: new customers and a new kind of muse. "There is nothing like this in all the world," he told *Women's Wear*. "No more perfect setting could be known for beautiful women and lovely frocks, than this. I predict that Palm Beach will shortly, if indeed it is not already, be not only the most beautiful resort in the world but the greatest center for the study of styles and the greatest inspiration to the designer and colorist." By the following winter he had expanded his store off Lake Trail Drive at the prime corner of Sea View and Palm Beach Avenues, in an attractive Mediterranean-styled shopping complex designed by Addison Mizner, the community's pre-eminent architect. Bendel later promoted resort wear and the resort itself in a winter 1925 issue of *Vogue* with a painted illustration spread on "Palm Beach Coats, Capes and Frocks" showing three stylish women posing under palm trees with the ocean in the background.

In the mid-1920s, Bendel's reach expanded with a store on a prominent corner of downtown Palm Beach, winter playground for the wealthy.

An unattributed 1920s "bathing costume" offered by Bendel's.
The drawing is part of the Bendel sketch collection of the Brooklyn Museum.

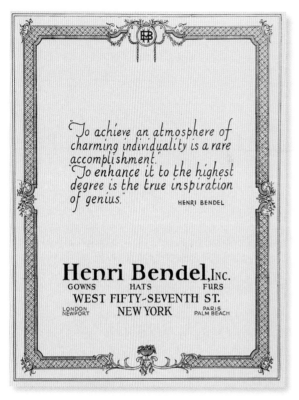

Bendel made news beyond the fashion pages in June of 1923 with a remarkable announcement—that he was giving his employees a stake in the company. Quite a stake: 45 percent of the store's full $4 million worth of capital stock. It would be distributed over five years, in quarter-million-dollar lots. The first $250,000 would be earmarked for eighteen employees who had been with him between fifteen and twenty-five years. "My purpose," he said, "is to perpetuate the house, as well as to reward its employees for faithful services which have made possible its upbuilding. Many firms enjoy their heyday and go to smash. I hope that the division of stock will keep up the interest of employees, making the business perpetual."

"Originally I planned to turn over, in my will, a part of the business to my employees," he added, "but have decided to carry out the scheme now, so that I can get pleasure out of it too." Granting stock to employees wasn't a new concept, but to offer such a large, valuable parcel, and to nearly 1,800 people, put Bendel in the forefront of corporate profit sharing. (The following year he would embrace unionized fur workers, which he had previously resisted under an "open shop" system, thereby falling in line with other garment industry employers.) Henri's stock gift signified both his generosity and his business foresight; the loyalty it engendered would pay long-term dividends for him and the store. And, as in his taking guardianship of Florye and Henri II, he had an eye on his legacy.

ABOVE: An ad offering up a style maxim from Henri

BELOW: A sketch of a fringed navy day dress from Chanel's fall 1920 collection

Still, the now fifty-six-year-old Bendel wanted no one to construe the stock sharing as a signal that he might be contemplating any changing of the guard, nor capitulating to his age. He would continue to run things from the top while also minding the front door, just like the Henri figure in the Stettheimer painting: anticipating another fall with a fall collection, another spring with a spring sale, welcoming new customers, new styles, and open to whatever the future might blow in. "I have no intention of retiring," he told the newspapers, cannily preempting idle speculation. "I intend to keep in harness until the end."

Planning his summer schedule of 1923, Henri decided to take Henri II, now fifteen, along to Europe, the boy's first time abroad. Although Bendel expected to do some business in Paris, this nearly two-month trip would be mostly a vacation, an excursion up and down France and into Switzerland, Spain, and the British Isles. John Blish and Abraham Bastedo would accompany them. They all departed on a foggy June 23 on the White Star Line's *Majestic*, as always in first class. Little Henri's crammed travel diary records many details of the trip, including his sense of excitement and the fun of the voyage (despite some early seasickness). "We started the day off by going swimming in the pool, which was very beautiful. Mr. Bastedo got the deck chairs after a little fighting with the deck steward. . . . Went all over the boat today and it certainly is wonderful. Mr. Bastedo beat me badly in some shuffleboard. . . . Uncle Henri met some friends and he and Mr. Bastedo have to play cards this afternoon." On a Sunday they attended an Episcopal service onboard; Little Henri appreciated that it was abbreviated.

Henri and Abraham on a beach, possibly in Europe, in the mid-1920s

The Majestic Hotel in Paris where Henri stayed with his nephew on their long summer trip to Europe in 1923

MAJESTIC HOTEL — PARIS - Avenue Kléber

In Paris they stayed "in a lovely suite of rooms" at the elegant Majestic Hotel, near the Arc de Triomphe. The three men and the lad plowed through the galleries at the Luxembourg and Cluny museums, likely the Louvre too; visited Napoleon's tomb; attended the theater; and dined at such fashionable spots as the Café de Paris and the Hotel Ritz. They made day excursions to the palaces of Fontainebleau and Versailles—in his diary, Little Henri marveled at the fountain of Apollo at Versailles "whose water shoots the highest of any in the world!" Then they radiated south. At the famous spa at Vichy Uncle Henri "took the waters" and saw an opportunity to lose a few pounds (this was becoming constant challenge for Bendel) signing on for the facility's health program. "It's a strict regimen," noted Little Henri. "All his food is weighed. He's always hungry but he eats fruit which he is allowed."

In Biarritz the foursome switched hotels because Big Henri didn't care for the one they were booked into. Little Henri and Bastedo swam in the ocean there. In St. Sebastian, Spain, they caught a glimpse of the king in his car, and they took in a bullfight, with the queen and queen mother in attendance. The gory action in the bullring, made worse by a bull mortally stabbing a horse and *nearly* mortally stabbing a bullfighter, drove them to flee the moment it ended and left Little Henri shaken. "It is too cruel for any person unused to such things," he earnestly told his diary.

Back in France the group toured Chantilly and other châteaux-rich areas, as Bendel could never get enough of beautiful houses. After seeing the Château de Blois, in the Loire Valley, Little Henri noted, "part of it was copied by the Vanderbilts whose house is on 57th Street, across from Uncle's store."

For all the grandeur and beauty that they took in, the men also saw the deep scars of the still-fresh war, such as the shattered cathedral at Reims, and the eerily deforested Belleau Wood, scene of heavy battle, now marked by some fifteen thousand crosses. "The Germans have black crosses," wrote Little Henri. He had heard that beautification plans were underway "but work is slow as there is still some [mustard] gas there."

Bringing along a keen, enthusiastic ward to share Europe with must have elevated this trip for Henri and would've given Mr. Blish and Mr. Bastedo a fresh focus. The group likely became energized by the youth's presence; Henri II was still a wide-eyed boy, yet old enough to value the history and aesthetics of the Continent and disciplined enough to sit patiently through long lunches and perhaps gossipy conversations that held little interest. As Bendel himself toured from one château to the next, he must have felt a connection with the European gentry for whom family lineage was paramount, knowing that he now had a lineage of his own and both children amply provided for. The vacation had an air of celebration and of pages turning. The year had already seen Florye married and now Little Henri was marking a classic milestone for families with wealth enough to travel abroad: the first grand tour.

Having Continental cachet not only suited Henri, it defined his brand. An ad for his "*parfums*" in *Town & County* magazine in December of 1924 listed outposts in Paris, London, Newport, and Palm Beach, in addition to the New York flagship store. (London and Paris addresses were business offices, not shops.) In December of the following year *Town & Country* ran two big photos of the film actress Lady Diana Manners (Lady Diana Cooper to her fellow English socialites) bundled in furs from Bendel before she departed New York City for England. A Bendel lady, this sort of press implied, was not only beautiful and famous and even titled, but she possessed a well-worn passport.

Actress and blueblood Lady Diana Manners posed in Bendel coats for *Town & Country* before sailing to England in 1924.

AN ENGLISH BEAUTY IN AMERICAN CREATIONS

Photo by Nicholas Muray

LADY DIANA MANNERS

Lady Diana Manners, the Madonna of "The Miracle" (Lady Diana Cooper, wife of Alfred Duff Cooper, D.S.O., in private life), was photographed, just before she sailed for England, wearing these luxurious fur coats and accessories from Henri Bendel. At the left the Broadtail wrap with the deep chinchilla collar and cuffs makes a point of an attached scarf of charmeuse and silver brocade. The straight line coat of dark Eastern Mink is also a very special creation of the house, as are the hats. A vulture Brush trims the black velvet model

33

In contrast to his journeys abroad and sojourns to America's toniest resort towns, trips back home to Louisiana scratched a different itch for Henri, his yearning to reconnect with family and the low-key, small-town southern culture that had nursed him. In the winter of 1925, after enjoying some time in Palm Beach, Henri, Abraham, and John headed to Lafayette and spent about a month at the home of his sister Louise and her husband, Myrtil Meyer, a house he commissioned to be built for them. Before leaving for New Orleans on his way back to New York he gave an interview to the local *Daily Advertiser* and shared his desire to acquire a getaway place near Lafayette. "I have to go back to New York to take up business matters . . . but I'm coming back . . . whenever I can manage to do so and in fact I think I'm going to fix me up a hunting and fishing camp down in this section of the country and take special advantage of all the opportunities offered along that line." The paper noted that Bendel spent part of this vacation on "some outing trips," presumably to scout properties. His honest enthusiasm for fishing and hunting is unknown, but such an endorsement of cherished southern Louisiana pastimes, not to mention the folksy phrase "fix me up," would have played well to the local readership, and Henri knew how to play to his audience. Marveling at his success, the article reported that Bendel's employee roster had grown to 1,800, or 2,000 when one counted

ABOVE: A very French-sounding ad in *Town & Country* (1924) for Bendel's perfume, lipstick, and powdered rouge. BELOW: Bendel frocks specifically geared to southern tastes and temperatures, featured in *Harper's* (1920)

"branch houses and others connected with the firm." By way of explaining his need to get back to New York, Bendel remarked that "the fashion world is one in which rapid changes predominate and it requires constant attention and a careful system of organization . . . [and it's] especially necessary that we keep in touch with the fashion developments [in] Paris."

A few months later, in early summer, Henri renewed his commitment to Lafayette by donating a lavish crystal beaded gown valued at $800—more than $13,000 today—to be auctioned off at the Radio Trade Ball benefitting the Elks Lodge. To drum up interest in the event, Town's Style Shop on Jefferson Avenue, downtown Lafayette's main commercial street, put the dress on display in their window.

A great-niece's vivid account of another of Henri's trips south, this time to Texas, captures his devotion to his extended family but also his somewhat intimidating reputation in the eyes of his kin.

"Uncle Henri is coming!"

Marjorie Arsht recalled the enthusiasm muddled with fear in her mother's voice when news broke of Bendel's impending visit to the sleepy town of Yoakum, Texas. Marjorie was a girl of maybe nine or ten; this would have been sometime in the mid-1920s. Arsht's mother, Myrtle Levy Meyer, was Henri's niece, the daughter of his sister Lena. "Uncle Henri Bendel, a famous New York couturier, was the most important person in my mother's family," wrote Arsht in her 2006 memoir *All the Way from Yoakum*. (She would go on to become a prominent Houston philanthropist and Republican Party political insider). "All babies' names were first submitted to him for approval, and anyone getting married had to pay a prenuptial visit to him either in New York or Connecticut or Louisiana. . . . [He] sported a tiny Charlie Chaplin moustache, was short, round, and slightly balding. If he hadn't been rich and famous, I don't suppose anyone would have noticed him. New Yorkers believed Henri Bendel to be a Frenchman, perhaps because of the spelling of his name and perhaps because he loved everything French. No one seemed to know or remember that he was a Jew from Lafayette, Louisiana."

Arsht writes that "everyone seemed vague about the existence of Uncle's Henri's wife, saying only that she died in childbirth. In any case, Uncle Henri wasn't lonely. Two tall, very handsome men . . . lived with him in his various residences. One or the other or both always traveled with him. I particularly liked Mr. Blish, but only Mr. Bastedo came with him on this trip to Yoakum. . . . By the time I began to wonder how he managed his unconventional lifestyle . . . it was too late to ask. I suppose his wealth, fame and generosity trumped any objection to his sexual [orientation]."

A Lanvin look in *Harper's*

A gathering in Lafayette at the home of Henri's sister Louise Meyer and her husband, Myrtil, possibly in 1925. FROM LEFT: Ike, Henri, John Blish, young Marjorie Meyer, Lena Levy, Louise, Abe Bastedo, and Myrtil.

The household "bustled with excitement" and industry before his arrival. Floors were scrubbed, counters scoured, and each prism from the dining room chandelier that had been a gift from Henri was removed, cleaned in ammonia water, and put back in place. Marjorie's mother anxiously focused on meal preparation. "In typical Louisiana superlative, the fire under the roast had to be low, low, low, and the food had to be served hot, hot, hot. Because he was arriving at noon, Mama planned a feast—but then every meal of his day-and-a-half visit was a matter of grave concern."

"Since no one had died, I never really knew why he came," writes Arsht, "but it was a memorable visit nevertheless. Just before he left, he said to Mama—and not in a stage whisper, either—'Myrtle, you have to do something about Marjorie. She is entirely too fat!' Humiliated, I cried the rest of that day." Eventually she would come to recognize that for all his blunt imperiousness her uncle "was a generous man, extending gracious hospitality to all the siblings, nieces and nephews and their children who made pilgrimages to visit him in New York." Not too many years after her girlhood mortification over his comment about her weight, Marjorie would be quite the beneficiary of that generosity.

And, after all, giving advice and voicing strong opinions had become Henri's trademark. By the mid-1920s Bendel carved out time to pen a nationally syndicated column, radiating out to hundreds of papers across America through the NEA news service, where his crisp assessment of trends and

"Many firms enjoy their heyday and go to smash. I hope that the division of stock will keep up the interest of the employees, making the business perpetual."

—*Henri Bendel*

decisive instruction on dressing had the weight of sacred tablets thrown down from the mount. "I dislike the sheath gown on the youthful figure," he opined in one, in 1925. "The slender waistline is much too lovely a line not to be emphasized. Nothing is more attractive for youth than the bouffant frock with its molded bodice and full wide skirts." Another declared that "the debutante should not be in a hurry to grow up, so far as her gowns are concerned."

He loved the epigrammatic turn of phrase with a nifty kicker. "Keeping cool in August is usually the crucial test of chic," he wrote. "August days and August nights are the hardest of all the year to gown. One must not only manage to feel cool. There is the responsibility of looking cool at the same time." A minor update, in 1925, on the demise of ensembles arrived punctuated by a wise-owl truism about why certain trends expire: "For the ensemble costume that was the rage this spring, the future is not so promising—at least not for the ensemble as we now conceive it with matching coat and dress. In the first place, women have tired of it. That, you know, finishes any mode."

In 1926 Bendel seemed all too happy to lay flowers on the grave of one of the early twenties' most defining trends, the flapper look. "If the flapper were not a dead issue, so far as style is concerned, she would be after this season," he said dryly. "For the abbreviated, blunt and graceless attire she affected has departed from the mode." Take *that*, Miss Flapper.

Vogue showed a black velvet and chiffon Chéruit dress imported by Bendel in 1925.

CHAPTER 9

LAUREL TREES
AND LAURELS

$\mathcal{A}$IMING TO KEEP UP WITH NEW TRENDS and women's still-in-progress fashion liberation, and having long argued that women drove fashion movements, Bendel reiterated that last position in a syndicated newspaper column he penned in December 1926 headlined "Women Set Styles, Not Designers." Laughing, as it were, at the Victorian era with its "bustles, hoopskirts, false curls and stupid little gewgaws" and contrasting these with the "classic draperies" of ancient Greece, and the rich hued silks and satins of the French court, he concluded that today's women were simply expressing themselves, even if unconsciously. "The Victorian woman did not realize what she was shouting to the world with her attire. And in fact, it didn't shout until after that era had passed. So today it is not an accident that a woman registers in her clothes her independence of thought and action, her wit and her ability to think in a straight line." Designers create, he argued, "not from their own instinct or inspiration. The unseen hand that shapes the mode is a feminine hand that knows what it wants." Steering the column to specific fashion (after all, he had to sell dresses, not just philosophize) he invoked three women designers—Vionnet, Chanel, and Lanvin—who, in his opinion, "most subtly understand women's subtle intellect" and who "represent the modern woman's triumph over sentimentality and the mere externals of clothes. Claiming their complete disregard of all tricks and obvious vanities, they proclaim their independence."

And he recognized the practical aspect of the sea change: women's roles and activities were shifting, not just for working women but for so-called women of leisure, too. In a 1927 column about what he termed "semi-dress" (more casual day dressing), Bendel observed that women need to be able to change quickly more than once in a day for various occasions. "There is little patience with the involved frock that has elaborate closings and requires a maid's attendance." Nor, he imagined, was there any patience for dressing in a state of pain. "Since women have learned that comfort and style may be reconciled, they demand comfort in every particular. No fashionable woman will tolerate a hat that is not perfectly

OPPOSITE: A semi-enclosed cloister opening onto the terrace frames a beautiful view at Laurel Lake Lodge in Stamford, Connecticut.

THE MORNING HERALD, GLOVERSVILLE AND JOHNSTOWN, N. Y.

Fashion Talks With Hats

"Hats are barometers for the mode," said Henri in a syndicated newspaper column in 1929.

fitted and hence perfectly comfortable, or will she wear small shoes for appearance's sake. She will not suffer any longer for style, because her intelligence tells her this is not necessary or desirable."

In acknowledging the passing of the era of the highly decorative hat—"furbelowed" in the language of the day—that had put him on the map back on Ninth Street in the late 1800s, Henri pointed to women's new interests and activities as one reason for its demise. "There may be a few places where the frilled and furbelowed hat may be worn, such as garden parties and the like," he had told the newly retitled *Women's Wear Daily* the previous summer, "but the hat of bygone days will not return, in my opinion, for many, many years, if at all. The sports influence cannot be ignored. Look at the statistics of automobiles now driven by women, and those who are playing golf. It is not a question of different hats so much as different places at which to wear them and even at the places where the frilly hat might be worn, it will be of simple adornment."

"Golf may be good for the nation," he concluded, "but not for the furbelowed hat."

Yet there was still a time and place for dressing to the nines, and, for that, certain women continued to look to the beacon of French couture. But had Henri stoked the desire to the detriment of his own interests? More and more designers and dress shops in America were selling French copies or couture-inspired designs, and Henri, feeling the heat of competition, appealed to women directly to judge his product superior. "In the 25 years we have been in business we have given full credit to French genius, and we continue to do so," he said in that same *Women's Wear Daily* article. "We acknowledge Paris as our inspiration, and, as such, like to feel that we are the interpreters of correct French styles in America. We founded the business on this policy, and as long as I am alive it will so continue." He echoed the sentiment in his own ad for the store a few years later, according to fashion historian Caroline Rennolds Milbank, declaring "[it is] impossible to truly copy a French model unless one copies its spirit, too. So truly Parisian in spirit is the House of Bendel that it is only natural that women who understand the art of reproducing French fashions should prefer them as Bendel's recreates them."

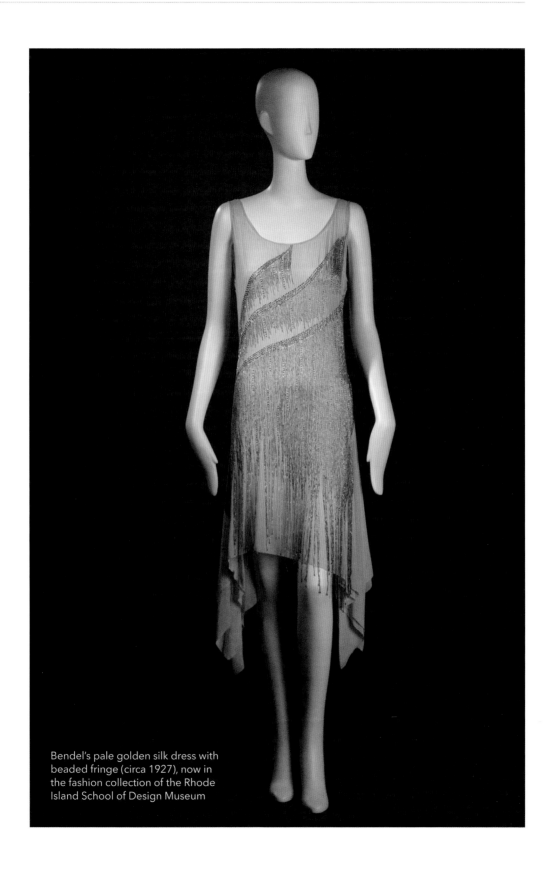

Bendel's pale golden silk dress with
beaded fringe (circa 1927), now in
the fashion collection of the Rhode
Island School of Design Museum

> "He couldn't stand anything that didn't please his eye."
>
> —*great-niece Elene Davis*

To what degree Bendel and the store may have been feeling squeezed is unknown, but in the late winter of 1927, a rumor went around that Henri was "to retire from active participation in the business," according to *Women's Wear Daily,* selling his interest but "with the understanding that the name was to be continued." A store executive quickly denied it, saying, according to the paper's paraphrasing, "that Mr. Bendel is still a comparatively young man and no such thought is in his mind." Just a month later Bendel himself refuted what sounded like an even worse version of the speculation, that the store's very existence may have been in jeopardy. The short but prominently placed item in the April 9 issue of *Women's Wear Daily* read: "Denying that the firm of Henri Bendel had ever been considering going out of business or selling out to other factors [entities], Henri Bendel stated last night, on the eve of sailing for Europe, that the rumor was without foundation." But was it altogether? Had profit margins shrunk? Had the store become a lure for larger retailers or financing firms looking for acquisitions? And had Henri, inadvertently or by design, signaled some interest in slowing down or cashing out? By all visible indicators the store was

In the mid-1920s Bendel and John Blish took Henri's sister, Lena, to Venice, Italy, where they boated (RIGHT) and fed pigeons in San Marco square (OPPOSITE).

still in expansion mode, and Henri was still its minder-in-chief, continuing to travel to Europe on its behalf.

And in his private life Bendel was expanding as well, but in ways that would offer periodic respite from business. He had the urge to retreat, for the second time, from the bustle of the city and create a secluded paradise echoing ages gone by, filled with treasures of antiquity and surrounded by glorious nature. Two paradises, as it happened.

The first would be in his homeland. As he had hinted on that trip to Lafayette in 1925, he wanted a place of his own there—"an ambition he began to dream during his boyhood days," according to the *Daily Advertiser*—and in 1927 he acquired approximately 185 acres of land adjacent to the Vermilion River, just outside what were then the town boundaries of Lafayette. It was a verdant and hilly area (hills being relative in the low prairies-and-marsh topography of South Louisiana), and it possessed a dramatic history of which Henri may have been only dimly aware. Most of the land had once been a part of the Walnut Grove plantation, a cotton-growing outfit owned in the early-mid-1800s by Jean Joseph Sosthène Mouton, the great-grandson of Vermilionville founder Jean Mouton. As laid out in Jeanette Plauché Parker's book *Bendel Gardens: An Historic Treasure in Lafayette, Louisiana,* in 1863 advancing Union troops battling Confederates along the river set upon the plantation. Jean Joseph, a Confederate major, was away fighting; his wife, Henriette Odéide Mouton, and their children were expelled as the property was seized and—whether by design or from crossfire from the nearby battle— the large house burned to the ground. After the war different parcels of the land passed through various owners. Henri bought three contiguous tracts.

He aimed to build a manor house there, sited approximately where the plantation house had once stood, on high ground with an ideal view of a bend in the river, not far from the Pin Hook bridge (today spelled Pinhook). He envisioned a wooded, rambling estate landscaped in a naturalistic but orderly fashion, enhanced by specimen trees and native flowering shrubs. As Lafayette didn't possess nurseries at that time, Henri's banker brother Ike combed the state on his behalf seeking worthy flora. Over several years, Henri would oversee the planting of more than three thousand azalea shrubs and seven hundred camellia trees. In fact, he planned to call his new home the Camellias.

Some of those winter-flowering beauties would be grown by Edward Avery McIlhenny, the scion and president of Tabasco who converted part of his family's large pepper-growing estate on Avery Island, thirty miles south of Lafayette, into an elaborate public garden. An explorer and naturalist, McIlhenny loved plants and flowers as passionately as Bendel did, and he grew—sometimes grafting—dozens and dozens of camellia cultivars with names like Gloire de Nantes, Duc de Orleans, and one called Dr. Oldwig Thayer originated by McIlhenny himself. He subtly layered flowers into landscapes the way a dressmaker might blend fabric colors for effect, attuned to nuance—and to his client's tastes. "I did not send the rose wisteria," he wrote Henri, "as [it has] a lavender cast . . . and I'm afraid would not please you. The pink wisteria I am sending is a true flesh-pink, and a beautiful variety."

A Beautiful Residential Scene, Lafayette, La.

7A-H2583

Little surprise the men struck up a casual friendship, fellow South Louisianans of great professional accomplishment with hyper-tuned aesthetic sensibilities.

A Louisiana journalist writing about Henri's gardens some years later described azaleas of every color, including "shades of pink, yellow, salmon, tea rose, and peach." She also noted that "to abet this riot of beauty, there are hedges of blue phlox, vines of purple and white wisteria, taller hedges of bamboo, jasmine and hollyhocks, dogwood and honeysuckle, red bud, stalwart pines and cypress trees, [and] budding magnolias," and she concluded that "Only a person who knows harmony—who feels emotionally the joys of the artistic creation of a beautiful pattern or design—could have arranged such a landscape." Many of the magnolia trees were planted along both sides of a winding path from the entrance to the property all the way back to the river; this was laid out to create an *allée* intended to shade a planned road to the yet-to-be-constructed mansion, which was expected to cost $250,000 to build—well over $4 million if it were erected today.

Knowing how long such a project would take, Bendel decided to first build a smaller house that he could use in the interim. Not too small, of course. He commissioned a New York architect to design a "commodious lodge" in the Spanish villa style, with cream-colored stucco walls and red roof tiles. Sited just past the entry to the property, the house featured a large central living room with a fireplace, a big dining room off the living room, and two bedrooms. Adjacent to the spacious kitchen was a butlery for dishes

A picture-almost-too-perfect postcard of the Camellia Lodge in Lafayette and (OPPOSITE) images of Henri's much-loved local flowers, the azalea and the camellia

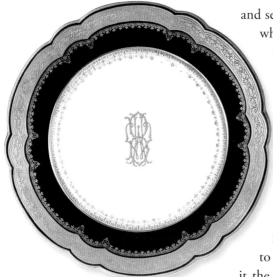

and serving pieces. Mrs. Elisabeth Denbo Montgomery, who would later attend beautiful dinner parties there, reported that Henri "was quite an entertainer."

In coming years Bendel expanded the house, according to Mario Mamalakis in her book *If They Could Talk: Acadiana's Buildings and Their Biographies.* This included adding a patio off the living room, which Henri eventually glassed in; a side porch with arches akin to the front entry; and an upper sun deck that was later converted into another bedroom. Two more bedrooms were added in the rear, including one for a butler, and the original garage was expanded to accommodate Bendel's Rolls-Royce. (Legend has it the car featured a rigged up "air-conditioning" contraption involving a fan and a tray of ice, an accommodation to the sultry climate.) Completed in 1928, and lavishly landscaped with magnolia trees—many of which are still standing today—and dozens and dozens of camellia and azalea bushes, Henri dubbed the picturesque house the Camellia Lodge.

For the entrance to the estate Bendel commissioned a set of elegant wrought iron gates from Stewart Iron Works of Covington, Kentucky, a firm that had fabricated benches for New York's Central Park, light fixtures for the US Capitol, and prison cells for Alcatraz (and who are still in business today). The double gates, wide enough for a car or truck, sported a smaller side gate on each end for foot traffic, all set between simple but imposing rectangular posts covered in stucco to match the house.

ABOVE: A fine china plate from France featuring Bendel's initials HWB in a dramatic monogram

BELOW: The gates to the property with the lodge visible behind it

FACING THE PLAZA ON PALM BEACH AVENUE

Marcus & Co., Henri Bendel, Delman's Inc., and Miss L. Brogan occupy the beautiful shops above.

In May of 1928, as the Camellia Lodge was being readied, Henri sailed for Europe on the RMS *Majestic* and stayed about six months, an unusually long stint. Bastedo went over to France that June and returned to New York in September. When Henri returned on the SS *Leviathan* in mid-November, he reported a "trend in elegant clothes" to *Women's Wear Daily* and in January of 1929 devoted one of his syndicated newspaper columns to hat trends, including a novelty called a scarf hat.

That winter found Bendel in Palm Beach, opening a new shop that sold everything from gowns and wraps to sportswear, lingerie, and accessories. Next, he and Abraham headed to Lafayette and spent two months in their new winter house. It was a chance for Henri to have a more leisurely reunion with his sister Louise, who had recently lost her husband Myrtil Meyer, and their brother Ike. (Widowed Louise and Ike, a bachelor with a reputation for courting but not marrying various women, would soon share a large house that Henri commissioned for them in town, adjacent to the campus of Southwestern Louisiana Institute, the local university.) The *Daily Advertiser*, chronicling his visit and his ongoing plans for his future manor house along the Vermillion River, noted that he was "accompanied by his friend and companion, A. B. Bascedo [*sic*], who is a famed and talented organist. A pipe organ will be one of the features of Bendel's new home."

The paper mentioned that Henri was recovering from illness but did not say what it was. Had he extended his recent stay in Europe because he felt

A newspaper sketch offered a glimpse of the posh shops on Palm Beach Avenue, including Bendel's new boutique.

A 1932 Bendel ad in *Harper's* touting Palm Beach-worthy resort fashion

too sick to travel back home? Had he perhaps been seeking extra rest or some therapy abroad? He offered the reporter only an optimistic response to their concern. "I feel sure this fine climate is going to make me well," he said.

Singing the praises of Louisiana broadly, he declared that he wanted to bring friends from the East and other parts of the country and, in the words of the paper, "interest them in the opportunities offered by his state." Imagining growth in industry and tourism, which he hoped to encourage, he deemed Louisiana underexploited. "The east and the north, particularly the east, are over-prosperous," he observed. "The wealth that is being created in eastern financial circles is almost inconceivable. But there must be an outlet. And the eyes of financiers are turning south. What state has a better chance to share in this wealth than Louisiana, or what part of the state than this section?" Making another comparison, he invoked Florida, already a tourist mecca, but took a strange swipe at the Sunshine State, peculiar given how often he praised it and profited from it. From the *Advertiser*:

> "People go to Florida," [Bendel] said, "because it has become a popular fad to do so. Of course there are attractions there, the great hotels, the beaches, the climatic conditions. But at the same time, I have found Palm Beach a sort of artificiality, an unnatural, high pitched vein of life. Even the wealthy, those who go to Palm Beach as a matter of course, seem to be growing tired of it. Now consider Louisiana, with her settings of beauty, the charm of her people and the many other things she has to offer. In Florida you have to buy flowers from hothouses. Here," and he held in his hand an azalea, his favorite flower—"you find the real thing."

It's a safe bet he never would have made such comments to a Florida newspaper! Henri was no doubt genuine in his dreams of a Louisiana tourist and industry boom, but he also appears once again to be playing to his audience, ladling kindness and compliments (at Florida's expense) upon his hometown like a smooth southern guest—and a public relations pro—might be guilty of.

In the early spring of 1929, back East where the azaleas weren't yet in bloom, Bendel oversaw the start of his next epic creation: a nearly 10,000-square-foot, twenty-plus-room mansion in Stamford, Connecticut, about an hour and a half drive from New York City. North Stamford was a prosperous, woodsy enclave of quaint old houses plus newer large estates of the robber baron variety. He had acquired an eighty-acre property on the edge of town that had originally been owned by George Blickensderfer, inventor of the first portable typewriter. More recently it had served as a private hunting camp called the Forest Lodge, which Bendel had visited and would now have razed. There was a spring-fed pond that over the years both neighborhood kids and Olympians-in-training had used for ice skating.

According to Henri Bendel II, who in the early 1960s shared some recollections about the house, his uncle Henri had been inspired when an antiques dealer from London had taken him to the English village of Maidenhead, not far from Windsor Castle, where he toured two pristine examples of Tudor architecture: Shoppenhangers Manor and Ockwells Manor. Bendel commissioned an architect friend named Perry Barker to loosely model his new house on those. Since the late 1950s, the mansion has

been the central building of the Stamford Museum, who remain custodial to the history and lore of the home, and an article in a 1961 edition of their bulletin relayed that "Bendel had more imagination than to copy either manor exactly. Instead, he took what he liked from each, then adapted and improvised the rest."

With a slate roof, half-timber gables, cathedral-arched and steel-framed windows, polygonal chimneys, oversized stone fireplaces, and a dramatic, wide stone staircase, the house cut an imposing figure. Inside it offered gracious—if somewhat dark and Gothic—living, with five bedrooms for family and guests plus four more for live-in staff, as well as two apartments over the garage, also for staff. A large music room appears to have been modeled on Ockwells's great hall, but according to the Stamford Museum's bulletin, Bendel "decided the ceiling should be five feet higher to provide the best acoustics for his immense pipe organ, so he ordered the change." When he moved in, Henri hung tapestries in that room to soften the sound.

Outside, a menagerie of roof gargoyles, stone lions, and cavorting fountain horses guarded the immediate grounds, which were also peppered with statuary that Henri had procured abroad, including four human figures representing the four seasons, three of which were nineteenth-century copies of a famous set from seventeenth-century Italy

Top: Little Henri posing in Stamford, Connecticut, in front of a house of his uncle's that predated the mansion Bendel would soon build on the property

Bottom: Henri and guests in front of the wisteria-draped gazebo at Stamford. Far right is his sister Emma Falk Mayer, and to the immediate left of Emma is her daughter, Florye Loewenstein.

(the fourth is thought to be original). One of Henri's most piquant flourishes: a limestone wellhead from a seventeenth-century Capuchins monastery in Bologna, Italy, placed in a stone cloister just off the house.

It took some forty workmen including stone masons, carpenters, plasterers, and plumbers nearly two years to complete the job, which was made extra challenging as Henri decided he wanted to exploit native granite boulders from the property and have them cut into useable pieces. "We tried to talk Mr. Bendel into buying stone already cut and much less expensive," recalled Robert Small Jr. decades later; Small had been the then-twenty-five-year-old head of the construction crew. "But he wanted stone from the property. Later, when he felt the pinch of the Depression, he finished up with some commercial stone from [nearby] Old Greenwich." Chestnut trees on the property provided some of the building lumber and old chestnut boards from the dismantled Forest Lodge that had been painted over were sanded, refinished, and deployed as decorative paneling.

According to Henri II, his uncle had many young laurel trees brought in to line the driveway, which led to the house being christened Laurel Lake Lodge. It was "the epitome of the American 'castle' of the time: distinctly continental, sumptuous, and refined," to quote from the website of the Stamford Museum.

At a Stamford gathering of friends and family, perhaps on Easter Sunday judging by the outfits, Mr. Bastedo posed with two unidentified women.

An Old-World Cocoon in Connecticut

A cloister-style courtyard with a wellhead from a Capuchins monastery in Bologna, Italy

With a Tudor façade punctuated by Gothic architectural flourishes, Bendel's nearly 10,000-square-foot, twenty-room Laurel Lake Lodge reflected his wide-ranging tastes inside and out. Renaissance tapestries mixed deftly with Central European and Asian rugs, Louis XIV furniture, and sterling silver Victorian tea services. Medieval Christian icons held the gaze of a marble head of the Roman god Janus and that of a Buddha carved into an ivory tusk. For Henri there was equal beauty in both a centuries-old red-velvet-and-gilt-wood Madonna shrine and a hand-crafted mahjong set from the Far East. In proscenium-shaped bookcases with thick molding, tomes

A piazza-like approach to the house with a neo-Italian Renaissance fountain, a copy of one presented to a spa outside Florence by the king of Italy. Its pieces were shipped over and reassembled stone by stone.

Venetian urns atop posts marking the entrance to the rear drive conjured European villa style.

on fashion and painting squeezed in with Shakespeare, Cervantes, Dickens, Kipling, and Wilde. Guests dazzled by the profusion of art and artifacts of silver, damask, and fine porcelains were in essence traveling to other continents and long-ago eras, with Henri as guide, and all for the price of a train ticket to North Stamford.

Nature-lover Henri, who sited his bedroom to look out at the lake, put as much effort into the exterior realms of the estate, starting with the layout of approaches and pathways, all lushly landscaped and punctuated by striking antique statuary, often of animals, including gargoyles on the roof. A marble-and-iron gazebo he had enjoyed at his house in Kings Point was dismantled, stored, and reinstalled here. As Americans of new wealth were copying the dramatic homes and gardens of titled Europeans, Henri's elegant property held its own.

TOP: One of two lions guarding the rear courtyard, replicas of those by the famous neoclassical Italian sculptor Canova.
BELOW: The Italian fountain featuring bas-relief horses

All the home's fireplace surrounds, like the one in the living room, came from England.

As in dressmaking, scale and proportion were of paramount concern to Bendel. The lodge achieved desired grandeur by way of several huge common rooms (including his concert-ready music conservatory) with high and sometimes vaulted ceilings. In contrast, smaller rooms with cozy, comfortable seating—plus hundreds of objects to delight the eye—created a sense of intimacy.

No matter how lively the dinner conversation might get around the Louis XIII dining table, thick rugs, elaborate drapes, and mounted tapestries would have softened the voices.

LEFT: In the music room a high vaulted ceiling—painted "medieval blue" between natural wood beams—and a large chandelier drew the eye heavenward while the big pipe organ led the ear in the same direction.
RIGHT: The chestnut-paneled living room with its imposing fireplace surround

The entrance hall doubled as room for cocktails, and a tapestry curtain separated it from the dining room with theatrical panache.

In effect it was a sort of museum in Henri's time; neighbors and other guests of his frequent parties marveled at the profusion of sixteenth-, seventeenth-, and eighteenth-century art, intricate sterling silverware, rare books, exquisite old china, Renaissance Christian iconography, and such fine antique furniture as a pair of French Regency armchairs in *petit point* and *gros point* needlework and a Louis XIV walnut wing chair in verdure tapestry. In fact, tapestries—some hung, others screen-mounted or framed—appeared in most every room, including the large one from Gobelins that had hung at Kings Point and several rare ones by Dutchman Johann Van Tiegen.

Christmas parties at "the lodge" "were the talk of the town," according to the museum website, and a neighbor recalled that back when she was a teenager, she and a group of carolers were invited into the house where they sang while Abraham played the great Estey organ that had once lived at Kings Point, and then everyone partook of an elaborate spread of holiday delicacies.

Bendel was creating not one but two Shangri-las, one northern, one southern, and these weren't his only major real estate investments. In March of 1929, six months before the Wall Street crash that would plunge the nation

Henri reading in the sunroom of Laurel Lake Lodge

into the Great Depression, he made news by purchasing 10–12 West Fifty-Seventh Street, the building he had been leasing since he opened his store there in 1913, for nearly $2 million (he had bought No. 14 in 1916 when he expanded). Now Henri owned his entire physical store and the ground beneath it, not just the brand within.

In the next few years, the store and its allure would continue to grow, at least outwardly. In August of 1931 it added new and distinct departments for gloves, scarves, and hosiery, and that same year it installed a ready-to-wear department—the term for lower-priced dresses that were made in quantity, in set sizes, requiring little or no alterations and ready to be bought "off-the-rack." In actuality Bendel's had carried some ready-to-wear since as early as 1910 but expanding such within-reach categories made sense as the Depression put a dent in at least some of Bendel's shoppers' budgets (what would later be called the "lipstick effect" was the theory that in an economic downturn buyers forewent big-ticket items for small luxuries), although, not unlike today, there remained in New York and beyond a stratum of rich people so rich that they were unaffected by the Depression, and they helped keep all of the high-end stores afloat. Regardless, ready-to-wear—the continuation of a national trend toward ease and democratization in fashion—was a wave Bendel had to ride.

"I despise the American *prêt-à-porter,*" Henri said privately to his great-niece Marjorie Meyer, using the French expression, "but with these times customers want a cheaper ready-to-wear line for their daughters going to college."

Still committed to custom-fitted dresses and fine stitchwork, Henri required top-notch seamstresses and he found one, remarkably enough, on a visit back home. Mary Rose Sibille had studied business at Southwestern Louisiana Institute (now the University of Louisiana at Lafayette) and been a yeomanette in the US Naval Reserve in Virginia during World War I, where she met her husband. In her late thirties, back in Lafayette and raising two children, Rose had parlayed

Bendel Buys Buildings Housing 57th St. Store

Specialty Shop Acquires 10 and 12 West 57th Street in Large Realty Transaction

Henri Bendel, Inc., has just acquired 10 and 12 West 57th street, which together with 14 West 57th street, it has been occupying for a number of years. The Bendel firm already owns 14 West 57th street. Although the amount of money involved in the transaction was not made known, it is estimated that an expenditure of close to $2,000,000 was made in the acquisition of the properties.

The structures at 10 and 12 West 57th street are nine stories high and the building at 14 West 57th street is 10 stories high. No changes in the Bendel home are contemplated, it was said.

Henri Bendel, president of the firm, is said to be responsible for the establishment of the 57th street section as what is sometimes referred to the Rue de la Paix of New York. Seventeen years ago, Mr. Bendel established headquarters on that street and during the past few years a migration of the high grade specialty shops to that section has been in progress.

The Bendel business occupies 12.500 square feet of space in the above structures, with a frontage of 72 feet on 57th street.

L. J. Phillips & Co. was the broker in the transaction and Nathaniel D. Reich, of Strauss, Reich & Boyer, acted as attorney for the buyer.

Mr. Bendel is at present in Louisiana, following a sojourn of several weeks in Palm Beach, where he went to attend the opening of the company's store. He is expected to return in about two weeks.

A 1929 *Women's Wear Daily* article about Henri purchasing the buildings he had been renting since 1913

Bendel's Snootier Side

From Gretta Palmer's 1930
tongue-in-cheek
A Shopping Guide to New York

"In the same patrician class is the establishment of Henri Bendel (pronounced as if he were an Englishman) at 10 W 57th St. This house has a maddening tendency to play favorites among its customers, who eat it up. They have in stock some of the most superb dresses from the French houses every season, but unless they are assured of your lineage you will not be allowed a peek at them. One reason for this is their earnest wish to safeguard their best customers from the embarrassment of meeting the same dress at [the races in] Aiken [South Carolina]. Indeed, if they know all about you and your plans, they can manipulate the model so that no one will suffer the indignity of seeing anyone wearing a duplicate of her own dress. Another reason for Bendel's renown is their remarkable flair for whisking out imports for a few intimates before they have appeared in the Paris collections of the designers themselves. For years I have scoffed at this claim, but they have finally convinced me that it is true. Bendel's has probably as many members of the Social Register on their list as anyone, if that sort of thing impresses you, and they never depart from their standards of well-bred, slightly cautious, chic."

a talent for sewing into part-time work, and one of her clients was Henri's sister, Louise Meyer. Bendel met her and was so impressed with her skill that he offered her a job in New York and moved her and her family up in 1930. According to Sibille clan history, under Henri's employ Rose sewed dresses for such disparate luminaries as the actress Joan Blondell, writer Alice Longworth (Teddy Roosevelt's daughter), and the Queen of Siam—not to mention various Astors and Vanderbilts.

By the end of 1931 Bendel was ensconced in Laurel Lake Lodge, along with Abraham and Little Henri. There's no evidence that John Blish remained in the domestic mix, and nothing has emerged to even hint at how his relationship with Bendel may have shifted or when he left the store—possibly several years prior. As someone who had lived, worked, and traveled with Henri for the better part of three decades, Blish's departure had to have changed the timbre of Henri's daily life. On whose accord did he leave? We can only wonder. In any case, records show that John Dennison Blish died in Clifton Springs, New York, near Rochester, on August 9, 1933, at the age of seventy-seven. From their earliest acquaintance at Altman's department store in the late 1800s, through their discreet domestic arrangements and Blish's public role at the store, John and Henri had been crucial pillars of each other's world.

Henri traveled to Paris in the summer of 1932 and by 1933 he had rented a new furnished apartment in Manhattan, at 400 East Fifty-Second Street, presumably for staying in town after late dinners or trips to the theater when he didn't feel like making the ride back to Connecticut or when he had a particularly early morning appointment. This may have been a short rental, just a year or two, because eventually he settled into a spacious apartment at 399 Park Avenue, at the corner of 54th Street, in the heart of Midtown.

In late 1933 Henri's long, deep dedication to France was reciprocated: the nation bestowed upon

HENRI BENDEL

Black On White: White On Black

A Bendel's ensemble—perhaps designed in-house—in a striking editorial photo in *Harper's* in 1932.
The photographer, Toni von Horn, was one of very few female fashion photographers then;
she camouflaged herself with the name Toni to better secure work.

NOVEMBER 1, 1933 47

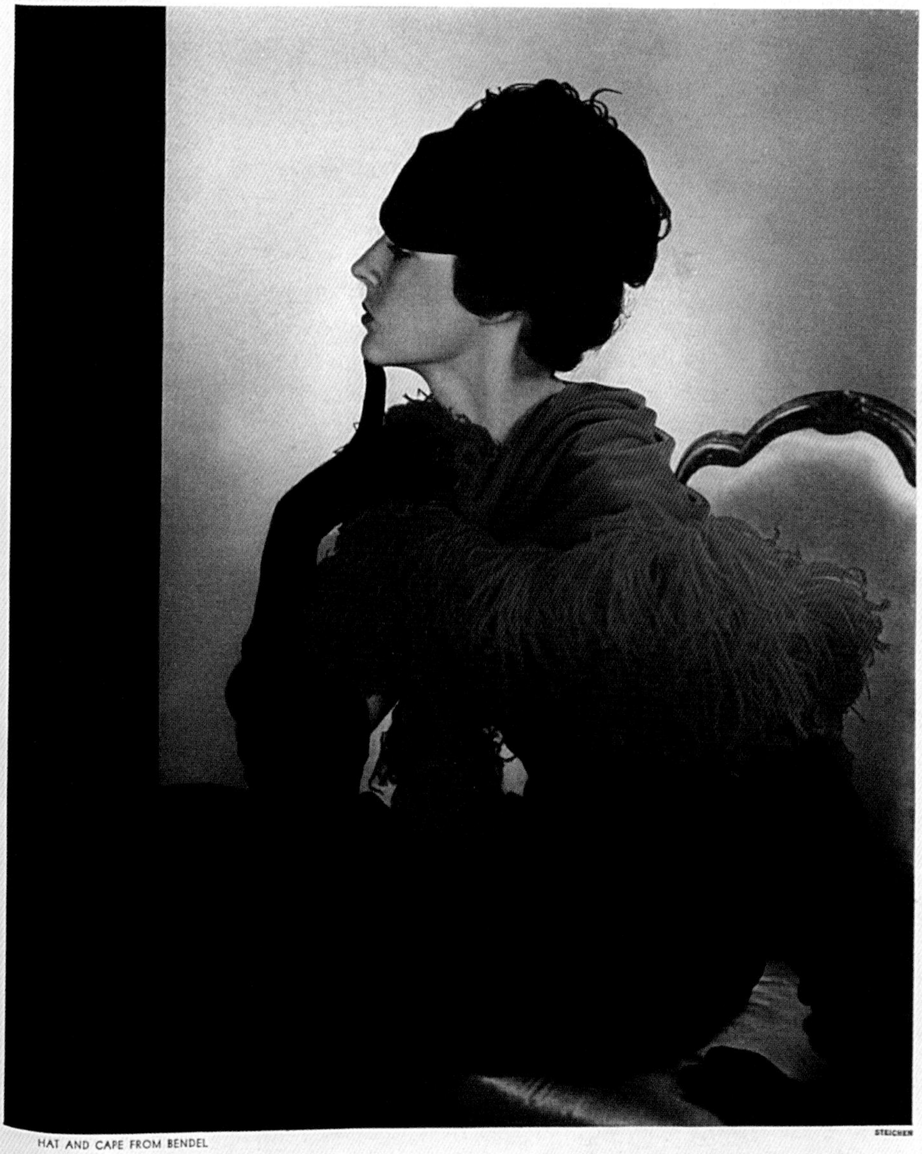

HAT AND CAPE FROM BENDEL

STEICHEN

Theatre hat—engagingly small

When you go to the theatre in a hat (and every one will, these nights)—let it be something small and extravagantly feminine and ostrich bedecked such as this one, which makes you think of Fritzi Scheff, and after-theatre suppers at Delmonicos, and ladies stepping out of hansom cabs in 1900. It is of velvet, as is the colourful cape, short and ostrich-edged. Chair from Lavezzo

A dramatic hat and theater cape from Bendel took center stage in the deftly lit photo by master lensman Edward Steichen, shooting for *Vogue* in 1933.

him one of its highest honors, the Legion of
Honor, in recognition, according to the *New
York Times,* "of his sponsorship of true French
fashion in the United States." *Vogue* raised
a glass to his achievement in their February
1934 issue:

> Mr. Henri Bendel from now on will be
> seen with a little red ribbon in his lapel,
> for the French government has given him
> the Légion d'Honneur in recognition of
> his devotion to the cause of French art
> and industry in this country. Mr. Bendel
> was a pioneer in Fifty-Seventh Street. His
> was the first shop to be opened there, and
> for 27 years Henri Bendel has occupied
> a place of peculiar prestige, both with
> the American couture and with the great
> houses of Paris. Personally speaking, we
> feel that a quarter-century of dressing
> women beautifully is in itself ground for
> any medal, crown, or Order of the Bath.

The following autumn he received an honor of a different sort, a uniquely
American one, when the Cole Porter musical *Anything Goes*, about shipboard
shenanigans and romance, opened on Broadway, starring Ethel Merman. In
the rousing number "You're the Top," a classic list song with lines like "You're
the Colosseum / You're the Louvre Museum / A melody in a symphony by
Strauss," Henri found himself in the company of superlatives:

Henri's apartment
building at 399
Park Avenue

> *You're a Bendel bonnet,*
> *A Shakespeare sonnet,*
> *You're Mickey Mouse!*

Forever after, in endless recordings, live cabaret croonings, and thousands
of stagings of the popular show, the song would keep Henri Bendel in the pan-
theon, snug in his stanza beside the Bard of Avon and the world's most beloved
rodent. In the words of another song Merman popularized, who could ask for
anything more?

CHAPTER 10

GOING HOME

$\mathcal{B}$ENDEL HAD ACQUIRED MANY LABELS over the years, from merchant and milliner to dressmaker, designer, importer, couturier, costumer, arbiter, expert, and chief. And by the mid-1930s he both owned and transcended them all. He was a luminary beyond the fashion world, a name recognized across the country—*the* Henri Bendel.

Gratifying as that was, Henri, now in his midsixties, still entertained challenges aplenty, and every day was not a Cole Porter musical. For starters, there were serious headwinds at the store. In 1933 the company's capital stock had decreased in value from $3,650,000 to $715,000, which a spokesperson for the store explained to *Women's Wear Daily* "merely represented a writing down of the value of certain assets carried on the books of the corporation for a long time." But by 1934 and 1935, the cumulative effect of the Depression on women's spending habits, the proliferation of competing high-end dressmakers, and a battering by unions and trade groups—empowered by President Roosevelt's National Industrial Recovery Act (NIRA) of 1933 and its attendant National Recovery Administration (NRA), which established codes regarding trade practices including employment quotas and minimum wages—had the store in straits. "Calamitous," Henri admitted later, after the Supreme Court struck down the act, and as the store erased red ink from his ledgers.

"The good intentions which lay back of this law were completely nullified by the law itself and by the methods by which it was administered," he argued to *Women's Wear Daily* in 1935. "Let me give you a specific example: before the [NIRA] we never employed more than eight porters. Today we employ nine. During the [time of the act] we had to have 20 porters, more than twice as many as we have ever needed during the most prosperous times of our business, and the same increase in personnel and the same restrictions in management applied to almost every other department in our business. The rise in our overhead was appalling and seriously endangered the organization and the employment of hundreds of skilled workers and trained salespeople."

OPPOSITE: An oil painting of Bendel in his later years, artist unknown, which lives at the Lafayette Museum

159

"Had the [act] continued," he said flatly, "it was my firm intention to sell my business to my employees and to retire on my modest savings. Business had become intolerable under those conditions."

Beyond business worries, Henri was tormented, at least intermittently, by very poor health. The *New York Times* had made mention of his being ill when it wrote about his receiving the Legion of Honor from France, and the subject became public again in the spring of '34 when *Women's Wear Daily* ran an item about Henri "continuing to show progress" after having been confined to his home due to illness. No specifics were offered. "With the advent of more favorable weather," the trade paper said, no doubt echoing some store representative, "it is expected that Mr. Bendel's recuperation will be greatly spurred." This was sheer spin—sunny skies might lift his spirits but not his underlying condition. The reality was that Bendel had been suffering from ulcerative proctitis, a form of ulcerative colitis, and it was severe enough that in October of 1934 he underwent a colostomy. Never in Henri's lifetime was this made public. Decades later his great-niece Elene Davis recounted hearing that he

Buddy Schmulen sailing for Europe with Henri's great-niece Marjorie Meyer on the *Berengaria* in June of 1933

spent "a lot of time" at the prestigious Mayo Clinic in Rochester, Minnesota. His having ulcerative proctitis would explain previous bouts of sickness, and, as with any chronic illness, had to have been not only a physical hardship for Henri, but emotionally draining too.

Still, Bendel must have felt well enough just prior to that, in the late summer and early fall of 1934, to host Marjorie Meyer, his great-niece from Yoakum, Texas, when she returned to the United States after spending a year in Paris attending the Sorbonne Institute. She was about to start classes at Columbia University in New York City. The year before, Henri not only paid for her first-class crossing on the RMS *Berengaria*, but he also dispatched her cousin Buddy— Leon Schmulen, his lieutenant at the store—to accompany her on the trip. Henri clearly saw something special in Marjorie and may have felt extra doting after his sister Lena—Marjorie's grandmother—passed away in 1929.

Now that the young woman was in New York, Henri planned to keep an eye on her and give her spending money as she started school.

In her memoir, Marjorie recounts seeing the Connecticut house for the first time when Buddy drove her up the long driveway and she marveled at its style and stature, likening it to that of a château. "Inside, the impression continued," she wrote, "with ornate French furniture, every piece an authentic antique. Some of the pieces were probably still upholstered in their original fabric. Certainly the satin damask covering some of the sofas was worn to shreds. I thought it was pretty awful to have shabby old furniture, but I realized whatever Uncle Henri had was expensive, so I didn't offer my opinion." She marveled that each of the five bedrooms had its own dressing room and bath, and some had adjacent little sitting spaces. The room Bendel picked for her was drenched in chintz. "Blue and white flowered material draped the windows, papered the walls, and covered the upholstered chairs. A downy quilted coverlet of the same material lay upon the bed. I felt like a princess."

A straw and silk Bendel hat, circa 1935, now in the collection of the Metropolitan Museum of Art, New York

Two looks for autumn of 1934 from the influential couture house Schiaparelli

The next day Big Henri had Little Henri take Marjorie to Manhattan to pick out fall clothes for school from Bendel's Young-Timers boutique. (Little Henri, she later noted, "was 28 and anything but little.") That's when Big Henri made the disparaging comment about cheaper ready-to-wear. "Actually, what Uncle Henri called 'cheaper' appeared pretty expensive to me," she wrote. "Some of the clothes cost almost a hundred dollars, and I gladly took everything that was offered: a new cloth coat, some sweaters, skirts, suits, and dresses." She knew better than to reach for a shorter skirt, something above the knee. "Uncle Henri would've disowned me."

Seeing how Marjorie had been careful with her money in her year abroad, instead of giving her a monthly allowance while she attended school, Henri decided she'd get $500 now and another $500 at midterm. "I thought he was the most generous man in the world." She savored a trip with him into Manhattan for dinner and the theater; they took in the popular Kaufman and Hart play *Merrily We Roll Along* about a successful man who abandons his values and his relationships, told backward from his middle-aged dissolution to his idealistic youth. No one could accuse Henri of such a fate.

While she was in school in Manhattan Marjorie was often invited by Bendel to spend weekends in Connecticut and bring a friend. Once, when she had to decline, as she had plans to weekend at a house in Garden City, Long Island, with the family of a girl she'd met at the Sorbonne, she got an eye-opening lesson in not-so-subtle suburban prejudice.

"Don't you know they don't allow Jews in Garden City?" Henri said to her, matter-of-factly.

Marjorie couldn't believe it. "Are you sure?" she asked. "It's only a few miles from Great Neck, where Aunt Fanny and Buddy live. How could that be?"

"Well," said Henri, "that's the way it is. Jews live in some towns and not in others."

He was quick to call out the unwritten code, but his apparent resignation to it was perhaps typical of the age. And though he worshipped as a Christian and had the wealth and standing that gave him entry into most every enclave of private and public life, as a Jew by birth and upbringing, the inequity had to be galling and painful whether he showed it or not. In fact, his regular trips to France and other parts of Europe—he and Abraham went over again in the fall of '34—would've made him more clear-eyed than many Americans about the political and fanatical forces that were swirling in Italy, Germany, and beyond, with omens of worse things to come.

The next year he glancingly—almost cryptically—spoke of this to *Women's Wear Daily*. "Europe is filled with a strange and weird and dangerous

An undated photo of Henri, looking gaunt and unhealthy, outside Laurel Lake Lodge in Stamford with Bastedo and unidentified guests; the young man may have been an employee.

military ardor," he said. "The masculine idea is permeating a certain phase of fashion where degeneracy rather than art is the standard. The over-emphasis on military force is perhaps responsible for this." His main points were of fashion, not fascism, as he went on to decry man-tailored jackets and slacks on women. But the phrase "dangerous military ardor" cut deeper than style concerns. Henri the Europhile had seen something behind the glory of the Continent's fashion, art, and history of empire building. Something darker.

Beyond the disturbing movements abroad, the national fatigue of the ongoing Great Depression, and the challenges at the store, 1935 was tough on Bendel personally. His sister Fanny Schmulen, who lived in Great Neck, passed away at the end of February. (Her husband, Gus, had died back in 1932.) And then in June he lost his younger brother Sam, who lived in Monroe, Louisiana. Of his seven siblings, now only Ike, Louise, Rose, and Emma remained. Having stayed so close to all his family, Bendel, at sixty-seven, must have felt not only deeply saddened but attuned to his own mortality.

Five days before Christmas that year, he gave *Women's Wear Daily* a remarkably long and roaming interview—the one in which he spoke about the National Industrial Recovery Act and his having considered selling the store, and about the militarism in Europe. He sounded like a lion in winter,

A 1935 Bendel's ad in *Vogue* featuring a Chanel dress

The influence of the Fashion Originators Guild, which was created to dissuade unlicensed copying, extended to garment labels.

battle weary but standing proud. His interrogator was Morris De Camp Crawford, editor of *Women's Wear* whom Bendel had befriended and come to trust; even so, Henri's candor and volubility were striking. He hit some familiar grandiose notes about quality, standards, and what Bendel's customers expected, but he also pulled back the curtain on his business and lowered his guard a bit, owning the frustrations and fears he had recently experienced.

Among many topics, he addressed conflicts with the Fashion Originators Guild of America, an alliance of dress- and fabric-makers who had banded together in 1932 to discourage copying, which they called piracy. They demanded strict allegiance from sellers and manufacturers, establishing a boycott against outfits that wouldn't comply with their rules about who could buy from whom. So called "red-carded" vendors shouldn't be carried by stores, or the stores would be penalized. The group's aggressive activism defended designer and garment makers' rights, but it waded into murky waters both legally, as fashion doesn't fall under laws akin to patent or copyright, and practically, as dressmaking always builds on popular looks and it's hard to adjudicate what is a replica and what is merely similar. Besides that, merchants such as Bendel who were opposed to certain strictures of the guild argued that these practices had the unwanted effect of calibrating market prices in an arbitrary and artificial way. It was holding businesses hostage, they felt.

Henri was glad to see the guild lose some of its teeth with the Supreme Court ruling against the National Industrial Recovery Act, but he aimed to keep a civil tone in the interview, knowing he still had to work with many members. "For 40 years the House of Bendel has stood for the basic principles of style protection which is the foundation of the Fashion Originators Guild program," he said.

> It is not egotism on my part when I say that the name Henri Bendel stands for honest dealing with its customers and with its sources of supply. . . . No creator of style, either in fabrics or in apparel, is the worse for my being in business and, regardless of whatever action they will take toward me, they will always find me in the same frame of mind. I was an enemy of style piracy before the Guild was even a dream. I will not copy and I will not permit myself to be copied if I can protect myself. I will not undersell and I will not permit any merchant to undersell me.

At times in the conversation, he exhibited bald defiance. "I will run my business as I have always run it," he said, "to suit the tastes and convenience of my clients. I earnestly hope for a continuation of the present friendly relationships with all of our many sources of supply but I am amply prepared to protect my own position. I feel that the Guild leaders, as individuals at least, now regard me as a constructive influence and will never force me from the present position of friendly relations."

Admitting that just the previous spring his business was in "a most calamitous condition . . . as bad as in 1934," Bendel was happy to report that things were greatly improving, even if "it is true that collections are a little slow." He said that his bottom line was up 40 percent since the spring after the store reduced its profit margins and, he noted, "our credit risks are the soundest in the world." He allowed that the challenges had taken a toll and threatened the very existence of Bendel's, but he implied that he would rather fall on his sword than compromise his values. "These have been anxious times for all of us," he said. "It has not been easy to keep up standards. But how can I tear down a lifetime of effort at the call of a temporary emergency? If I had to go down in the storm of this financial crisis I determined to go down doing the best I knew how. I determined that the last garment sold in the store should be the best I could make or buy for that price, and I determined to sell it at a fair and equitable price."

Then he was quick to drop gloomy thoughts of what might have befallen the store and instead project the buoyant persona that had defined him for so many decades. "All this is now past history," he assured Mr. Crawford. "The turn has come; confidence and enthusiasm have been restored and once more business is a pleasure; an exciting, entertaining and daily delight." It was in this optimistic frame of mind that Bendel threw himself into the familiar rhythms of Christmas and looked to a hopefully brighter new year.

In the winter of 1936, he and Abraham traveled to Lafayette. He visited with family and tended to his property, honing plans for his still-on-paper mansion by the river. E. A. McIlhenny, corresponding about orders placed for

> "It is a motto of the house—never to follow but always to lead, and for that one must keep thinking and be ever on the alert. One lapse and the other fellow is ahead."
>
> —*Henri Bendel*

CATHEDRAL, LAFAYETTE, LA.

56451-C

The Cathedral of Saint John in Lafayette, near where Henri grew up and adjacent to the Cathedral School where he was invited to speak to students

grafted camellia shrubs, as well as for bamboo and wisteria, suggested that Henri also plant live oaks, to be spaced seventy-five feet apart, saying they would enhance his existing allée of magnolia trees and "give dignity to the approach to where your house is to be built." But Bendel was not consistently in good health, likely owing to his gastric issues. "Unfortunately I have been ill all week and scarcely able to go out," he wrote to McIlhenny in mid-February. "It would've been a great pleasure to lunch with you and Mrs. McIlhenny but I cannot always make plans."

Still, his renown had made him an in-demand guest, and he felt well enough around that same time to accept an invitation to visit the Cathedral School (for boys) and its sister institution, Mount Carmel Academy. At Cathedral, just around the corner from the clapboard house in which Henri had grown up, at an assembly of more than fifty students from various French classes organized by the Alliance Franco Louisianne, he received accolades from Brother Alexander, the principal, and V. F. Mouton, the French Consular Agent, followed by readings, recitations, and songs, all in French. The *Daily Advertiser,* writing about it on February 20th, 1936, reported that Mr. Mouton "referred to Mr. Bendel's early days in Lafayette and his devotion and love for his native city" as well as his receipt of France's Legion of Honor. "Mr. Bendel urged the continued study of the French language and emphasized his appreciation for the kind reception accorded him."

At nearby Mount Carmel, Henri was welcomed by Mother Superior Gabrielle. "Mr. Bendel recalled interesting memories of the childhood days of his sisters when they attended Mount Carmel and paid a special tribute to Mother Hyacinthe, Mother Patrick and Mother Clair. The pupils of Mount Carmel rendered a program of old French songs, including 'Sur le Pont d'Avignon' and 'Savez-Vous Planter les Choux.'"

Savez-vous planter les choux
À la mode, à la mode?
Savez-vous planter les choux
À la mode de chez nous?

Do you know how to plant a cabbage
In the fashion, in the fashion?
Do you know how to plant a cabbage
In the fashion that we do?

Bathed in this admiration and nostalgia for his youth, in his beloved hometown where time could seem to stand still or even drift backward, listening to American students singing French songs with perfect pronunciation, did Henri see the arc of his life bending into a graceful circle? Did he maybe smile inwardly at the phrase that echoes throughout the tune—"à la mode, à la mode"?

In the fashion, in the fashion . . .

Was it not a most apt refrain for the guest of honor?

Over the years, Bendel nurtured new friends in Lafayette. Back in January 1930, he and Abraham visited with Beverly Stephens, wife of Edwin L. Stephens, president of Southwestern Louisiana Institute (now UL Lafayette) and visiting dignitary Dr. Albert E. Winship of Boston, the editor of the *Journal of Education*, in the president's garden. (Dr. Stephens took the picture.)

Bendel taking in the beauty of his azalea bed in Stamford, Connecticut, and (OPPOSITE) the *New York Times* account of his funeral in Manhattan

Bendel stayed in Lafayette just another few weeks, long enough to see his bounteous azaleas start to put on their shameless fuchsia-pink-purple-coral-white show. Then he and Abraham headed back to blustery New York, back to work.

Henri was in the city, in his apartment on Park Avenue, on the evening of March 22, 1936, a Sunday, when just after sundown he was seized by a heart attack. He died on the spot. The coroner's report identified "coronary artery thrombosis of the heart (general arterial sclerosis)" as the primary cause—the parenthetical phrase "general arterial sclerosis" was written that way by the coroner, who also noted Bendel's colostomy as a contributing condition. Obviously Henri didn't see his end as imminent, but for whatever reason, two months prior, on January 17, he had filed his last will and testament.

The *New York Times* reported the news of his passing the next morning, calling him a style leader whose "taste and keen sense of what the New York woman wanted led to his steadily increasing success and the eventual addition of his stock of almost everything that 'the well-dressed woman' would wish to buy." The obituary invoked his role in turning Fifty-Seventh Street into the "Rue de la Paix of New York," recalled his 1923 gift to employees of 45 percent of $4 million worth of capital stock, and wrote that he was a widower survived by four siblings—which was a failure to account for niece Florye, nephew Little Henri, and companion Abraham. The *Times,* incidentally, said Bendel was sixty-nine when in fact he had turned sixty-eight exactly two months earlier.

Women's Wear Daily's long tribute recounted Henri's start in wholesale in the late 1800s, and his move to Fifth Avenue when he didn't have money to advertise and had to rely on his window displays, which he executed himself. "Mr. Bendel's passing," the trade paper wrote, "has drawn many expressions of sorrow from the creators of this famous thoroughfare where his smart good humor and stimulating competition will be missed."

"Mr. Bendel," the paper continued, "once said he could count among his customers many who had patronized him for three generations—mother, daughter, and grandchildren. Through this long service [he] came to occupy a unique position in the confidence of socially prominent families. For to him they turned for all their important functions—for weddings, debuts, anniversaries and so on—and frequently Bendel was the first to know about them." Maurice Renter, chairman of the Fashion Originators Guild of America, the organization with which Henri had once been at odds, told the paper that Bendel "exemplified the best in qualified retailing, and by sticking closely to the finer types of merchandise succeeded well in impressing his personality on retailing. He showed conclusively that those who know and appreciate the quality market in New York City can carve out a niche for themselves. His passing will leave a void in the ranks of high grade retailing."

500 ATTEND RITES FOR HENRI BENDEL

Friends From Many Walks of Life at Services for Women's Shop President.

More than 500 friends, customers and employes attended funeral services yesterday afternoon for Henri Bendel, founder and president of the women's specialty house of Henri Bendel, Inc., at the Campbell Funeral Church, Broadway and Sixty-sixth Street.

Mr. Bendel, who died on Sunday of a heart attack at his home, 399 Park Avenue, was 69 years old. He came to New York from Lafayette, La., in 1899 and moved to his present place of business, 10 West Fifty-seventh Street, about twenty-five years ago. As a reward to his employes, Mr. Bendel left 45 per cent of $4,000,000 in company shares to them.

The ceremony was conducted by the Rev. Dr. Alexander McKechnie, pastor of All Saints' Church, Great Neck, L. I., where Mr. Bendel was a member of the congregation for many years.

'Henri Bendel was

Bendel and Bastedo's shared grave on a hill in stately Kensico cemetery in Valhalla, New York. Henri had conceived of the copper sculpture of a mourning woman, and it was fabricated in France. Abraham's name was added after he died in 1953.

Down in Lafayette the *Daily Advertiser* referred to Bendel as "an internationally known fashion designer" and wrote that he "always took a great interest in Lafayette and Southwest Louisiana and looked forward eagerly to his visits here for the renewal of his many acquaintanceships. He had made extensive plans for the development of his large estate here, but these had been deferred owing to general conditions, and also to Mr. Bendel's ill-health. . . . Mr. Bendel's estate, with its most attractive lodge and beautifully landscaped grounds, is one of the special points of interest to visitors here especially during the season when the azaleas and other flowers are in bloom."

That Wednesday some five hundred mourners, including friends, employees, and even devoted customers filed into the Frank E. Campbell Funeral Home chapel then located at Broadway and Sixty-Sixth Street on the Upper West Side of Manhattan for the afternoon service. Ike and Louise had come up from Lafayette and presumably Henri's sisters Rose Kahn and Emma Meyer were there as well. The Reverend Dr. Alexander McKechnie of All Saints' Church of Great Neck officiated and during his homily praised Bendel as "a Christian gentleman who always lived with his God [and who] was loved for his generous spirit by everyone who came in contact with him." The music was selected from Henri's favorites including Handel's "Largo," Edward F. Johnston's "Evensong," and "Andante Cantabile" by Tchaikovsky. A Black gospel quartet sang the spirituals "Lead, Kindly Light," and "Going Home."

Then about 150 of the assembled made the hour-long drive up to Valhalla, New York, in Westchester County, where Henri was interred at bucolic Kensico Cemetery. Later, a permanent monument was erected there, a large copper likeness of a robed woman solemnly tossing roses upon the granite crypt. Henri had conceived of her himself; the artfully detailed figure was sculpted and cast in Paris.

The subsequent reading of Bendel's will revealed that his gross estate totaled over $1.2 million, "a respectable sum in the Depression year of 1936," as Lafayette historian Alvin Bethard observed. Mr. Bastedo would inherit the lion's share, and the stone lions—$200,000 and the use of Laurel Lake Lodge in Stamford for life, plus half of Henri's common stock of Henri Bendel, Inc. And, it was stipulated, the right to be buried with Henri. After Abraham died in 1953, he was indeed interred at Kensico and the single name Bastedo was chiseled into the granite, just below the name Bendel, in lettering of equal size.

Henri II—Little Henri—inherited $100,000 "plus income from 15 percent of common stock of Bendel Inc until sold, then all of principal, and the balance of the stock undistributed," as reported in the *New York Times*. All Bendel's surviving siblings and some of his nieces and other nephews received smaller bequests, including cash, stock, and land interests in Louisiana.

The morning after Henri's funeral and burial, Henri Bendel the store opened its doors for business. It would continue to do so nearly daily for the next eighty-three years.

CHAPTER 11

BENDEL'S AFTER BENDEL

$\mathcal{I}$N CREATING BENDEL'S, HENRI HAD BUILT A TEMPLATE for sophisticated fashion retail that would prove surprisingly resilient. But to survive, the store had to adapt, and in fits and starts it did. Going forward it came to bear the imprimaturs of the people and corporations who led it, as well as reflect evolving times, tastes, and industry forces. The balance of Bendel's long run divides fairly neatly into three main eras: the family-dominated period from the time of Henri's death all the way through the mid-1950s; then twenty-nine years under president Geraldine Stutz and (for most of those years) the company Genesco; and finally, the thirty-three-year stretch from 1986 until 2019, after the store was bought by The Limited corporation. Each period had its hallmarks—from elegant propriety to edgy high fashion with clever merchandising, then a step toward mass appeal with branches around the country, which, just prior to the end, came to rely on accessories, cosmetics, and a large degree of flashiness.

And each era had its challenges and setbacks. For many years the store ran in the red, and several times it nearly succumbed, always to be scooped up and resuscitated. For each leader who stepped in to save it—or refused to kill it—there must have been a conviction that despite underlying deficiencies it was a brand with such history, customer loyalty, and positive associations that there was value in the name alone. That romantic, nearly blind faith in the moniker "Henri Bendel" carried the store far but couldn't carry it forever.

Before the curtain came down, and even in the toughest times, Bendel's would hit dazzling highs in its merchandise, marketing, and mystique. It would attract new generations of stylish women and celebrity clientele, and it would make a mark, as Henri had, by introducing and nurturing exciting new designers. The store's reach would expand too, first in select full-size

OPPOSITE: A tree of Bendel boxes in the flagship store in New York
ABOVE: A twenty-first-century Bendel's shopping bag

An older shopping bag

Opposite: A 1940 Bendel's ad in *Vogue* "for boudoir and bath" products with fabled model Lisa Fonssagrives, photographed by George Platt Lynes

satellite stores in several big cities, then finally in small stores tucked into high-end malls across America.

If the hypothetical loyal Bendel's shopper could time travel, she might not recognize—nor approve of—Bendel's from one era to the next, save for the brown and white stripes (and even they changed a bit), but she would have to admit that for the most part, with a few missteps, it had clung to its aura of luxury and stylishness and to some ineffable spirit that declared *ours is a store unlike the others.*

As for who would run Bendel's in the immediate aftermath of Henri's death, presumably a succession plan prioritizing his life partner and nephews had been in place. In early April of 1936 it was announced that Abraham Bastedo was elected president of Henri Bendel, Inc.; Henri Bendel II, who was twenty-eight, would become vice president and treasurer; Leon Schmulen, secretary; and Gaston de Clairville, who had been the store's head of millinery, was named vice president and general manager. In the first decade and a half of the post-Henri years, Bendel's appears to have chugged along smoothly, gauging by old advertisements and editorial coverage, with its same dedication to tailored, tasteful fashion and its wide offering of standard accessories. New looks and products emerged with changing times and styles, not so much in response to a changing of the guard. The men in charge had been trained by Henri and steeped in the ethos of the store for decades and well understood that much of Bendel's appeal was quiet consistency; they didn't care to fool around with a winning formula.

Bendel's continued to distinguish itself with importations from the likes of Molyneux, Chanel, Balenciaga, and Schiaparelli, as well as with French copies. "Our clients were, and to a degree still are, steeped in the Paris tradition," said Leon Schmulen, "and still sigh for the old days of the [couture] openings." But over time it increased its offerings of American designs and original house-brand creations, particularly during World War II when, once again, Parisian dresses were few and hard to come by. The late '30s and '40s saw Bendel's

EBRUARY 15, 1940

GEORGE PLATT LYNES

Beauty by Henri Bendel . . . the same traditional perfection that has long distinguished our Fashions now identifies our Boudoir and Bath Preparations. Available in fine shops throughout the country. Illustrated brochure on request.

Henri Bendel
10 WEST 57
NEW YORK

The film star Margaret Sullavan in a Bendel gown of white faille shot by acclaimed lensman George Hoyningen-Huene for *Harper's Bazaar* in 1936

AND MISS SULLAVAN AGAIN, IN A SWEEP OF WHITE FAILLE SHOT WITH PINK METALLIC THREADS.

THE EVENING GOWN, HENRI BENDEL.

image enhanced in magazine editorial spreads and its own ads by new artful, high-glamour photographers such as George Platt Lynes shooting both professional and celebrity models. In 1939, for example, Horst P. Horst photographed the famous debutante Brenda Frazier in a Bendel dress for *Vogue*, and in 1940 that magazine featured a full-page photo by Horst of the movie star Joan Bennett in a dark lamé dress from Bendel's. A *Harper's Bazaar* spread from 1942 set in the American West and photographed by Louise Dahl-Wolfe showed editor Diana Vreeland posing in a Bendel's suit

Grey Broadtail...a Bendel Original
from our collection

Joan Bennett in Lamé

Photographed in a dramatic dress a medieval heroine might have worn—Joan Bennett, whose new picture, "The Son of Monte Cristo," has just been released. The dress—mauve lamé and black rayon velvet. Henri Bendel. Jewels from Flato.

ABOVE LEFT: Model Lisa Fonssagrives in a fur coat, photographed by George Platt Lynes for *Vogue* in 1943

ABOVE RIGHT: In 1940 Horst captured movie star Joan Bennett wearing a gown of mauve lamé and black rayon velvet.

RIGHT: A "red heads for autumn" illustration of three bright Bendel hats, in *Vogue*, 1939

THREE HATS FROM HENRI BENDEL

Red heads for autumn

In 1942, *Harper's Bazaar* editor Diana Vreeland sported a Bendel suit in a fashion layout shot out west by noted photographer Louise Dahl-Wolfe. It was a rare modeling turn for the legendary fashion arbiter, who would one day launch the Metropolitan Museum of Art's famed costume collection.

in front of an old stagecoach station—a rare modeling moment for the future style doyenne.

By the late '40s and early '50s, Schmulen, who had been with the store since he was a teenager, assumed a front-of-house, elder statesman role, akin to that of his late uncle. Schmulen's great-nieces Barbara and Valentine Hertz, whose father David Bendel Hertz was the son of Leon's sister, Wilhelmina (Wilhel) Schmulen, recall the excitement, when they were young, of putting on their smocked dresses and patent leather Mary Jane shoes and going to the store with their mother or grandmother to visit Uncle Bud. Even though they grew up in New York City, "we'd never seen anything like Bendel's," says Barbara Hertz Burr, now a pediatric psychiatrist in Boston and the older of the sisters by three years. "It was bright and pretty, with pretty clothes and perfumed air. It seemed like a fairyland."

Her sister, Valentine Hertz Kass, former program director at the National Science Foundation in Alexandria, Virginia, recalls one particular visit, when she was about eight, when she sat quietly on a chair in the bridal department and observed her great-uncle assist a bride and her mother as the bride tried on gowns. "I was impressed with how calmly and patiently he helped them," says Kass. "I thought he was wonderful." The girls saw a lot of Schmulen away from the store too, and at holidays and on birthdays he was generous, once bringing them black velvet ice skating outfits with matching muffs, plus the skates to go with them, and on another occasion giving them a light-up world globe. Barbara recalls Uncle Bud being "sweet and doting, always affectionate" and he offered their family a discount on clothing when they came to the store.

A 1954 ad in *Vogue* showed a gown of silk faille taffeta "from our Immediate Wear Collection"– Bendel's new term for ready-to-wear.

Despite the warm customer service, the up-to-date fashion, and the glamour, by the mid-1950s Bendel's was financially shaky. Nicholas Parker, a Texan who had recently been the vice president and merchandising manager at Neiman Marcus in Dallas, came along with an offer to buy the store—including branches in Palm Beach and Southampton, New York. He paid over a million dollars to purchase the outstanding stock from the trustees, led by Leon Schmulen and Henri Bendel II, who were quite ready to sell. Henri II exited in 1955 and launched Belgian Shoes, a small

Bendel Original

from our Immediate Wear Collection. Silk faille taffeta with swathed shoulder drapery of matching silk satin...the billowing skirt, capriciously pocketed. In pale pink, hydrangea blue, navy, black...$275.

NOVEMBER 1, 1954

Henri Bendel
10 WEST 57
NEW YORK 19 NY

Henri Bendel II when he was an executive at the store in the late 1940s or early 1950s (the woman with him was most likely his secretary).

line of chic, high-end loafers favored by fashion insiders—and unfashionably fashionable Manhattanite Greta Garbo—which is still a coveted brand. (Little Henri died in 1997 at the age of eighty-nine and his only child, John Bendel, took over Belgian Shoes until his sudden death in 2013.) Leon Schmulen stayed on as a Bendel's employee until 1957—the last family member connected with the store—then jumped to nearby competitor Bergdorf Goodman as their "roving ambassador of fashion" until he passed away in 1961.

In a wonderful exit flourish, around the time of the sale of Bendel's to Parker, the family members donated more than seven thousand fashion sketches to the Brooklyn Museum of Art—a vast trove that chronicles not only what Bendel had been selling, but also the work of the most important French couturiers from the first half of the century, which fashion students and historians still benefit from today. (Over two thousand of them can be seen on the museum's website.)

Upon taking over, Parker said he planned no big changes other than the expansion of some departments. After the acquisition he campaigned for the city to make aesthetic enhancements to Fifty-Seventh Street, which he called a "faded lady," wanting shade trees and sidewalk cafés for a "Parisian atmosphere," according to the *New York Times*. He also proposed banning trucks. Neither of those ideas gained traction, and in any case Parker's tenure was short-lived. As the store was losing about $850,000 a year on 3.5 million volume it became ripe for a buyer with deeper pockets.

Genesco (once General Shoe Co.) was a huge shoe manufacturing company based in Nashville and run by W. Maxey Jarman, the Tennessee-born, Ivy League-educated son of the company's founder. One of its subsidiary companies was I. Miller, a distinguished New York shoe line. Jarman had enough confidence in a relatively young vice president there named Geraldine Stutz that he gave her an extraordinary opportunity. Stutz had started out as shoe editor at *Glamour* magazine before being hired by I. Miller, where she rose quickly through the ranks. (It was there that she pounced on a just-starting-out artist to draw whimsical illustrations of shoes for ad campaigns—Andy Warhol.) After Genesco bought Bendel's in 1957, Jarman hired the thirty-three-year-old Stutz as president, making her only the third woman—and the youngest by far—to run a major women's department store, after Hortense Odlum of Bonwit Teller (tenure from 1934–1940) and Dorothy Shaver of Lord & Taylor (1945–1959).

According to the *New York Times*, "Jarman decided that the Bendel's turn-around required drastic measures and installed Stutz at the helm . . . with free rein to reform the store as she saw fit." He gave her five years to erase the red ink, which she did—almost to the day—with a 1963 profit of $8,000 on sales of $5 million. Stutz didn't have much business experience, but she had taste, courage, and one big edge over the competition: as she told fashion columnist

The Bendel's storefront with its two distinct striped-awning entrances in the early 1960s.

Doing It Her Way

From "Gerry's Little Store on 57th Street" by Ann Crittenden, *The New York Times*, April 24, 1977

" And the woman is 52-year-old Geraldine Stutz, president of the high fashion women's specialty shop that she designed with a taste so sure and so strong that items gathered under Bendel's roof seem automatically to signal "This Is In"—a benediction that falls impartially on everything from $1500 clinging silk tunics to $15 tee shirts and the crusty croissants set out for hungry shoppers in a boutique called E.A.T.

The secret of Stutz's survival lies in combination of taste and absolute self-confidence in what she wants Bendel's to be. She single-mindedly set out to create a store offering 'not something for everybody, but everything for a special kind of customer,' as she put it in a recent interview.

[And] there have been enough women who wanted the kind of avant-garde but never-too-far-out clothes that Bendel's offered to enable the store to become a sort of laboratory of fashion ideas, many of them copied later by much larger stores.

'She promoted a new mobility of departments and emphasis on fleeting images and flexibility,' notes Mildred Custin, a fashion consultant and former president of Bonwit Teller. 'This pointed the way for stores like Bloomingdale's.'

Miss Stutz attributes much of Bendel's success to a philosophy that comes close to the now-familiar concept that small is beautiful. 'The bigger store, the blander. Size and character are not compatible,' she says flatly."

Geraldine Stutz in the 1950s at the start of her long and influential role as president of the store

> [Stutz has] "a taste so sure and so strong that items gathered under Bendel's roof seem automatically to signal 'This Is In.'"
>
> —*New York Times*

Marilyn Bender of the *Times* in the mid-1960s: "Andy Goodman [president of Bergdorf Goodman, a traditional rival of Bendel's] and all those boys are more experienced than I, but they are not a woman. I am. I am the customer." Trusting her gut and empowering her lieutenants, Stutz created a store for a new kind of shopper—questing, fashion-forward, and young at heart if not literally young. "We picked a customer to concentrate on," she told Bender. "She's 20 to 60, depending on her point of view, but she's hip. And she is not going to grow old with me."

Raised in Chicago where she attended Catholic school before going off to Mundelein College to study theater, English lit, and journalism, Stutz brought Phi Beta Kappa smarts and dramatic flair to Bendel's, "and transformed [it] into a mirror of her uncompromising fashion-editor taste," as the *Times* wrote in 1977. She famously reconceptualized the first floor into an arcade of twelve individually styled and cleverly named boutiques running along a large U-shaped corridor, designed by architect H. McKim Glazebrook. Stutz dubbed this fanciful environment the Street of Shops, devoted not to dresses but to accessories and beyond. There was Shoe Biz for shoes, Scentiments for perfumes and soaps, The Leg Shop for hosiery, The Gilded Cage for makeup, and so on. Soon after, Stutz augmented apparel with jewelry, stationery, and linens, and she featured vendors such as Frank McIntosh, purveyor of stylish housewares; Lee Bailey, with his signature contemporary tableware and kitchen accoutrement; and the deluxe potpourri and candles company Agraria, whose boutique was located at the entrance. "Fifty-seventh Street was heaven," designer Michael Kors—another Stutz discovery—told *Vogue*.

Stutz in the Street of Shops in the early 1980s. The mini-stores-within-the-store concept was her game-changing idea.

And the Award for Oldest Oscar Dress Goes to . . .

❝Watch the Academy Awards show this weekend. I think you'll find it fascinatin.' I found an old Fortuny dress ol' man Bendel made for me thirty years ago, and it didn't need alterin' at all—I think you'll find it very interestin'."

—Actress Ruth Gordon to Bendel's president Geraldine Stutz, a few days before the seventy-two-year-old thespian and fashion enthusiast accepted the best supporting actress Oscar in 1969 for her role in *Rosemary's Baby* (as recounted by restaurateur Faith Stewart-Gordon in her memoir *The Russian Tea Room: A Love Story*)

Ruth Gordon after her big win

"I smelled the Agraria potpourri wafting out of Henri Bendel, but I just thought the street smelled good."

"Geraldine had a vision," said Jean Rosenberg, who was the vice president and merchandising director at Bendel's from six months before Ms. Stutz's arrival in 1957 to their joint departure nearly thirty years later, in 1986. "It was for a particular kind of New York woman, where she could find a uniformity of taste and a certain amount of comfort in a smallish environment, where everything in one store was to her liking."

Having boutiques or designer-specific zones within stores has been the industry standard for decades; back then it was novel. Stutz invented it. And Street of Shops was an instant hit. "It was brilliant," says author and fashion leader Fern Mallis, who in the '70s was an editorial assistant and who would go on to launch Seventh on Sixth, which brought all the fashion shows under one tent in Bryant Park. "Shoe Biz was incredible. And Bendel's had the best hosiery department, every color in the rainbow."

Stutz took that same sense of adventure and playfulness in Street of Shops up to the higher floors. The classicism of the old Bendel's kept a foothold on the second floor, with evening wear and furs, but one flight up, on three, Bendel's Cachet beckoned with contemporary sportswear. Savvy on four unleashed the younger, edgier styles, which became one of Bendel's most profitable departments. Lingerie and bridal were found on the fifth floor, and on the sixth floor Stutz added a hair salon in 1965. Working off the mantra of "Well, what would *I* like?" she had it decorated in peach and green with trellises and wicker furniture and flower-printed wallpaper. An early fitness enthusiast, in the mid-1970s Stutz installed a small spa and gym at the store; she even had it outfitted for the latest exercise innovation, Pilates equipment, and Joe Pilates himself oversaw the installation and posed shirtless for the press while exercising in his Wunda chair.

"She had a whim of iron," says designer and cosmetics creator Linda Rodin, who worked as a stylist for the Bendel's catalog in the early 1980s. And no details of display, marketing, or PR were too small to escape Stutz's attention; she even wrote much of the ad copy. Says Rodin: "She put her stamp on everything."

"The store is my theater and my show, and I am the producer and director," Stutz would tell *Fortune* magazine in 1980, when she was into her twenty-third year of tenure.

Window displays at Bendel's became a prime example of such theatricality—playful and sometimes edgy. In the early 1960s they were created by a charismatic prodigy fresh out of Parsons School of Design, Joel Schumacher, who would go on to a legendary career directing films like *St. Elmo's Fire*, *The Lost Boys*, and two Batman movies, among many. "Bendel's was then the jewel of all stores, probably in America," he would later say. In the 1970s Robert Currie was Bendel's display director in charge of what

"10 West 57 was like a nightclub and a candy store," says Robert Rufino, Bendel's visual director, who, along with his mentor Robert Currie, came up with dramatic and sometimes racy window displays in the 1970s and early '80s.

Actress Ingrid Boulting modeled for *New York* magazine the 1969 bohemian chic of Zandra Rhodes, a then twenty-seven-year-old London designer embraced by fashion-forward Bendel's.

Bendel's offered this 1960s ruffled chiffon dress by British designer Jean Muir, now in the costume collection of the MFA Boston.

Architectural Digest called "the humorously chic windows," and he groomed Robert Rufino to take up the mantle, deploying "street theater" design, with, as the *Times* noted, "slightly decadent models posed in tableaux, including one particularly soignée murder." (Rufino went on to big jobs at Tiffany & Co. and in magazines.) "It was a ritual every Thursday night to walk over and see the new window displays," recalls Mallis.

As seismic cultural shifts of the mid- and late-1960s reverberated up to high-end fashion, Stutz made equal impact by launching rising British and European stars such as Jean Muir, Sonia Rykiel, Chloé, and Vicky Tiel. "Bendel's was also the first store to go heavily into European ready to wear," wrote the *Times*, "partly because the small operation couldn't afford to buy in the volume demanded by Seventh Avenue designers, and partly because of a preference for the soft, young, close-to-the-body look of European clothes."

New American designers, too, proved to be important, including future legends Perry Ellis and Ralph Lauren. Stutz also helped to break racial boundaries; she was so enamored of the pioneering Black American designer Stephen Burrows that in the early 1970s she made him creator of a Bendel's house line of dresses and also offered him an in-store boutique called Stephen Burrows World for his own line. "You felt like you'd made it, buying Stephen Burrows at Bendel's," says Mallis. California designer Holly Harp, whose batik and hand-dyed dresses had wowed the likes of Bette Midler and Janis Joplin, had her own dedicated niche on the second floor in the mid-1970s. By 1978 Ralph Lauren's eponymous line and a second one of his, Lauren Country, each had dedicated spaces on the third floor.

Some of Bendel's discoveries literally came in off the street. Early on Stutz implemented "open see," a once- or twice-monthly open call for unknown designers to show their wares to Bendel's buyers. And in an almost unprecedented policy, Stutz offered favored designers such as Muir not only their

ABOVE: Trailblazing Black designer Stephen Burrows (in 1971) who had his own boutique in Bendel's and (BELOW) his mod color-block knits let loose in Central Park

Geraldine Stutz (FOURTH FROM RIGHT), flanked by some of the designers she promoted, in 1973. FROM LEFT: Don Kline, Lee Bailey, Viola Sylbert, Dick Huebner, Ralph Lauren, Holly Harp, and Carlos Falchi.

own boutiques but also fabrication services on premises, in some of the same upper-floor workrooms where Henri's designers and seamstresses had labored in his day. Broadway costumer Donald Brooks used Bendel's to execute dresses he designed for Diahann Carroll for the musical *No Strings* in 1962, and in the '70s Burrows whipped up many of his colorful, energetic outfits on-site.

So did dressmaker Stan Herman, who did an exclusive line for Bendel's in the late sixties. "Bendel's had a renegade personality, and it found the young customer," recalls Herman, who went on to a career designing uniforms for such companies as FedEx and McDonald's, and who in 2022, at age ninety-four, celebrated thirty years of selling clothes on QVC. He vividly remembers Stutz—Gerry (sometimes spelled Jerry) to friends and colleagues—looking manicured and worldly in a turban. "She had a light touch and great taste. And she was fun, she wanted to mingle with different kinds of people."

Conversely, regular customers sometimes found themselves perusing merchandise next to such familiar faces as Yoko Ono and Lauren Bacall. Gloria Steinem shopped at Shoe Biz, as did Cher (who also modeled Bendel's clothes in an issue of *Vogue*). "Cher was in there all the time," recalls Mallis. Lena Horne and Susan Sarandon were Bendel's enthusiasts. First Lady Jaqueline Kennedy wore long gloves from the store to a White House state dinner, and Elizabeth Taylor ordered lacy slips to be delivered to her hotel suite.

FASHION TO ENJOY— THE PRICE IS RIGHT— THE GIRL IS CHÉR

$13,300 for the bracelet shown twice, opposite, on the arm of Chér— she of Sonny and—with her own glorious hair wrapped around as a backdrop. The fashion here, dazzlingly enjoyable. You get: 164 diamonds set in a domed oval of platinum, a few spilling out in charming sprinkles at the sides. Total caratage, 16.93. All, the centrepiece of a smashing design by David Webb, done in solid 18-karat gold with a heavily chased Etruscan finish. Durable—could last a couple of lifetimes. Washable. Won't shrink. A good catch. And, by that second lifetime its value could well increase.... Considering all this, the tab figures. Right? Right.

$123 to acquire this joy—a long look of black glossy jersey to wear, as Chér does, in stark outline on a marvellous figure, or to decorate with your own inventions in glitter. This look breaks into two: a long-sleeved leotard with low neck, a long wrapped skirt to tie on at the hips. By Jon Haggins, of Encron polyester jersey (Stretchnit fabric). At Henri Bendel; Joske's Houston. More enjoyable fashion at a price, worn by Chér, on the next eight pages. All coiffures by Suga.

In an eight-page fashion layout shot by star photographer Richard Avedon for *Vogue* in 1969, Cher—a Bendel's shopper herself— sported a jersey leotard top with matching tie-on skirt, both by Jon Haggins and sold at Bendel's.

"Barbra Streisand loved Bendel's," says Herman. Writer Lisa Birnbach (*The Preppy Handbook*) remembered seeing disco goddess Grace Jones in the store and on another occasion watching composer Burt Bacharach purchase a present for his wife, the actress Angie Dickinson. "I bought a Stephen Burrows cocktail dress there right after college and I used to get my hair cut there," she recalled. "In the seventies when department stores were kind of fussy, Bendel's was cool."

The designer and entertainer Isaac Mizrahi got a taste of Bendel's allure in the mid-1970s when he was a student at the High School of Performing Arts in Manhattan. He went in with a model friend of his whom he likens to "early Carrie Bradshaw" from *Sex and the City* (fictional Carrie shopped at the store too). Isaac's pal went wild for a red leather motorcycle jacket. "She spent like her entire month's salary, but it was fabulous," he says. "At Bendel's you didn't feel like you were buying something even close to on promotion or on sale. That was where you went to buy clothes *not* on sale. You could rest assured you were getting something that you *should* pay full price for." On the other hand, he notes, "Bendel's wasn't a rich-people-only, privileged place. It was just very smart and carried very, very good stuff. It was about knowing—knowing the best."

In 1977 Bendel's sales were up—it was doing around $10 million annually—but its parent company Genesco was hemorrhaging money, "with a drop in earnings from $11 million in the first half of fiscal 1976 to $810,000 in 1977," according to the *New York Times*. In 1980 Stutz gathered a group of foreign investors and for a reported $8 million they bought Bendel's outright, with Stutz holding majority interest. This made her the first woman to own a major New York fashion store. (An insider told Sally Robbins that Stutz wanted to change the name to hers.)

But by the mid-1980s Bendel's narrow profit margins had left it vulnerable. Enter Leslie Wexner, the forty-four-year-old founder of The Limited corporation, at the time a 2,682-store conglomerate based in Columbus, Ohio, and valued at $3.1 billion. Wexner made his mark with The Limited women's apparel store and its model of within-reach fashion replicated in hundreds of malls across America, which revolutionized fashion retail, streamlining the supply chain and maximizing volume. He followed that with more mid-priced mall brands such as Express, Lane Bryant, Lerner New York, and others. He was known as "a tenacious and exacting individual," good at aiming high, breaking molds, and trusting his instincts. "Les's vision and strategic agility are among the best in the business," says Philip Monaghan, a former marketing executive who for part of his years at Limited Brands worked specifically for Bendel's. "His chutzpah and big-picture thinking are remarkable."

"The whole experience of Henri Bendel was extraordinary, the whole feeling of it."
—*Isaac Mizrahi*

HENRI BENDEL

for the cream-of-its-class lauren look, be a real sport/ and race on in to ralph's own shop on 3 at 10 west 57th street/

Gösta Peterson shot print ads for Bendel's in the late 1970s and early 1980s, including this one from '78 featuring Ralph Lauren sportswear.

Wexner's initial goal: reinvigorate the store, then clone it in a handful of top-tier markets. He was said to be eyeing Chicago, San Francisco, Beverly Hills, and even London and Paris.

Fairly desperate, Stutz and her investors agreed to sell for $2.4 million in cash, plus a promissory note for $800,000. Whatever Wexner's long-term strategy, he apparently gave Stutz the impression that she had a future there and that things would continue to run under her direction much as they had been. But it soon became clear that he and his management team had different goals, foremost being beyond-the-horizon growth. Immediately everything from sales strategy to accounting and computer systems started changing, at the hands of executives who showed no sentimentality about Gerry's baby or the clients who liked Bendel's curated, insider-y feel. After ten months of struggling to even get Wexner's attention, Stutz gave her notice. It was the end of her brilliant twenty-nine-year run.

Remaining long-term staffers felt at sea. "Behind those baffled and hurt feelings is a fascinating takeover tale at perhaps the most glamorous store in America," wrote Jesse Kornbluth in a *New York* magazine cover story titled "The Battle for Bendel's." He called it "a case study worthy of the Harvard Business School of what happens when the mass-market culture of mideighties retailing engulfs a one-woman enterprise renowned for its quirky individualism." Talking to Kornbluth, The Limited executive Tom Hopkins, who led the transition team, was blunt in his assessment of the tension between the old and new regimes.

A 1990 *New York Times* Sunday style supplement featured color-block dresses by Tom and Linda Platt available at Bendel's.

Two cotton jersey color-block dresses by Tom and Linda Platt: left, $240, and right, $250. Henri Bendel. To order at Saks Fifth Avenue. Gloves: La Crasia. Hose: Gamine. Earrings: Stuart Freeman.

"The atmosphere was very divided here," Hopkins says. "Some people thought we were liberators, others that we were an occupation army. Some people wanted Bendel's to go back ten years, to that simpler time before Bergdorf's out-Bendelized Bendel's. And there were people—at all levels— who were institutions here who were screwing the business every day."

In December of 1986 Bendel's named Mark Shulman, thirty-seven, the new president; he had been president of Ann Taylor and the merchandising manager of I. Magnin, the upscale California-based department store chain. Shulman told *Women's Wear Daily* he wanted to make the store "a paradise for women to shop in." Bendel's, wrote the trade paper, "has slipped in its image" since the '60s and '70s and Shulman "conceded that while the store may have been the most avant-garde of its time, he is not certain that its approach to merchandising and presentation is satisfactory for women of today. . . . 'We want to broaden our base,' he said." This meant adding merchandise, such as price-friendly house-brand cashmere sweaters and more hosiery and lingerie, and reconfiguring the layout of the store for greater volume and easier navigation. Among many modest-sized changes, a cashmere "shop" replaced the stationery vendor. Sales increased a bit, but in 1987 *Women's Wear Daily* noted that "as of yet [Bendel's] does not have the excitement of its early years, nor is it a moneymaker . . . for the last several years it has been operating at a loss under both Limited and Stutz managements. Poor performance has been attributed to a sparse presentation on the upper floors, lack of markdowns with merchandise that lingered too long on the racks, ambiguous assortments, and a loss of identity in the face of increasing competition."

Undaunted, Wexner and Shulman boldly adjusted the formula of the store, pledging that, in time, Bendel house-label merchandise would grow to represent 70 percent of their inventory, from 20 percent, in addition to that sold in the designer department Fancy, where shoppers could still find Oscar de la Renta, Thierry Mugler, and Karl Lagerfeld (who later reinvigorated Chanel). For the first time since Stutz took over in the '50s, Bendel's offered sizes up to 14. (Gerry famously had a bias toward slender fashion.) According to *New York*, Shulman and Wexner conceived of vaulting expansion—they eventually hoped to see Bendel's in forty markets. That ambitious goal would never be met, but by 1990 Bendel's had new, full-sized outposts in Chicago, Boston, and in Wexner's hometown, Columbus.

A figure from a 1990 Bendel's ad that ran in *Vogue* conjured a bygone era, to play up the store's classic heritage.

The flagship store on the west side of Fifth Avenue between Fifty-Fifth and Fifty-Sixth Streets, luring new customers in the twenty-first century

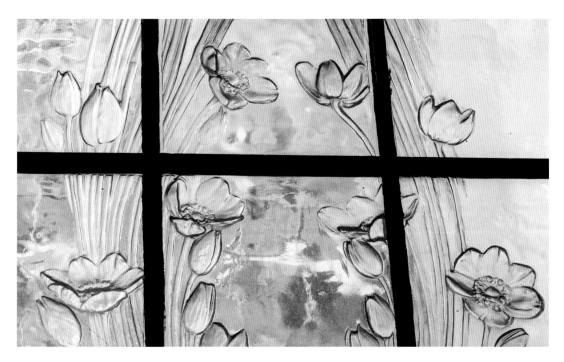

Several years and a few delays after announcing a desire to move to a bigger space, in 1991 The Limited relocated Bendel's New York flagship around the corner to 712 and 714 Fifth Avenue between Fifty-Fifth and Fifty-Sixth Streets—the former Rizzoli bookstore (712) and the old Coty Building (714), combined and expanded at the foot of a mixed-use high-rise. This afforded the store far more room—80,000 square feet, including 40,000 square feet for selling on five levels, with a dramatic 55-foot central atrium. The Coty Building, a former perfumery, had just been saved from destruction; when the tower was proposed, the Municipal Arts Society and other conservation groups rallied to protect it because of its unique three-story windows that François Coty had commissioned from iconic French glass designer René Jules Lalique in 1912. The art nouveau windows depicting interlocking vines and flowers had been covered up, and in taking a thirty-year lease (at a very low rate) Bendel's agreed to restore the windows and open them to the public. The Lalique windows, viewed up close from the second floor, became a focal point of the store and garnered as much press as the move itself, even drawing Jackie Kennedy Onassis to the opening gala, a benefit for the Municipal Arts Society of which she was a patron.

(Top) A detail of the Lalique windows at 714 Fifth Avenue and (above) Jacqueline Onassis, whose historic preservation group helped save those windows, flanked by society benefactor Brooke Astor and Bendel's owner Leslie L. Wexner at the 1991 opening gala for the relocated store

From a fashion and merchandising perspective, the 1990s into the early 2000s was a period of experimentation and innovation at Bendel's, bolstered by the dramatic new space and by designers either launched or picked up by the store's buyers who, struggling to compete with larger chains like Saks Fifth Avenue and Neiman Marcus for the biggest name designers, took the opportunity to nurture up-and-comers. On the stylish-but-somewhat-conservative end of the spectrum were offerings from Emanuel, Zoran, Victor Alfaro, and Michael Kors, then trendier designs from the likes of Dolce & Gabbana, Dries Van Noten, Ann Demeulemeester, Cynthia Rowley, and Marc Jacobs. Even *enfant terrible* Jean Paul Gaultier had a place at the table, along with his fellow Frenchman Claude Montana. The new guard also included fashion-forward modernists Issey Miyake, Comme des Garçons, and American designer Anna Sui, who launched her haute hippie dresses at Bendel's. *Women's Wear Daily* reported that a 1992 Todd Oldham one-day trunk show with a personal appearance by the designer, to celebrate the first anniversary of the opening of the new location, yielded $95,000 on sales of his playful, hand-painted and -beaded outfits. Bendel's had buzz again.

Cosmetics became a growth category for the store with lines by Trish McEvoy, Laura Mercier, Bobbi Brown, and MAC. Main floor, in-store makeup artists made Bendel's a first stop for women on their way to parties or events.

Bendel's ran an ad in *Vogue* in 1991 shot by Horst and featuring model Elaine Irwin (back when she spelled it Erwin). It promoted new satellite stores in Chestnut Hill, MA; Chicago, IL; and Columbus, OH, home base of The Limited.

HENRI BENDEL
New York

Romancing rock 'n' roll:
Sui modeled her modern-
day dandy after music-
scene idols like Jim
Morrison, Jimi Hendrix,
and Mick Jagger. Velvet
frock coat (about $665),
leather vest (about
$195), tapestry pants
(about $265), and poet's
blouse (about $200).
Henri Bendel. Coat and
vest also at Macy's
Herald Square, McLean
VA. In this story: hair,
Sam McKnight; makeup,
Kevyn Aucoin. Details,
more stores, see In This Issue.

Fashion Editor: Grace Coddington
Photographer: Penn

499

In a 1992 *Vogue* spread shot by veteran fashion lensman Irving Penn, Naomi Campbell
works a modern-day dandy ensemble by Anna Sui that was sold at Bendel's.

ABOVE: Bendel's cosmetics department was the site of star-studded events such as the crowning of pitch-model RuPaul as MAC Cosmetics' "First Face of MAC" in 1995.

BELOW: The debut of the late Kevyn Aucoin's eponymous line; the celebrated makeup artist, like Henri, hailed from Lafayette, Louisiana.

In 1994 MAC launched its "Who is the MAC girl?" campaign at Bendel's, featuring drag recording artist RuPaul; after that, sales of Viva Glam lipstick raised the first $1 million for the MAC AIDS Fund. And Bendel's devotees treasured the store's brown-and-white-striped cosmetic pouch, a constant dating back decades.

Nineteen-ninety-five saw the birth of the Bendel Girl in advertising and display—girls plural, actually—fanciful pen and watercolor illustrations of stylish youngish women gallivanting around New York with Bendel's shopping bags and hatboxes in hand. The Bendel Girl was the creation of French-born illustrator Izak Zenou, who drew thousands of variations on the theme for more than twenty years. In addition to style, Bendel's was now selling fun.

Still, as *Women's Wear Daily* put it in 1995, "recapturing the magic of the old store [has been] difficult," and profits remained elusive. New president Ted Marlow said optimistically, "We will find a niche. . . . We probably share a lot of customers with Neiman's, Saks, Bergdorf's, and Bloomingdale's, but they come to us for something different." The Limited was still thinking growth, and announced hopes for a fifty-unit, $500 million chain by the year 2000. The next year *Women's Wear* relayed that "half a decade after closing its legendary store on

Izak's shop-happy
Bendel Girls

West 57th Street—a store so special that shoppers grow misty eyed talking about it— Henri Bendel will attempt to evoke its spirit in Troy, MI and Paramus, NJ." But by early 1998, with Bendel's continuing to underperform, rumors of the store folding or being sold were rampant. According to *Women's Wear,* the brass were mulling how employees might be absorbed into other divisions.

Even Geraldine Stutz weighed in, saying to the trade paper, "The Limited chose . . . to over expand and lose some of the character . . . it became a higher-priced Limited or Limited Express. . . . I sold the store in 1985, and within a year it was no longer my Bendel's. . . . My philosophy for Bendel's was that small is special and big is bland. Specialty stores like Bendel's existed and prospered by being small enough to have a totally individual character.

"What I regret today," she continued, "is that there may be no Bendel's for somebody to turn around as I turned around the old-time Bendel's. Any name with the kind of reputation and history from the turn of the century as the store of style, not just fashion, deserves to survive."

ABOVE: Bendel's on Fifth Avenue

BELOW: A modern Bendel's hatbox

The store did not fold in '98 but having had disappointing sales of only $83 million in 1997 with a $28 million loss, Limited Brands (as the company was now called) decided to close the Bendel outposts in Chicago, Boston, Detroit, Columbus, and Paramus. Bendel's might have closed altogether but for a far-below-market-rate rent tied to a nearly impossible-to-break lease on the Fifth Avenue store; essentially, they couldn't afford *not* to keep it going, at least until they figured out something better to put in the building. Bendel's was once again a one-store affair, and new general merchandise manager Ed Burstell, a nine-year Bendel's vet who had led the prized cosmetics department, reverted to strategies more in the Stutz mode: He upped the percentage of designer labels after a house line failed to catch on. He hooked cool, emerging talents such as Vivienne Tam and Isabel Marant, brought back "open see" days, expanded some specialty departments, including jewelry and shoes, and according to *Women's Wear Daily,* "was instrumental in elevating the profile of Bendel's again to a level of visibility not seen since the early Eighties."

Still, in 2004, with wan sales numbers nowhere near his goal, Wexner rolled the dice once more on expansion, but with a completely different model: many small Henri Bendel shops in high-end malls, each with average space of just 1,500 to 2,000 square feet. The New York flagship would remain but reflect the chain's new focus on beauty, lingerie, and accessories, with more Bendel-branded products. A prototype was launched in Easton Town Center in Wexner's hometown of Columbus, where he had previously test-driven new

A Bendel's store in the International Plaza mall in Tampa, Florida

businesses in The Limited's stable. The rollout continued over the next few years, with stores opening in San Diego, Boca Raton, and Miami. In 2009 six more were set to launch starting in Troy, Michigan. Eventually there would be twenty-eight around the country (later reduced to twenty-two).

By 2009 Bendel's stopped selling apparel altogether. "Fashion isn't where we're seeing our growth," President Ed Bucciarelli told *Women's Wear*. He argued that smaller stores with a narrow product line would be "viable in every 'A' mall in the country." He even predicted potential international opportunities. (In 2007 Limited Brands sold their now-lackluster Limited chain in order to focus on Victoria's Secret and Bath & Body Works, their biggest profit drivers; the corporate name changed to L Brands.) Problem child Bendel's reduced its flagship store selling space from three floors to two, with merchandise and display now in sync with the mall stores: just jewelry, beauty and fragrance products, and accessories—everything from handbags and gloves to hairpieces and Wellington-style boots. Most of the merchandise sported Bendel's logo and brown and white stripes. "There's lots of iconography," said Bucciarelli. "And Izak illustrations of fashionable young women in the windows. It's set up like a candy store . . . everything appeals to a younger customer."

Whether this branded-bling mall model could have been sustainable is debatable, but outside forces were fighting success. In the late aughts and early teens, the fashion retail industry was in crisis as online shopping, soaring rents, and fierce competition were rewriting the rules. "As retail experiences its most traumatic period in a generation," wrote *Women's Wear*, "the new Bendel's represents yet another counterintuitive move by the legendary Wexner as he concentrates his empire [including Victoria's Secret] on beauty and innerwear [lingerie and underwear]. [But] the refocusing gives Bendel's another chance to be the cash cow Wexner always wanted." The dramatic changes repelled most of the old Bendel's enthusiasts but drew in a new group of shoppers, including more tourists and younger women who liked the pizzazz and the label. This was bolstered by lively, playful window displays, in-store events, and de facto prime time product placement—Bendel's

Handbags (TOP) and jewelry (BELOW), along with other accessories, became the brand's stock-in-trade after they stopped selling dresses.

The girls of *Gossip Girl* loved shopping at Henri Bendel, and the store returned the affection in a new-season-launch window display in the late summer of 2008.

The girls of *Gossip Girl* loved shopping at Henri Bendel, and the store returned the affection in a new-season-launch window display in the late summer of 2008.

was a favored stop for teen shop-'til-you-droppers Serena and Blair on the TV hit *Gossip Girl*. By 2014 Bendel's had stopped selling third-party merchandise altogether; everything was house line, most with the Bendel name or initials seared on the product; the name more than the item, it seemed, was what customers came for.

As changing shopping habits and economic hardship continued to pummel fashion retail in the late twenty-teens, even L Brands' once white-hot Victoria's Secret was struggling. With Bendel's revenue for 2018 totaling $85 million with losses around $45 million, and Wexner aiming all resources at VS, he could no longer justify propping up Bendel's. In September of 2018 L Brands announced that it would be closing all twenty-two Bendel mall stores, the online business, and the flagship store in Manhattan. Everything. By January of 2019 Henri Bendel—after a 123-year run—would be no more.

"This decision is right for the future growth of our company, but not easy because of the impact to our L Brands family," said Wexner in the press release. "I want to thank our Bendel associates for their dedication to this iconic brand and to our loyal Bendel customers." (However, it's important to note that as of 2024 Bath & Body Works—previously known as L Brands—still holds an active trademark of the Henri Bendel name and brand.)

Industry insiders and former execs weren't surprised. "Over 30 years, at least $300 million was pumped into Henri Bendel and the business never earned anything," says L Brands alum Monaghan. "It was not one of the company's biggest failures, but it was always a distraction and a headache."

But to the public—even, or especially, people who hadn't set foot in the store in more than a decade—the news came as a startle and brought out real emotions. "Shoppers Mourn the End of Henri Bendel," read the headline on the *Town & Country* website. "Henri Bendel, the brand, died today," said the *New York Times,* which also took a skimming interest in Henri himself and his previously unchronicled private life, noting Bastedo's inheritance and burial with Henri. The *Wall Street Journal* recalled the store as a "pioneer" and "mainstay" in New York City, and "the first to hold a semi-annual sale and the first to stage a fashion show." Real-life Bendel Girls who hadn't known the store's illustrious history but loved the accessories and the vibe took to Twitter to commiserate. "Will always treasure my Henri Bendel items," a woman named Archie tweeted. "Really a sad day."

Subsequent articles placed Bendel's folding in the context of the general garment industry tumult. The sprawling Fifth Avenue flagship of venerable Lord & Taylor closed just prior to Bendel's announcement (the chain remains), and 2019 would see Barneys call it quits altogether—a store that since the 1980s was perhaps the most fashion-forward, top-end department store in America, the closest analogue to Bendel's in the '60s and '70s. "The increased corporatization of high-end fashion, the incursions of private equity, with its

"Henri Bendel is going dark"–the first sentence of the September 14, 2018 *Women's Wear Daily* article announcing the impending closing of all Bendel stores, set for the following January

2   SEPTEMBER 14, 2018

WWD

BUSINESS

L Brands Closing Henri Bendel

- The Victoria's Secret parent described the shuttering of all 23 stores as an effort to increase shareholder value.

BY DAVID MOIN AND EVAN CLARK

Henri Bendel is going dark.

Owner L Brands Inc. said late Thursday that it has decided to shut down the division. Bendel has for years suffered losses which can be attributed to management changes, flip-flopping merchandising strategies and attempts at expansion. Ultimately, the business proved to be more of a distraction for L Brands than a growth opportunity.

The company said all 23 Henri Bendel stores, including the Fifth Avenue flagship as well as the Henri Bendel e-commerce Web site, will close by January 2019, though new merchandise will continue to arrive through the holiday season.

"We are committed to improving performance in the business and increasing shareholder value. As part of that effort, we have decided to stop operating Bendel to improve company profitability and focus on our larger brands that have greater growth potential," said Leslie Wexner, chairman and chief executive officer of L Brands. "This decision is right for the future growth of our company, but not easy because of the impact to our L Brands family. I want to thank our Bendel associates for their dedication to this iconic brand and to our loyal Bendel customers."

When L Brands, formerly called The Limited, acquired Henri Bendel in 1985, Wexner predicted that Bendel could

ultimately become a $1 billion luxury business. The goal never came close to reality. On Thursday, the company disclosed Henri Bendel's revenues for 2018 would total about $85 million while operating losses would come in around $45 million. The costs to close the business have yet to be tallied.

One of the most serious challenges Bendel faced under the Limited ownership was procuring upscale brands and designer lines, the kind that were sold at nearby Bergdorf Goodman and Saks Fifth Avenue. With a lack of luxury offerings from the market, Bendel found itself pursuing alternative strategies and

struggled to find its identity, changing its merchandising focus over the years. In 2014, the company cut off ties with third-party vendors, and has of late been selling accessories under the Bendel label, as well as beauty products. Last year, WWD reported that Bendel was once again considering opening its doors to brands other than its own.

But by shedding Bendel, L Brands will be able to put more effort into turning around its now struggling Victoria's Secret business.

When Wexner decided his company should purchase Bendel in the mid-Eighties, he relocated the business from its modest

but long-standing location at 10 West 57th Street to a much more spacious and location on Fifth Avenue. Wexner created a true and lavish flagship for Bendel, with six levels and 80,000 square feet housed at the base of a $200 million mixed-used tower at 712 Fifth Avenue, with a hotel, apartments and offices. The Bendel flagship is between 55th and 56th streets on Fifth Avenue, opposite Trump Tower.

The store was founded by Frenchman Henri Bendel in 1895 as a hat shop on East Ninth Street in Manhattan. The business relocated to 57th Street in 1912.

Under the management of the late, legendary Geraldine Stutz, and as a single-unit operation, Bendel became a chic, international fashion destination filled with avant-garde designer collections. It was best known for its innovative "Street of Shops" on the ground floor, housing an eclectic and cutting-edge array of products in a range of categories. The format was widely copied by many retailers for years but those knock-offs never captured the cachet or spirit of what was Bendel, which employed Andy Warhol as an illustrator in the Sixties.

Stutz ran the business since 1957, became an owner along with other investors, and sold the store to Limited in 1985.

L Brands said that its associates staying with the business through January will be offered retention bonuses. At the point when associates' positions are eliminated, they will be invited to interview for open positions within the company or will be offered separation pay and job search support services.

Aside from Victoria's Secret and Bendel, L Brands also operates Pink, Bath & Body Works and La Senza and operates 3,084 company-owned specialty stores in the U.S., Canada, the U.K. and Greater China, and its brands are sold in more than 800 additional franchised locations worldwide.

Bendel's in Fiction

Beyond Cole Porter's shout-out in the song "You're the Top," Henri and his store have turned up in popular culture dozens of times over the years. Some highlights:

BUT GENTLEMEN MARRY BRUNETTES, Anita Loos's 1927 sequel to her bestselling novel *Gentlemen Prefer Blondes* about fortune-seeking single ladies. Loos purposely misspells some proper nouns such as Florenz Ziegfeld and Rolls-Royce—but not Bendel.

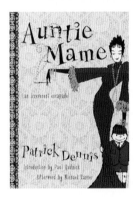

AUNTIE MAME, Patrick Dennis's cheeky 1954 faux memoir of indomitable Mame Dennis.

> "Auntie Mame's last stop in the garment industry was at Henri Bendel's, where, thanks to a beautiful figure and a long friendship with Mr. Bendel, she modeled tea gowns for just over a week. But on the day her elegant posterior was pinched by a dirty old man of untotaled buying power, there was an ugly contretemps and her services were dispensed with. Mr. Bendel wrote Auntie Mame a touching letter, saying he felt terrible about the whole thing, but that she was, after all, a Lady and too fine a woman to be a mere clotheshorse."

ROSEMARY'S BABY, Ira Levin's 1967 bestseller (which later became a hit movie), a creeping-dread tale of modern-era Manhattan Satan worship.

> "She stopped to look in Henri Bendel's windows, because she didn't want to think any more about witches and covens and baby's blood and Guy being over there."

NO STRINGS, the Richard Rodgers Broadway musical. According to Marilyn Bender's book *The Beautiful People,* Bendel's in-house designer Donald Brooks dressed Diahann Carroll "in the [Geraldine] Stutz-Bendel's ladylike look of 1962, which consisted of low-heeled lizard shoes, an alligator bag with chain handles, white gloves, pearls and a scoop-necked evening dress with a sash at the waist that was pure Mainbocher."

MANHATTAN, Woody Allen's black-and-white valentine to New York City (1979). In the opening sequence, underscored by Gershwin's "Rhapsody in Blue," workers and shoppers strut beneath Bendel's twin brown-and-white-striped awnings on Fifty-Seventh Street.

SEX AND THE CITY, Bendel's wasn't her go-to style emporium, but in at least one episode of the era-defining TV series (1998–2004) writer and fashion fiend Carrie Bradshaw (Sarah Jessica Parker) couldn't resist.

13 GOING ON 30, the 2004 movie comedy in which teen-in-an-adult-body Jenna (Jennifer Garner) goes on a Bendel's bender.

GOSSIP GIRL, Blair Waldorf (Leighton Meester) and her posh posse of Upper-East-Siders were such Bendel's girls that in 2008 the store cohosted the TV series's season two premiere party and created a special window display.

> "Fifth Avenue will live, with or without Bendel's. But, for those of us who grew up believing that the place was a symbol of fortunate and fashionable adulthood, those brown-and-cream stripes deserve a proper eulogy."
> —*Sloane Crosley in the* New Yorker

demand for bigger and bigger profit margins, share blame for the current state of affairs," wrote Ginia Bellafante in the *New York Times,* who noted that "there are very few models in New York anymore for what Henri Bendel was."

Her *Times* colleague, style writer Vanessa Friedman, argued that it was appropriate to lament the passing of Bendel's and of other old-line stalwarts:

> What were these grand department stores but monuments to our shared history, repositories of group memory? That's why, whenever the end of the department store comes up, people immediately begin to quote everything from Émile Zola and "The Ladies' Paradise" to Judith Krantz and "Scruples." It's why Midge Maisel was given a day job working the switchboard at B. Altman.
>
> They represented not only consumption, but also much more: the way New York became a city of aspiration, invention and reinvention. They were about communion and the treasure hunt for identity, rites of passage individual and generational. In their walls, memories lie. Losing them, we lose a piece of our own past too.
>
> Few stores embodied it as much as Bendel's.

Women's Wear Daily reminded its readers of the Stutz years when the store was "a chic international fashion destination filled with avant-garde designer collections." But perhaps in a rush to get the news out, the usually fastidious trade publication erroneously said that "the store was founded by Frenchman Henri Bendel."

Maybe Henri's Francophile ghost inserted himself into the fact-checking that day. In any case, it wasn't the first or last time Mr. Henri Bendel would be mistaken for a Frenchman. Almost certainly he would've considered it a compliment.

CHAPTER 12

LEGACY

$\mathcal{D}$OWN SOUTH AND BACK EAST HENRI LEFT FOOTPRINTS—bolder in some spots, fainter in others. His imprint in fashion history books, sadly, is fainter still. Yet his impact on American fashion and retailing is no less substantial for being less chronicled.

In Manhattan one can trace Henri's path via a few residential buildings and store locations still standing, but as of 2024 his pioneering emporium at 10–14 West Fifty-Seventh Street was on borrowed time. Flanked by the rubble of several razed limestone stalwarts from the early twentieth century to the west, and the behemoth Crown building to the east on the corner of Fifth Avenue (which several years ago gained a residential and office tower above it), the two once-joined buildings sat empty, awaiting their likely fate, presuming a fifty-two-story mixed-use skyscraper courtesy of Solow Realty and Development and designed by Skidmore, Owings & Merrill proceeds apace. In their last retail incarnations, No. 10 had been a Club Monaco clothing store, and Nos. 12–14 had been an antique seller called Metropolitan Antiques. Strollers can spot other vestiges of old Fifty-Seventh Street, the "Rue de la Paix of New York," but the number of those stone buildings is dwindling, and it requires a patient eye to absorb their architectural panache, dingy and shrunken as they are in the shadows of glass-and-steel giants.

BELOW: The store's longtime home at 10-14 West Fifty-Seventh Street in 2024, shrouded and gutted in preparation for a skyscraper to be built on the site

As of this writing—five years after Bendel's closed—the store's last incarnation, the 712 Fifth Avenue flagship was still empty, awaiting a new tenant. The former Coty building's landmark status—granted

209

The emptied-out flagship store at 712 and 714 Fifth Avenue shortly after the closing in 2019. It was still unoccupied as of 2024.

primarily for its Lalique windows—plus its street-level niche in the fifty-two-story luxury office tower built behind and above it (called simply 712 Fifth) should keep its lovely old façade intact for quite some time.

Today Bendel's former mansion at Kings Point, Long Island, serves as the main administrative building of the United States Merchant Marine Academy, called Wiley Hall. After automobile baron Walter Chrysler died in 1940, what he had dubbed Forker House (his wife Della's maiden name) and all its property were acquired by the academy, and over the years a large campus sprung up, composed of structures of various styles that serve as classrooms, training facilities, housing, dining halls, a chapel, and such. But the white beaux arts house retains its commanding stature, still the king of its green hill. A canon sits on the front lawn facing the Long Island Sound; uniformed cadets can be seen crossing the grounds on their way to class or drills; the swimming pool down near the sound is used for training. Unlike in Henri's time, vessels of various sizes and purposes anchor at a large floating dock. In the distance, New York City's skyline juts out from the southwest horizon.

The house from the outside looks much as it did in Henri's day, having been only lightly modified. Inside, though now filled with working offices and decorated with plaques and artifacts of a nautical military nature, the central living spaces retain most of the home's original detailing such as the sweeping marble stairway, carved and painted wood ceilings, decorative tile floors, and massive stone fireplace surrounds imported from Europe, all of which conjure Bendel's Old World splendor. The muraled ceiling of the former card room seems as fresh and audacious as when it was first painted, but today its radiating pastel panels of flowering vines and mythological figures float above a no-nonsense office. The music room, now a conference room, still holds the marble casing of the large Estey organ that Bastedo played. The house is not open to the public, although visitors can take self-guided tours of the entire academy campus including the grounds surrounding Wiley Hall (there's also a separately housed academy museum).

The US Merchant Marine Academy on Long Island, where a number of Henri's architectural and decorative flourishes remain

Very much open to the public is Laurel Lake Lodge in Stamford, Connecticut, Henri's last country home, which was purchased by supporters of the Stamford Museum in 1955, two years after Abraham Bastedo died and the furnishings of the house auctioned off by Kende Galleries of

Bendel's house in Connecticut is now the Stamford Museum and Nature Center, where visitors can see some of Henri's sculptures and admire the fine architectural details of the home.

New York City. Operating today as the Stamford Museum and Nature Center, it offers revolving exhibitions of art in addition to hosting special events such as talks and classes and is also rented out for private functions. The expansive grounds are home to a working farm with vegetable gardens and animals, plus miles of walking trails. The new adjacent Knobloch Family Farmhouse offers educational programming especially geared to schoolchildren and doubles as another rentable events space.

Although there are no furnishings left in the old house from Henri's era, surrounded by the wood paneling, leaded glass windows, carved staircases, wrought iron gates, and other architectural details, visitors can easily imagine Henri and Abraham's life of baronial luxury. Some of Bendel's original statuary peppers the property, including the Four Seasons sculptures, which flank a

modern-era walkway up a hill to the main entrance. Behind the house along the driveway and parking area sits the large fountain with its bas-relief horses; though not currently in operation, it's a popular backdrop for wedding pictures. And nearby, the pair of regal gatepost lions still keep a relaxed watch.

In Lafayette, Henri's name resonates with many, even as his story is known to few. Although his family's store and opera house were torn down after World War II, and his childhood home razed in 1957, he's commemorated by the Bendel Gardens subdivision, developed on his former property, and its adjacent Bendel Road, a short but well-trafficked connector between key thoroughfares on the south side of town. The neighborhood abuts the Oil Center, a low-rise office and retail area developed in the 1950s when Lafayette became a center of petroleum engineering. (Now the fourth largest city in Louisiana with a population of around 120,000, it has long been considered "the Hub City" to outlying towns of Acadiana, enhanced by an extensive medical infrastructure, the thriving University of Louisiana at Lafayette, and robust tourism built on Cajun music and food.)

Back in 1933, perhaps owing to concerns about his own health and a desire to lighten his estate, Henri had donated the Camellia Lodge and its property to his life partner Abraham, "in consideration of the care, attention, and kindness shown to [me] . . . during the past years." When Bastedo decided to sell it in 1950 (less than three years before his own passing) a small group of Lafayette men led by real estate developer Leopold Weill teamed up with Houston oilman and investor David Bintliff, paying about $282,000 for the roughly 171 acres, in order to turn the land into a subdivision. According to Jeanette Plauché Parker, who delves deeply into the rich backstory of the neighborhood in her book *Bendel Gardens: An Historic Treasure in Lafayette, Louisiana,* Bintliff suggested they use as their model the luxurious River Oaks neighborhood in Houston, famous for its large houses, curving streets, profusion of specimen trees, and deep, graceful lawns. Landscape firm Hare & Hare and real estate developer J. C. Nichols, both of Kansas City and both of whom had worked on River Oaks, consulted on the Bendel Gardens project; and Howard A. Kipp, the chief engineer for River Oaks, laid out the plan along a "wavy grid" in order to create a less rigid, more naturalistic effect. The first lot was bought by local druggist Paul Béchet in 1951, and twenty-five more lots were sold that year. Eventually the subdivision would swell to more than three hundred lots.

Bendel Gardens hardly approaches River Oaks' grandeur—most lots are smaller, and few homes resemble those ten-gallon-hat houses in Houston—but the neighborhood has distinct charm, with winding streets weaving themselves inside the kidney-shaped enclosure of Beverly Drive, endless oaks, a number of bayou-front lots, and vestiges of Henri's original landscaping. A drive down serpentine Marguerite Boulevard reveals thick-trunked *Magnolia grandiflora* trees planted by Bendel for the *allée* leading to his never-built manor-style house. As Parker notes, they "remain a testament to his foresight and love of beauty."

Houses in the neighborhood run the gamut from simple brick ranch-style houses typical of suburban American homes of the 1950s and '60s to more expansive abodes. Distinguished Louisiana architect A. Hays Town contributed at least eight larger homes, working in different vernaculars, including his signature style that combined French, Spanish, and Caribbean elements and used such reclaimed materials as cedar beams and heart-pine floors.

Southern magnolia trees line Marguerite Drive in the Bendel Gardens subdivision; they were planted by Henri as an intended allée leading to the manor-style house he aimed to build.

Bendel Gardens residents Harold "Lefty" Lagroue and Dave Perkins were architects independently responsible for a number of more contemporary-style houses—today they stand out as fairly classic examples of mid-century modern architecture. The house Lagroue designed for the Azar family, directly across Marguerite from the Camellia Lodge, had a supporting role in the 2010 movie *Secretariat*, as the Colorado home of Penny Chenery (played by Diane Lane), owner of the legendary Triple Crown winner. (The Rocky Mountains in the background were added with CGI technology.)

Prominent past residents of Bendel Gardens include Louisiana Governor Kathleen Babineaux Blanco; the painter George Rodrigue, known for his folkloric renderings of early Cajun families posed amid dark oaks and for one ubiquitous blue dog; and the Honorable Kaliste Saloom Jr., a distinguished city judge and beloved friend to many whose widow, Yvonne, still lives in their home across the street from the riverfront site where Henri intended to build his mansion. Several years before he passed away in 2017 at the age of ninety-nine, Judge Saloom recalled how as a boy he had seen Bendel riding through town in his Rolls-Royce. (He also noted the mutual support between the Lebanese and Jewish families, who were crucial to Lafayette's development: "We were both outsiders," Saloom said.)

For decades the Camellia Lodge, passing through various owners, offered a charming welcome at one of the two entrances to the neighborhood, on the corner of Marguerite and Bendel Road. David Romagosa, who purchased it in 1994, had grown up in Bendel Gardens and recounted to Parker that as a boy he was intrigued by the house, which he thought had a "mysterious air" about it.

He and his wife, Mary, raised their children there and were planning to expand the structure in 2002 when inspectors determined that it was rife with termite damage. Despite hoping to salvage at least part of it, they ultimately deemed it necessary to tear it down. In 2009 they sold the empty lot to state congressional lobbyist and philanthropist Randy Haynie, the owner (as of this writing) who neatly maintains it. Several of the large magnolia trees planted there by Henri conjure his once-rural retreat, but as tall pines in the rear were recently cut down, the illusion is spoiled a bit by the Ochsner Lafayette General hospital complex looming behind it.

Henri's old stucco gateposts mark the Bendel Road entrance, and a number of matching fence posts still stand though many have been replaced by plain wooden ones. The elegant wrought iron gates that guarded the property in Henri's time passed through different hands after he died and not long ago were bought by a prominent Lafayette physician and entrepreneur who had them refurbished and installed at his new home in another part of town. The house itself is all but hidden from view but is so large and built in such a grand French chateau style that Henri himself might marvel at it.

Another house Bendel built in Lafayette in the 1920s, the one for his sister Louise and her husband, Myrtil Meyer—in which Henri stayed while he was in town overseeing the construction of the Camellia Lodge—still stands on busy Johnston Street (No. 1511). After Myrtil died in 1928, Louise shared the classical revival home with her bachelor brother Ike, who among other professional endeavors became chairman of the board of First National Bank of Lafayette.

The house in Lafayette that Bendel built for his sister, Louise, and her husband, Myrtil Meyer, was acquired by the University of Louisiana at Lafayette and now is the welcome center.

In 1955 it was acquired by the Southwestern Louisiana Institute (now the University of Louisiana at Lafayette), where it became known as the French House, a center for French language and culture studies—which would have pleased Henri to no end. It's now the office of undergraduate admissions and still referred to by some as the French House.

Less than a mile from there, at the corner of University and Lee Avenues, the great bronze angel Henri commissioned for the graves of his father, William Bendel, his mother, Mary, and his stepfather, Benjamin Falk can be seen from the street; it requires a trip inside the small, oak-shaded Menachim Aveilim cemetery ("comforting the mourning" in Hebrew) to take in the full drama and beauty of the mourning woman lying at the angel's feet. A number of Henri's Plonsky, Bendel, Falk, and Levy relatives are also interred there, including Henri's siblings Louise, Samuel, Lena, and Isaac (Ike).

In New York State Bendel himself rests alongside Bastedo beneath another figure of a mourning woman, this one tossing copper roses, on a high hill in the elegant Kensico Cemetery in the hamlet of Valhalla, in Westchester County. Befitting his renown, he is in stellar company—the meticulously manicured 460-acre property is forever home to such notables of the twentieth century as baseball champ Lou Gehrig, big band leader Tommy Dorsey, actor Danny Kaye, Russian composer Sergei Rachmaninoff, and actress Anne Bancroft, as well as many business leaders and philanthropists.

Angel and Mourner, the sculpture Henri commissioned, marks his parents' and stepfather's graves and dominates the oak-shrouded Menachim Aveilim cemetery in Lafayette.

Bendel's acquaintances Florenz Ziegfeld, the impresario, and his wife, actress Billie Burke whom Bendel had costumed, are also interred at Kensico, as is Henri's friend and top celebrity client, opera singer and film star Geraldine Farrar. A swell party, as cemeteries go.

Over the years descendants of Bendel's brothers and sisters have, in their low-key ways, kept Henri's torch burning. Elaine Cohen, a daughter of Henri's niece and ward Florye Bendel Loewenstein, was possibly the last living member of the Falk and Bendel descendants who met the man. Before she passed away suddenly in 2023, she hazily recalled a visit to the house in Stamford when she was about five; somewhere in a box or photo album she kept a photo of herself standing

The late Elaine Cohen, daughter of Henri's niece Florye Loewenstein, at home in Arizona

with two servants in front of the imposing Tudor-style entryway. When she was older (after Henri had passed away) Elaine and her sister Mary would travel from their home in Peoria, Illinois, to New York, where they'd reside at the Plaza Hotel and shop at nearby Bendel's—on one such excursion she procured a velvet gown and cape to wear to a fancy party. And she remembered trips to Lafayette, where her family would stay at Uncle Ike's house. Treasures that had once been Henri's, or china that he gave Florye when she wed, punctuated the decor of Cohen's home in Tucson, Arizona, including a three-panel antique tapestry screen mounted on the wall in her living room; an elaborate porcelain vase and other decorative ceramic pieces; and a pair of crystal decanters set into ornate silver sleeves. In her foyer hung a photo of her mother in the wedding dress that Henri himself designed.

Elaine's late uncle Henri Bendel II established Belgian Shoes in New York, which he oversaw in the same hands-on fashion of his uncle. "For 41 years he could be found in the front of the store talking to his customers," recalled his only child, John Bendel. In a 1983 Q&A in Andy Warhol's *Interview* magazine, Henri II was asked whom he most admired in business. "I guess the one person I have the greatest admiration for in my life is my grandmother [Mary Falk]," he said. "She had seven children by the first husband and one by

A sixteenth-century French tapestry depicting the Last Supper hung in Henri's Kings Point home and is now in the permanent collection of the Museum of Fine Arts in Boston. Other Bendel-owned tapestries are held by the Getty Museum in California.

Henri Bendel II
in 1980

the second husband—my mother. She raised them all including the senior Henri Bendel. . . . She [became] a very rich woman. She had farms and stores all in Southwest Louisiana. We're [adoptive] Cajuns. Henri Bendel, Sr. was a Cajun before me. The pronunciation is *Ben*del, it never was Ben*del*."

After Henri II passed away in 1997, John, who lived in Boston, inherited Belgian Shoes (which has since been sold). At clan reunions with various cousins, he took pride in the history of his great-uncle and his Fifty-Seventh Street store, recounting lore and dubbing a photo of Henri with his sister and nieces sporting old-timey swimming togs at the house on Long Island the "bathing beauties" picture. John believed his father always thought of himself as a country boy from the South, just as his uncle Big Henri did to some extent, even if both of their resumes said otherwise.

After John's death in 2013, his widow Diana Bendel took a deeper interest in her late husband's famous great-uncle and delved into old newspaper clippings and public records looking for clues, generously sharing her finds with this author. "I became fascinated," says Dee, who feels she's finally gotten some sense of Henri's personality. "He was fastidious, impeccable," she says, "and perhaps a little bit pompous." She admires his standards—"My father-in-law told me Big Henri was an astute businessman who believed in first class quality merchandise and service"—and his sense of connection to his past. "He loved his family and his Louisiana roots." But she notes, "it had to have been difficult being gay in that era. Perhaps his large and beautiful homes were like islands that protected him from the outside world."

John and Diana Bendel of Boston on a trip to Europe in the 2010s. John inherited Belgian Shoes from his father, Henri Bendel II.

Some of the Bendel-Falk family descendants visiting Lafayette in 1985, with Henri Bendel II seated in front (wearing tie)

With inherited land holdings in the Lafayette area, many of which passed down through Ike Bendel, dozens and dozens of Bendel-Falk descendants from all over the country have for decades met semi-regularly in Lafayette and immersed themselves in such Cajun traditions as boiled crawfish dinners, while sharing stories from their parents and grandparents about the enterprising progeny of Mary Plonsky Bendel Falk. "Many of us probably wouldn't even know each other if not for this legacy," says Susan Gillette of Dallas, the great-granddaughter of Henri's sister Rose, who has guided the Bendel group for years. "We love to tell the tales to the younger generation. We're proud of our heritage."

Finally, Henri lives on in the annals of American fashion and retail, if often glimpsed in fragments rather than fully revealed. "In his heyday," writes historian Sally Robbins, "Bendel's name was a byword for style and taste." As the *North Side Tribune* of Great Neck declared back in 1925, "to have a name stand for so much in the realms of fashion, where competition is keen and constant vigilance must be exercised, means that there is a splendid and reputable backing behind that name." As late as 1950 the Lafayette *Daily Advertiser* called him "a man renowned the world over as a genius of women's fashions." But in few compendiums of American fashion history—of which there are a slew—will you find "Bendel, Henri" in the index. This is likely owing to the fact that Bendel was not a designer foremost. He *had* designed, particularly hats, when he started out. But his primary roles became those of importer, merchant, and arbiter; he doesn't fit well into a strict list of most important designers per se, though he gave so many of those designers crucial exposure. "Henri Bendel influenced the development of fashion in America and American appreciation of European designers," wrote historian Rona L. Holub in American National Biography Online.

A 1938 silk evening ensemble
by Elsa Schiaparelli from the
permanent collection of the
Metropolitan Museum of Art

Recognition from the likes of Holub and from noted fashion historian Caroline Rennolds Milbank who wrote that Bendel was "universally acknowledged as a genius of taste and style" is rare and vital. Happily, various top museums hold Bendel-label hats, dresses, gowns, and costumes in their collections. In New York, these include the Metropolitan Museum of Art, Parsons School of Design, the Fashion Institute of Technology, the Museum of the City of New York, and the Brooklyn Museum (in addition to their vast Bendel sketch collection). Bendel garments can also be found at the Rhode Island School of Design in Providence and the Philadelphia Museum of Art. In 2010 the New York Public Library's performing arts branch at Lincoln Center featured an exhibit called "On Stage in Fashion: Design for Theater, Opera, and Dance," where Henri was the eldest states-man among the likes of Hattie Carnegie, Chanel, Mainbocher, Oscar de la Renta, Calvin Klein, Marc Jacobs, Miuccia Prada, and Isaac Mizrahi.

In that show the library viewed him strictly as a fashion artist. Yet it took more than an eye for de-sign for Bendel to achieve his full stature. But what exactly? "His admirers," wrote Frances Anderson, "attributed his success to quick perception, a sixth sense with regards to changing fashion trends, su-perb taste, infallible artistic judgment, a genius for administration, and courage in initiating hitherto unknown merchandising policies."

Henri himself took a humble stance regarding his accomplishments and, with the generosity for which he was known, shared credit. "It is with col-laboration of the people I have surrounded myself by, and by years of perseverance and experience, that I have achieved my success," he told the *North Side Tribune*. "Without them I could not have ac-complished the things I have." That unwritten roster would have to include Mr. Blish and Mr. Bastedo.

This perhaps is the Henri Bendel captured by Florine Stettheimer in her painting *Spring Sale at Bendel's*—discreet in aspect and manner, apt to

A Stephen Burrows knit jersey dress (late '60s) now at the Museum of the City of New York

Bendel's longest serving employee— by many decades— James "Buster" Jarrett posed with Geraldine Stutz in front of the store in the 1970s.

deflect the spotlight so it would shine upon his customer, or on the reader of his columns, or on his colleagues, but also firmly in control of the splendid show that was the store and the label Henri Bendel.

Well, in control *most* of the time. When James Jarrett, better known as Buster the doorman, was asked nearly forty years after Bendel's death— when Jarrett was in his seventh decade of service at the store—whether Henri had been an easy boss to work for, he asserted his loyalty but with a wink. "Off and on," he said. "When he was in Europe, I had it all to myself."

Creativity. Ambition. Hard work. An aggressive business instinct. These traits belonged to Bendel, as they do to many successful people and certainly to those who ascend in the competitive, quicksilver realms of high fashion. But Henri had an extra something—utterly organic and hardly secret— that fueled his rise and kept him on top, and that was his innate and boundless devotion to aesthetics—aesthetics of fashion and aesthetics of living. Above almost everything else, save for his family and his God. *La vie esthétique.* A life of art and artfulness, a sensitivity of perception, an *insistence* on beauty, whether carved in stone and wood, woven in tapestry, sewn into the lines of a dress, or crafted by nature into a perfect magnolia blossom.

Remarkably, he did not view this consuming passion, this *raison d'être*, as his alone, nor as the exclusive province of the wealthy, the urban, the elite, but rather something we all share—or should. "The desire for beautiful things, the ardent love of true fashions," he once said in his inimitably grand way, "runs like a strong river through all civilization. It cannot be turned off nor on at anyone's whim or will, and I will never lend my aid nor my reputation to regulate or to disturb this flow."

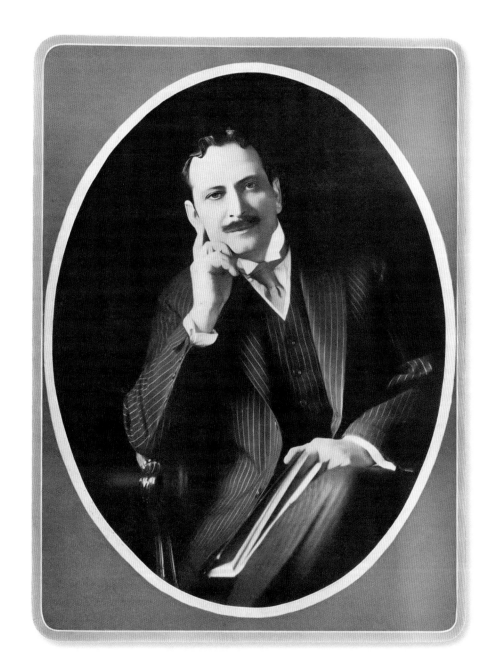

Very Truly Yours
Henri W. Bendel

AUTHOR'S NOTE

Long before I knew who he was, I'd lived in one of Henri Bendel's worlds. Growing up in South Louisiana on what had once been his property, I was surrounded by oak trees and camellia bushes that he planted. Was the magnolia tree in our front yard that we climbed one of his? Or maybe a wind-blown-seed descendant? Back then, Bendel Gardens was just the name of our subdivision, adjacent to Bendel Road. Not a person. It wasn't until I was older that I learned the man who built the Spanish stucco cottage at the entrance to the neighborhood was *the* Henri Bendel of the famous women's clothing store in New York. Later, living in Manhattan and working not far from Bendel's, it would strike me from time to time: I bet few who shop there know who he was or where he came from. Even in Lafayette, I rarely heard him mentioned.

Then, some years ago, my friend Karen Jones brought him up, having seen his portrait at the Lafayette Museum. She felt Henri was in hiding—even literally, as the large oil painting had been found in the attic of the museum's Creole cottage—and thought someone should write about him. Spurred by her enthusiasm and some online digging she'd done, I got more interested and was soon struck by how little chronicled he was. No one had published a full-length book, nor even a comprehensive biographical article in a national magazine. Over the years, I came to understand why. Leaving behind no memoir and no diaries, and with letters to family and friends long lost, Bendel was elusive to say the least. Getting his story seemed so daunting that more than once I put the project down and doubted I'd ever write this book. But whenever I'd tell someone a little about him, they'd be intrigued. I knew I had to keep trying, and UL Press's invitation to create the book with them felt like a natural fit, a chance to bring Henri home.

Happily, between the public record—from fashion coverage to short sketches of his rise from humble roots to great success, and especially his syndicated pronouncements on styles, and interviews in which he articulated his attitudes toward merchandising—and later from stories I heard from his descendants, another portrait came out of hiding: that of a man of tremendous creativity, with a tireless work ethic and a passion for beauty and art in myriad forms. Also, of someone whose sexuality and unusual domestic arrangements likely led him to keep his private self under lock and key. I hope he'll forgive this intrusion upon that privacy, which might now be appreciated as an act of overdue liberation.

How to consider a nearly-lost figure once renowned—and one with an almost perverse devotion to long-ago eras and manners—from a modern vantage? Hacking through hyperbole and myth about Bendel, it seems fair to say that though he held women on a pedestal (and they returned the favor), he was also a product of nineteenth- and twentieth-century attitudes about women's and men's roles. It's a fine line between decreeing what a woman must and *must not* wear, and sexist tyranny. In his defense, Bendel was a prisoner of his time, and of other societal constrictions. And selling hats and dresses to wealthy women, becoming rich and part of their rarefied, indulged circle, nurtured a decided snobbery in him that now can feel by turns amusing or appalling. I've wondered, would I have liked Henri? He reputedly had a great sense of humor, was gracious and charming. He could also be a prig, a fussbudget, and high-hatted. *Particular*, in the pejorative sense (well, I fear *I've* been accused of that). Regardless of his flaws, I admire the Henri I've come to know, for his vision, his ambition, what he was up against, for his loyalty to friends, family, and to his roots, and for his holistic view that the beauty one can find—or make—in fashion connects to wider spheres. We can all marvel at his greatest legacy, an ever-evolving store and brand that captured the patronage and imagination of many generations of stylish women of all backgrounds. The one and only Bendel's.

It's Henri's trajectory I find most compelling—for him to have gotten to the pinnacle of fashion merchandising, with a name and voice that reverberated even with average American women across the country, having started out in my sultry little corner of the world. What were the odds of it?

ACKNOWLEDGMENTS

*T*HANK YOU, KAREN JONES—your curiosity about Mr. Bendel was the spark for this. And thanks to your marvelous late mother, Denise Jones, a longtime French professor at UL Lafayette who led you to Henri's portrait that day.

Dr. Joshua Caffery who runs the Center for Louisiana Studies and serves as publisher of UL Press saw the potential in Bendel's story and lent hearty support. Merci beaucoup, Josh.

Bendel's great-nephew, the late John Bendel of Boston, in my sole phone conversation with him, gave me enough of a sense of Henri as a colorful, flesh-and-blood character to encourage the pursuit. After John passed away suddenly, his wife Diana Bendel became invaluable—first by introducing me to dozens of descendants of Bendel's siblings, then with her own intrepid digging borne of passionate interest, and finally in cheerleading my endeavor, becoming a friend along the way. Dee, I'm grateful—as I am to *all* the family members who shared stories and perspectives.

This book perches on the shoulders of Sally Robbins of New York City whose published 2014 lecture on Henri was a crucial early roadmap. Sally, who once aimed to do her own full-length Bendel book, nailed, in short form, the weight and drama of Henri's life and career. When we finally connected as my book was in the editing stages, we discovered we had trod uncannily parallel research paths. Her generosity in opening up her old file boxes yielded a few new treasures, including correspondence with two Bendel relatives who had died before I started my work and some great family photos. I was happy to crack open my draft to accommodate the finds. Her material and insights also validated things I had and provided some fact checking. Moreover, Sally's enthusiasm for what I was doing, being glad Henri's story might be told more fully, was a gracious benediction.

Devon Lord, editor in chief of UL Press, beyond greenlighting the book, brought precision, judiciousness, and a writer's knack for storytelling to the editing process, along with much bonhomie. Her equally cheerful colleague

Mary Duhé never blinked under a barrage of photo options and story components, smartly art-directing the book in a manner worthy of its stylish subject. Stephanie Durante helped me chase down and secure photos, a long and daunting project that she tackled with energy and ingenuity. To the three of you, a million thanks to go with the seemingly million emails we exchanged. And appreciation to Summer Greer at UL Press for contributing some extra photos.

Architectural historian Andrew Cronson, who has done his own extensive research into Bendel's first mansion, at Kings Point, Long Island, generously shared his findings and photos. Dr. Josh Smith and Veronica Barry of the US Merchant Marine Academy at Kings Point invited me to tour the house and offered research material with enthusiasm. At the Stamford Museum and Nature Center, great thanks to Jennifer Parry, Lucy Burdick, Pat Standaert, and their predecessor, Kirsten Brophy.

I'm grateful to Deirdre Lawrence, formerly of the Brooklyn Museum, for my first access to the Bendel sketches collection, and more recently at BM, to Abigail Dansiger and Monica Park. Thanks too to Cynthia Cathcart and Cole Hill at Condé Nast; Wendy Israel and Laurie Feigenbaum at Hearst; Kristen Knieper at ProQuest; Zach Stein at the Edith Garland Dupré Library at UL Lafayette and his predecessor, the late Alvin Bethard (who published his own article on Bendel's life); Bill Hooper, Time Inc. archivist extraordinaire; Neal Mayon at the Morgan City Historic Society; Jere Bacharach and Richard Eisner for some history of the Lehman family; Elizabeth Marchesani for photos and stories of the Bastedo clan; Nikki Hudson at Bath & Body Works, which holds the Bendel's trademark; Mary Jones at the New York Public Library; Phyllis Magidson, curator of costumes and textiles at the Museum of the City of New York; Hazel Clark at Parsons School of Design, and Shane Bernard with McIlhenny Co. of Avery Island, Louisiana.

Author and educator Jeanette Parker first came into my life over half a century ago as the principal of my elementary school (!) and reappeared when she was researching her book about (small world) the history of the Bendel Gardens subdivision. We traded findings and pondered Bendel conundrums, and beholding her dizzying industry and deep passion was a lesson they don't teach in first grade.

Speaking of Bendel Gardens, Brit Huckabay, dear friend and former BG mischief-maker, thank you for your artful photography.

For entrée, insights, research help, photos, feedback, and sundry other acts of assistance I'm indebted to Yvonne Saloom, Dan Hare, Jim Oberman, Patrice Adcroft, Irene Neves, Kevin Ryan, Louisa Ermelino, Candace Allenson, Dan Scheffey, Leslye Arsht, Lynn Davis Lasher, Susan Gillette, Jane Cohen, Philip Monaghan, Russ Sonnier, Steve Diamond, Louise Evans, Lisa Gabor, Sarah Rozen, Tom Lowe, Paul Roelofs, Fiona Donovan, Douglas Ross, Betsy Marchesani,

Fern Mallis, Stan Herman, Isaac Mizrahi, Linda Rodin, Billy Norwich, Barbara Hertz Burr, Valentine Hertz Kass, John Goodman, Susan Gillette, Christine Nuttall, Mark Welsh, Alice Ross, Deborah Hughes, Michelle Edelman, Rachael Goldberg, Pam Sommers, Donna Bulseco, Robert Rufino, and Izak Zenou, creator of the iconic Bendel Girl.

An in-memoriam thank you to those who offered personal recollections: Elene Davis, Betty Burnell, Adrian Goodman, Elaine Cohen, and the Honorable Judge Kaliste Saloom.

To friends and family who've listened to me talk about Henri for too long, I marvel at your fortitude.

And how I wish two beloved mentors, Novalyne Price Ellis and Jo Brans—masters each in writing and living life—could hold copies in their hands.

Last but never least, thank you, Jeffery McCullough for being a sharp-eyed first reader, and for keeping the faith—in this and in me.

—T. A.

SELECTED BIBLIOGRAPHY

Anderson, Frances. "Henri Willis Bendel, 1868–1936 : an appreciation." Unpublished manuscript, n.d., print.

Arsht, Marjorie Meyer. *All the Way From Yoakum: The Personal Journey of a Political Insider.* College Station, TX: Texas A&M University Press, 2006.

Bane, Scott. *A Union Like Ours: The Love Story of F. O. Matthiessen and Russell Cheney.* Amherst, MA: Bright Leaf, 2022.

"The Beautiful Shop of Henri Bendel." *The Illustrated Milliner* 8, no. 4 (April 1907): 63.

Bender, Marilyn. *The Beautiful People.* New York: Coward-McCann, Inc., 1967.

Bethard, Alvin Y. "Henri Bendel, 'Connoisseur of Style.'" *Attakapas Gazette*, Summer 1991, 83–87.

Blackman, Cally. *100 Years of Fashion Illustration.* London: Laurence King Publishing, 2007.

Bloemink, Barbara J. *Florine Stettheimer: A Biography.* Munich: Hirmer Verlag, 2022.

———. *The Life and Art of Florine Stettheimer.* New Haven, CT: Yale University Press, 1995.

Bradshaw, Jim. "Bendel Gardens Creator Earned Fame in New York Fashion Circles." *Daily Advertiser* (Lafayette, LA), June 5, 2002.

Brown, Henry Collins. *Fifth Avenue, Old and New.* New York: The Fifth Avenue Association, 1924.

Brown, Stephen and Georgiana Uhlyarik. *Florine Stettheimer: Painting Poetry.* New Haven, CT: Yale University Press, 2017.

Burns, Ric and James Sanders. *New York: An Illustrated History.* New York: Alfred A. Knopf, 2021.

Buxbaum, Gerda, ed. *Icons of Fashion: The 20th Century.* Munich: Prestel, 1999.

Cantu, Maya. *American Cinderellas on the Broadway Musical Stage: Imagining the Working Girl from* Irene *to* Gypsy. Houndmills, Basingstoke, Hampshire, England: Palgrave Macmillan, 2015.

Carter, Ernestine. *The Changing World of Fashion: 1900 to the Present.* London: Weidenfeld and Nicolson, 1977.

Chase, Edna Woolman and Ilka. *Always in Vogue.* Garden City, NY: Doubleday, 1954.

Citron, Alan B. "Lafayette 'Discovery' Drilled Down 50 Feet," This Week in Oil. *Daily Advertiser* (Lafayette, LA), October 29, 1949.

Crawford, M. D. C. *The Ways of Fashion.* New York: G. P. Putnam, 1941.

Devorkin, Joseph. *Great Merchants of Early New York: The Ladies' Mile.* New York: The Society for the Architecture of the City, 1987.

Ellenzweig, Allen. *George Platt Lynes: The Daring Eye.* New York: Oxford University Press, 2022.

Farrar, Geraldine. *Such Sweet Compulsion.* Richmond, VA: The William Byrd Press, Inc., 1938.

Finamore, Michelle Tolini. *Hollywood Before Glamour: Fashion in American Silent Film,* Houndmills, Basingstoke, Hampshire: Palgrave Macmillan, 2013.

Garelick, Rhonda K. *Mademoiselle: Coco Chanel and the Pulse of History.* New York: Random House, 2014.

Goldring/Woldenberg Institute of Southern Jewish Life, "Lafayette, Louisiana." Encyclopedia of Southern Jewish Communities. Accessed October 12, 2023, https://www.isjl.org/louisiana-lafayette-encyclopedia.html.

Goreau, Lorraine. "Lafayette Estate, Home of Fashion Arbiter Henri Bendel, to Be Sold." *Daily Advertiser* (Lafayette, LA), March 19, 1950.

Gray, Christopher, ed. *Fifth Avenue, 1911 From Start to Finish in Historic Block-by-Block Photographs.* New York: Dover Publications, 1994.

Hendrickson, Robert. *The Grand Emporiums: The Illustrated History of America's Great Department Stores.* New York: Stein and Day, 1979.

Holub, Rona L. "Henri Bendel." *American National Biography,* October 2008. https://www.anb.org/display/10.1093/anb/9780198606697.001.0001/anb-9780198606697-e-1701700.

Homberger, Eric. *The Historical Atlas of New York City.* New York: St. Martin's Griffin, 2016.

Kiesel, Jean S. *Images of America: Lafayette.* Charleston, SC: Arcadia Publishing, 2007.

Kornbluth, Jesse. "The Battle For Bendel's." *New York,* February 23, 1987.

L., Zach. "Forker House." Old Long Island (blog), April 17, 2010. https://www.oldlongisland.com/2010/04/forker-house.html.

"Laurel Lake Lodge." *The Spur,* March 1935.

Levy, Flora. "The Bendel Family." In *Some Early Families of Lafayette, Louisiana,* compiled by Quintilla Morgan Anders. Lafayette, LA: Galvez Chapter, NSDAR, 1969.

———. "The Levy Family." In *Some Early Families of Lafayette, Louisiana,* compiled by Quintilla Morgan Anders. Lafayette, LA: Galvez Chapter, NSDAR, 1969.

Mamalakis, Mario. *If They Could Talk: Acadiana's Buildings and Their Biographies.* Lafayette, LA: The Lafayette Centennial Commission, 1983.

Mateyunas, Paul J. *Images of America: Long Island's Gold Coast.* Charleston, SC: Arcadia Publishing, 2012.

Mears, Patricia. "Erté: Art Deco Master." In *Icons of Fashion: The 20th Century,* edited by Gerda Buxbaum. Munich: Prestel, 1999.

Mears, Patricia and G. Bruce Boyer, eds. *Elegance In the Age of Crisis: Fashions of the 1930s.* New Haven, CT: Yale University Press; New York: Fashion Institute of Technology, 2014.

Milbank, Caroline Rennolds. *New York Fashion: The Evolution of American Style.* New York: Harry N. Abrahms, Inc., 1989.

Montgomery, Elisabeth Denbo. *Personal Reflections of Early Lafayette.* Lafayette, LA: printed by the author, 1988.

Palmer, Gretta. *A Shopping Guide to New York.* New York: R. M. McBride & Co., 1930.

Parker, Dorothy. *Complete Broadway: 1918–1923.* Edited by Kevin C. Fitzpatrick. Bloomington, IN: iUniverse, 2014.

Parker, Jeanette Plauché. *Bendel Gardens: An Historic Treasure in Lafayette, Louisiana.* Lafayette, LA: Angers Graphics Press, 2021.

Parsons/The New School, Geraldine Stutz Fellowship. https://adht.parsons.edu/GeraldineStutz/.

Picardie, Justine. *Coco Chanel: The Legend and the Life.* London: HarperCollins, 2010.

Pouillard, Veronique. *Paris to New York: The Transatlantic Fashion Industry in the Twentieth Century.* Cambridge, MA: Harvard University Press, 2021.

Robbins, Sally. *Henri Bendel: From Louisiana Obscurity to Fame as Fashion Authority and Bon-vivant Icon.* Lafayette: The Flora Levy Lecture Series, University of Louisiana at Lafayette, 2013.

Roshco, Bernard. *The Rag Race: How New York and Paris Run the Breakneck Business of Dressing American Women.* New York: Funk & Wagnalls Company, Inc., 1963.

Sclare, Liisa and Donald. *Beaux-Arts Estates: A Guide to the Architecture of Long Island.* New York: Viking Press, 1980.

Seebohm, Caroline. *The Man Who Was Vogue: The Life and Times of Condé Nast.* New York: Viking Press, 1982.

Smith, Adam D, Susan I. Enscore, and Sunny E. Adams. "Character-defining Features of Contributing Buildings and Structures in the United States Merchant Marine Academy Historic District." Draft report for the US Army Corps of Engineers by ERDC (September 2013.) https://hdl.handle.net/11681/27476.

Smith, Cecil Michener, and Glenn Litton. *Musical Comedy in America.* New York: Theatre Arts Books, 1981.

Spencer, Charles. *Erté.* New York: Clarkson N. Potter, 1981.

Stein, Sarah Abrevaya. *Plumes: Ostrich Feathers, Jews, and the Lost World of Global Commerce.* New Haven, CT: Yale University Press, 2008.

Stewart-Gordon, Faith. *The Russian Tea Room: A Love Story.* New York: Simon & Schuster, 1999.

Storey, Shirley Lee. "Henri W. Bendel." Unpublished paper, Winter 1939. Special Collections, Edith Garland Dupré Library, University of Louisiana at Lafayette.

Trager, James. *The New York Chronology: The Ultimate Compendium of Events, People, and Anecdotes from the Dutch to the Present.* New York: HarperResource, 2003.

Valuable Furnishings and Art Collection at Laurel Lake Lodge. Auction catalog. Kende Galleries Inc.: New York, NY, 1949.

Wallace, Mike. *Greater Gotham: A History of New York City From 1898 to 1919.* New York: Oxford University Press, 2017.

Whitney Plantation. "Slavery in Louisiana." Accessed October 12, 2023. whitneyplantation.org/history/slavery-in-louisiana/.

SELECTED ENDNOTES

CHAPTER 1

"The great New York house of Bendel"—"Who's Who in the Mode: A Tale of Two Cities," *Vogue*, January 1, 1923, 70.

"I think it's high time American designers were thinking for themselves"—Sarah Addington, "The Metropolitan Creates a Super-Nursery," *New York Tribune,* August 15, 1915.

"universally acknowledged as a genius of taste and style"—Caroline Rennolds Milbank, *New York Fashion: The Evolution of American Style* (New York: Harry N. Abrahms, Inc., 1989), 117.

"genial dictator"—M. D. C. Crawford, *The Ways of Fashion* (New York: G. P. Putnam, 1941), 243.

"It's a fact that frills are finished"—"Notes From London and Paris," *Women's Wear*, January 5, 1914.

"Let me warn you that your evening and dinner gowns"—Henri Bendel, NEA Service, "Flapper Styles Will Be Passé After This Season, Says Bendel; Evening Gowns Much Longer and Show Softness," *Appleton (WI) Post-Crescent,* October 14, 1926.

"Paris couturiers are apparently repentant"—Bendel, "Flapper Styles Will Be Passé."

"Women make their battle with life much harder"—Hortense Saunders, "Charming, Feminine, Beautiful," *Lawrence (KS) Daily Journal-World*, March 4, 1925.

"There is not a gown leaves the shop"—*North Side Tribune* (Great Neck, NY), 1925, reprinted in "Success of Henri Bendel, Local Man, In Business, Fashion World, Is Told By New York Newspaper," *Daily Advertiser* (Lafayette, LA), April 14, 1925.

"Henri Bendel lent himself to the creation of myths"—Crawford, *The Ways of Fashion*, 243.

"Paris couldn't stop creating"—Addington, "The Metropolitan Creates a Super-Nursery."

'Now let me whisper a secret"—Mlle. Manhattan [pseud.], "Footlight Fashions," *The Theatre,* July 1916.

CHAPTER 2

"I just had a mighty fine visit"—"Henri Bendel, Owner of Big New York Fashion Firm, Still Feels Lafayette Is His Home," *Daily Advertiser* (Lafayette, LA)*,* February 26, 1925.

"When Mr. Bendel first saw the light of day"—*North Side Tribune* (Great Neck, NY), reprinted in "Success of Henri Bendel, Local Man, In Business, Fashion World, Is Told By New York Newspaper," *Daily Advertiser* (Lafayette, LA), April 14, 1925.

"I talk of Lafayette wherever I go"—"Henri Bendel, home for two months, pushes plans for fine residence near city," *Daily Advertiser* (Lafayette, LA)*,* January 23, 1929.

More than 330,000 African Americans were enslaved in Louisiana…—Whitney Plantation, "Slavery in Louisiana," accessed October 12, 2023, whitneyplantation.org/history/slavery-in-louisiana/.

"a great admirer of [Henry's] father"—Frances Anderson, "Henri Willis Bendel, 1868–1936: an appreciation" (unpublished manuscript, n.d.), print.

Falk "tended his ready-made flock well"—Lorraine Goreau, "Lafayette Estate, Home of Fashion Arbiter Henri Bendel, to be Sold," *Daily Advertiser* (Lafayette, LA)*,* March 19, 1950.

"As a child he liked to play"—Elisabeth Denbo Montgomery, *Personal Reflections of Early Lafayette* (Lafayette, LA: printed by the author, 1988).

Mary was quite a businesswoman—Flora Levy, "The Bendel Family," in *Some Early Families of Lafayette, Louisiana,* compiled by Quintilla Morgan Anders (Lafayette, LA: Galvez Chapter, NSDAR, 1969).

Siblings who were "full of fun"—Author correspondence with John Goodman.

A great-niece recalled family lore—Author interview with Elene Davis.

"were among the early members and benefactors"—Alvin Bethard, "Henri Bendel 'Connoisseur of Style,'" *Attakapas Gazette*, Summer 1991, 83.

By at least one account, the plantation store's name was Hiller—Anderson, "Henri Willis Bendel, 1868–1936."

CHAPTER 3

"A well-dressed woman nowadays is as fluffy as a downy bird"—Quoted in Sarah Abrevaya Stein, *Plumes: Ostrich feathers, Jews, and a Lost World of Global Commerce* (New Haven, CT: Yale University Press, 2008), 20.

"The world of women is composed of peacocks, butterflies and Jenny wrens"—Hortense Saunders, "Wear Clothes Correctly!" *Muskogee (OK) Times-Democrat,* December 2, 1924.

"probably to bolster their presence in their most important market"—Author correspondence with Richard Eisner.

in September 1890 . . . a blaze consumed a sizeable area of downtown—"Extensive Conflagration Involving Loss of Four Stores and Three Residences," *Times-Picayune* (New Orleans), September 17, 1890.

CHAPTER 4

According to Richard Eisner . . . Mitchell handled business in America"—Author correspondence with Richard Eisner.

"handsome assemblage of carriages"—"Henri Bendel: He has proved that American Women want 'Values,'" *Women's Wear,* March 27, 1914.

his partner, Julius Saur, ran off with company profits—"Petitions in Bankruptcy," *New York Times,* April 24, 1902.

"He has succeeded in building up a paying manufactory of pattern hats"—*Lafayette (LA) Advertiser*, November 9, 1901.

"The French are the greatest people in the world to invent names for colors"—"Naming the Colors," *New York Times*, September 4, 1904.

Mrs. Catherine Donovan . . . was known as the 'Dresser to the 400'—Sally Robbins, *Henri Bendel: From Louisiana Obscurity to Fame as Fashion Authority and Bon-vivant Icon* (Lafayette: The Flora Levy Lecture Series, University of Louisiana at Lafayette, 2013), 12.

Whom the couture importer Max Meyer would later recall as—M. D. C. Crawford, *The Ways of Fashion* (New York: G. P. Putnam, 1941), 106.

"Never before or since, except at one very fashionable wedding"—"Henri Bendel: He has proved that American Women want 'Values.'"

"recognized in Paris as a keen judge"—Crawford, *The Ways of Fashion*, 243.

CHAPTER 5

According to a 1925 profile of Henri . . . —*North Side Tribune* (Great Neck, NY), reprinted in "Success of Henri Bendel, Local Man, In Business, Fashion World, Is Told By New York Newspaper," *Daily Advertiser* (Lafayette, LA), April 14, 1925.

"For all these screen stories"—Geraldine Farrar, *Such Sweet Compulsion* (Richmond, VA: The William Byrd Press, Inc., 1938), 184.

Henri himself would one day refer to Mr. Bastedo as a "lifelong intimate friend"—Sally Robbins, *Henri Bendel: From Louisiana Obscurity to Fame as Fashion Authority and Bon-vivant Icon* (Lafayette: The Flora Levy Lecture Series, University of Louisiana at Lafayette, 2013), 12.

attraction to Mr. Bastedo cemented the conversion—Author interview with Elene Davis.

"We were, all of us, trained in Paris"—M. D. C. Crawford, *The Ways of Fashion* (New York: G. P. Putnam, 1941), 245.

Henri "saved her from embarrassment when she wore a similar dress"—Author interview with John Goodman.

"Mr. Bendel and Paris will always remain in the center of fashion"—"Paris Gossip," *Women's Wear,* January 27, 1915.

An interview in the New York Times *in the fall of 1912 captures this verbal highwire act*—"Shall American Women Follow Paris," *New York Times,* October 6, 1912.

"Competitors and friends alike sort of pitied him"—"Fifth Ave. Trade Centre Appeals to Realty Buyers," *New York Tribune,* February 13, 1916.

CHAPTER 6

"to the millinery firm of Henri Bendel"—"Real Estate," *New York Times,* August 25, 1912.

"I'd give it to my mother-in-law"—Sarah Addington, "The Metropolitan Creates a Super-Nursery," *New York Tribune,* August 15, 1915.

employee ranks had swelled to a remarkable 1,100—"Henri Bendel: He has proved that American Women want 'Values,'" *Women's Wear,* March 27, 1914.

Upon that milestone New York *magazine wrote a short piece on Jarrett*—"September Song," *New York,* September 27, 1976, 78.

Bendel made no attempt to obscure the provenance of particular dresses—"Henri Bendel: He has proved that American Women want 'Values.'"

"The growth of the Henri Bendel business has not been the overnight kind"—"Henri Bendel: He has proved that American Women want 'Values.'"

"Clothes should not reach their lowest ebb in the morning"—Hortense Saunders, NEA Service, "House Dress Needn't Be Dowdy," *Palm Beach (FL) Post,* September 1, 1925.

"The pajama is the ideal costume for the boudoir"—Hortense Saunders, NEA Service, "Pajamas Replacing Time-Honored Kimono" *The Bee* (Danville, VA), October 10, 1925.

"The scarf is a direct answer to that very harassing question"—Henri Bendel, NEA Service, "Small Things Make Costume," *Kenosha (WI) Evening News,* February 9, 1927.

"Accessories do come and go, flourish and die"—Henri Bendel, "Accessories Will Stretch a Meager Wardrobe And Gain Clever Effects," *Des Moines (IA) Evening Tribune*, January 14, 1927.

"Don't wear a white hat unless you are so beautiful"—Hortense Saunders, "If You're Heavy Don't Wear Wide-Brimmed Hats," *Meriden (CT) Daily Journal*, August 8, 1925.

"What the petite blonde can wear, the exotic brunette of Juno-like dignity should never consider"—Henri Bendel, NEA Service, "Dress to Suit Your Own Type," *Bakersfield Californian,* October 10, 1927.

"It is always smarter to be informally dressed for formal occasion"—Henri Bendel, NEA Service, "Two-In-One Costumes Smart For Summer Weekends," *Abilene (TX) Daily Reporter*, June 21, 1927.

"Outside of a musical comedy you cannot find a more captivating costume than [a bathing suit]"—Henri Bendel, NEA Service, "Why Beaches Are Popular! Bathing Togs Have Smartness, Intrigue, Femininity!," *Abilene (TX) Daily Reporter*, July 10, 1926.

"Nothing that is essentially correct gives the appearance of over-decorativeness"—Henri Bendel, NEA Service, "Intricate Trimming For New Costumes," *Santa Ana (CA) Daily Register*, January 17, 1929.

"Naturally when fabrics are so gorgeous lines must not be intricate"—Henri Bendel, NEA Service, "Styles Flash Gold and Silver," *Amarillo (TX) Globe*, February 2, 1927.

"Life can never be entirely dull"—Hortense Saunders, NEA Service, "Charming, Feminine, Beautiful," *Lawrence (KS) Daily Journal-World,* March 4, 1925.

"Such an investment might take from Henri Bendel the final decision"—"Henri Bendel: He has proved that American Women want 'Values.'"

"always received him in a private room to view her collection"—M. D. C. Crawford, *The Ways of Fashion* (New York: G. P. Putnam, 1941), 243.

In the summer of 1914, however, his time abroad proved to be an adventure—"Henri Bendel Brings Home Paris Models," *Women's Wear,* September 21, 1914.

"From time to time he had heard of the Austria-Hungary and Serbia trouble"—"Henri Bendel Brings Home Paris Models."

Bendel's dear friend Max Shwarcz . . . had perished onboard—Randy Bryan Bigham and Judith Tavares, "Mr. Maximilian M. Schwarcz," the Lusitania Resouce, accessed November 21, 2023, https://www.rmslusitania.info/people/saloon/max-schwarcz/.

Thus began the first Fashion Fête—"To Be Seen at Ritz-Carlton," *Women's Wear,* October 30, 1914.

In a newspaper article about the operetta Adele—"Tights Are Past, We Now Want Our Show Girls Not Only Dressed But Dressed In The Finest," *Pittsburgh Sunday Post,* September 20, 1914.

"Does Mr. Bendel say that New York will replace Paris?"—"Paris Gossip," *Women's Wear*, January 27, 1915.

"It's all nonsense to talk of 'American fashions for American women'"—"Whence Prestige Comes," *Women's Wear,* November 16, 1914.

But the crowning glory . . . was an Italianate roof garden—"Italian Garden Twelve Stories Above New York Street," *New York Sun,* July 25, 1915.

CHAPTER 7

That year Women's Wear *declared that Bendel was "the biggest buyer"*—"Paris Gossip," *Women's Wear*, January 27, 1915.

"Henri Bendel is ever in the van of the mode"—"A New Type of Frock," *Kansas City Star,* January 21, 1915, excerpting "With Father Knickerbocker's Daughters," *Vogue*, January 15, 1915.

His influence even reached abroad—"Henri Bendel, Specialty Shop Founder, Dies," *Women's Wear Daily,* March 23, 1936.

Mrs. Falk's obituary—*Daily Advertiser* (Lafayette, LA)*,* September 4, 1915.

Asked by the Trade Review *whether he planned to go to market in Paris in the spring*—"America's Leading Fashion Authority Defines the Style Trend," *Millinery Trade Review,* March 1916, 27.

"The feminine playgoer takes an added interest"—"Stage Frocks," *Harper's Bazar*, December 1915, 78.

As a reviewer of 1916's Our Little Wife *put it*—"'Our Little Wife's' Frocks An Aid to Heart Breaking," *Women's Wear,* November 25, 1916.

"About the most helpful thing that an actress can do for her audience"— Quoted in Donald Brooks, *Dorothy Parker: Complete Broadway 1918–1923* (Bloomington, IL: iUniverse, 2014), 218.

"the stage is the greatest factor"—*North Side Tribune* (Great Neck, NY), 1925, reprinted in "Success of Henri Bendel, Local Man, In Business, Fashion World, Is Told By New York Newspaper," *Daily Advertiser* (Lafayette, LA), April 14, 1925.

A year later Henri himself would reiterate the point, to Women's Wear—"American Women Will Remain Smartly Gowned," *Women's Wear,* May 18, 1918.

"For fall we don hats all wreathed with feathers"—Advertisement, *Dallas Morning News,* September 3, 1919.

"whenever a lady bought a fur coat"—M. D. C. Crawford, *The Ways of Fashion* (New York: G. P. Putnam, 1941), 243.

CHAPTER 8

Payment Overdue/Fritzi Scheff sued by costumer—"Sued By Costumer," *Washington (DC) Times* (Home Edition), December 10, 1914.

A complex, three parties real estate deal—"Henri Bendel Has Purchased Large N. Y. Apartments," *Daily Advertiser* (Lafayette, LA), February 14, 1923.

Dressmaking "like all art is autobiographical"—"Fashions From the New York Point of View," *Vogue*, May 1, 1922.

"the great New York houses probably reproduce greater numbers of many of their models"—"Who's Who in the Mode: A Tale of Two Cities," *Vogue*, January 1, 1923, 70.

"Henry [sic] *Bendel of New York, after seeing Palm Beach"*—"Social Notes," *New York Times*, January 25, 1923.

"There is nothing like this in all the world"—"New York Retailers Arrive in Palm Beach," *Women's Wear*, January 22, 1923.

Quite a stake: 45 percent of the store's full four million dollars' worth of capital stock—"Newspaper Specials," *Wall Street Journal,* June 21, 1923.

"I have no intention of retiring"—"1,800,000 Of Stock To Go To Employes [*sic*]," *New York Times*, June 20, 1923.

"I dislike the sheath gown on the youthful figure"—Hortense Saunders, NEA Service, "Emphasis Is On Youthful Frock," *Battle Creek (MI) Enquirer*, September 21, 1925.

"the debutante should not be in a hurry to grow up"—Saunders, "Emphasis Is On Youthful Frock."

"Keeping cool in August"—Henri Bendel, NEA Service, "Keep Cool . . . With Sheer White Frocks," *Pittsburgh Press*, July 22, 1929.

"For the ensemble costume that was the rage this spring"—Hortense Saunders, NEA Service, "Chiffon and Crepe Frocks Will Continue to Be Popular Says Henri Bendel," *Arizona Republican* (Phoenix), July 3, 1925.

"If the flapper were not a dead issue"—Henri Bendel, NEA Service, "Flapper Styles Will Be Passé After This Season, says Bendel," *Appleton (WI) Post-Crescent*, October 14, 1926.

CHAPTER 9

Bendel reiterated that last position—Henri Bendel, "Women Set Styles, Not Designers," *Syracuse Herald,* December 26, 1926.

In a 1927 column about what he termed "semi-dress"—Henri Bendel, "Semi-Dress is Popular for Shopping," *Syracuse Herald,* February 20, 1927.

"There may be a few places where the frilled and furbelowed hat may be worn" —B. J. Perkins, "Rock of Haute Couture Stands Firm in a Sea of Imitations," *Women's Wear,* July 9, 1926.

a rumor went around that Henri was "to retire from active participation"—"Deny Henri Bendel Is To Retire From Firm," *Women's Wear Daily,* March 3, 1927.

"an ambition he began to dream during his boyhood days"—"Henry Bendel Purchases Large New York Commercial Building," *Daily Advertiser* (Lafayette, LA), March 12, 1929.

A Louisiana journalist writing about the gardens some years later—Agathine Goldstein, "Artistic Genius of Henri Bendel, World Famous Designer, Penetrates Louisiana," *Alexandria (LA) Weekly,* April 20, 1935.

to design a "commodious lodge" in the Spanish villa style—"Designer Plans $250,000 Home Near Lafayette," *Times-Picayune* (New Orleans, LA), January 26, 1929.

The Daily Advertiser*, chronicling his visit and his ongoing plans*—"Henri Bendel, Home For Two Months, Pushes Plans For Fine Residence Near City," *Daily Advertiser* (Lafayette, LA)*,* January 23, 1929.

According to Henri Bendel II, who in the early 1960s shared some recollections about the house—"The Main Museum Building," *Bulletin*, Stamford Museum and Nature Center, Stamford, CT, December 1961–January 1962.

"We tried to talk Mr. Bendel into buying stone already cut"—Marie Updegraff, "Former Henri Bendel Estate: Man Who Built Museum Reminisces," *Stamford Advocate*, May 19, 1971.

a copy of one presented to a spa outside Florence—"Marcel LePiniec to Talk to Members of Garden Tour on Tuesday Afternoon," *Stamford Advocate*, July 12, 1935, 19.

He made news by purchasing 10–12 West Fifty-Seventh Street—"Bendel Buys Buildings Housing 57th St. Store," *Women's Wear Daily,* March 5, 1929.

Mary Rose Sibille had studied business at Southwestern Louisiana Institute— Robert Sibille, "Sibille Family, Narratives and Genealogy," December 1993. https://issuu.com/papa262/docs/sibille_narratives.

Vogue raised a glass to his achievement—"Vogue's Eye View of the Mode," *Vogue*, February 15, 1934, 25.

CHAPTER 10

In 1933 the company's capital stock had been decreased in value from $3,650,000 to $715,000—"Henri Bendel, Specialty Shop Founder, Dies," *Women's Wear Daily,* March 23, 1936.

"The good intentions which lay back of this law were completely nullified by the law itself"—M. D. C. Crawford, "Definite Change for Better Is Noticed by Henri Bendel," *Women's Wear Daily,* December 20, 1935.

"Europe is filled with a strange and weird and dangerous military ardor"—Crawford, "Definite Change for Better."

he gave Women's Wear Daily a remarkable long and roaming interview—Crawford, "Definite Change for Better."

"give dignity to the approach to where your house is to be built"—from the archives of McIlhenny Co. of Avery Island, Louisiana.

At an assembly of more than fifty students from various French classes—"Henri Bendel Makes Visit to Schools Here," *Daily Advertiser* (Lafayette, LA), February 20, 1936.

The New York Times *reported news of his passing*—"Henri Bendel Dies; Dress House Head," *New York Times,* March 23, 1936.

Down in Lafayette the Daily Advertiser *referred to Bendel as "an internationally known fashion designer"*—"Henri Bendel Dies Suddenly In East," *Daily Advertiser* (Lafayette, LA), March 23, 1936.

That Wednesday some five hundred mourners. . . . filed into the Frank E. Campbell Funeral Home chapel—"500 Attend Rites For Henri Bendel," *New York Times,* March 26, 1936.

CHAPTER 11

it was announced that Abraham Bastedo was elected president—"AB Bastedo New Head of Henri Bendel's," *Women's Wear Daily,* April 7, 1936.

"Our clients were, and to a degree still are, steeped in the Paris tradition"—M. D. C. Crawford, *The Ways of Fashion* (New York: G. P. Putnam, 1941), 245.

"we'd never seen anything like Bendel's"—Author interview with Barbara Hertz Burr.

"I was impressed with how calmly and patiently he helped them"—Author interview with Valentine Hertz Kass.

Upon taking over, Parker said he planned no big changes—"Nicholas Parker," Obituary, *New York Times,* June 10, 1970.

"Jarman decided that the Bendel's turnaround required drastic measures"—"Camelot on 57th Street: A History of Henri Bendel," Geraldine Stutz Fellowship/Parsons-The New School, 2016.

as she told fashion columnist Marilyn Bender of the Times *in the mid-1960s*—Marilyn Bender, "Bendel's President Sees Herself as Customer," *New York Times,* May 10, 1965.

"We picked a customer to concentrate on"—Bender, "Bendel's President Sees Herself as Customer."

"Fifty-seventh Street was heaven"—Dana Wagner, "Beauty Buzz: Fashion Scents," *Vogue*, September 2000, 670.

"Geraldine had a vision"—Eric Wilson, "Geraldine Stutz Dies at 80; Headed Bendel for 29 Years," *New York Times*, April 9, 2005, 9.

Stutz has "a taste so sure and strong"—Ann Crittenden, "Gerry's Little Store on 57th Street," *New York Times,* April 24, 1977.

Street of shops . . . "It was brilliant"—Author interview with Fern Mallis.

"She had a whim of iron"—Author interview with Linda Rodin.

"The store is my theater and my show"—Eleanor Johnson Tracy, et al., "The Merchant Princess," *Fortune*, August 25, 1980, 15.

"Bendel's was then the jewel of all stores, probably in America"—"Joel Schumacher on His Colleagues, His Critics, and His Sex Life," Vulture, June 22, 2020, https://www.vulture.com/2020/06/joel-schumacher-in-conversation.html.

"the humorously chic windows"—Rosemary Kent, "Décor For Dining," *Architectural Digest*, November/December 1975, 176.

"slightly decadent models posed in tableaux"—Crittenden, "Gerry's Little Store on 57th Street."

"Bendel's was also the first store to go heavily into European ready to wear"—Crittenden, "Gerry's Little Store on 57th Street."

"Bendel's had a renegade personality"—Author interview with Stan Herman.

"I bought a Stephen Burrows cocktail dress there"—Author correspondence with Lisa Birnbach.

"She spent like her entire month's salary"—Author interview with Isaac Mizrahi.

"a tenacious and exacting individual"—Susan Alai, "Bendel's Chief Sets New Route," *Women's Wear Daily,* December 18, 1986.

"Les's vision and strategic agility are among the best in business"—Author correspondence with Philip Monaghan.

"Behind those baffled and hurt feelings is a fascinating takeover tale"—Jesse Kornbluth, "The Battle For Bendel's," *New York,* February 23, 1987, 26.

Shulman told Women's Wear Daily *he wanted to make the store "a paradise"*—Alai, "Bendel's Chief Sets New Route."

"As of yet [Bendel's] does not have the excitement"—David Moin, "Bendel's: On the brink of change," *Women's Wear Daily*, June 30, 1987.

a 1992 Todd Oldham one-day trunk show … yielded $95,000—Maryellen Gordon, "Todd Oldham's Trunk Show Scores in Bendel's Atrium," *Women's Wear Daily*, May 13, 1992.

"recapturing the magic of the old store [has been] difficult"—David Moin, "Henri Bendel Outlines An Ambitious Vision: 50 Units in Five Years," *Women's Wear Daily*, October 16, 1995.

"half a decade after closing its legendary store"—Sharon Edelson, "Bendel's: The Limited Version," *Women's Wear Daily*, July 1, 1996.

The brass were mulling how employees might be absorbed—Sharon Edelson, "Bendel's Holds Breath As The Limited Rates Its Underperformers," *Women's Wear Daily*, February 12, 1998.

Ed Burstell "was instrumental in elevating the profile of Bendel's"—David Moin, "Wexner Buoys Bendel's," *Women's Wear Daily*, July 21, 2004.

"Fashion isn't where we're seeing our growth"—Sharon Edelson, "Bendel's New Strategy: Accessories and Beauty the Keys To The Future," *Women's Wear Daily*, May 1, 2009.

"As retail experiences its most traumatic period in a generation"—Edelson, "Bendel's New Strategy."

"This decision is right for the future growth of our company"—David Moin and Evan Clark, "L Brands Closing Henri Bendel," *Women's Wear Daily*, September 14, 2018.

"Over 30 years, at least $300 million was pumped into Henri Bendel"—Author interview with Phillip Monaghan.

"Shoppers Mourn the End of Henri Bendel"—Megan Friedman, "Shoppers Mourn the End of Henri Bendel…" *Town & Country*, September 14, 2018.

"Henri Bendel, the brand, died today"—Choire Sicha, "The Very Open Hidden History of Henri Bendel," *New York Times*, September 14, 2018.

The Wall Street Journal *recalled the store as a "pioneer"*—"Henri Bendel to Close After 123 Years," *Wall Street Journal*, September 13, 2018.

"The increased corporatization of high-end fashion"—Ginia Bellafante, "Henri Bendel and the Death of Luxury," *New York Times*, September 24, 2018.

Vanessa Friedman argued that it was appropriate to lament the passing of Bendel's—Vanessa Friedman, "New York's Lost Department Stores," *New York Times*, January 16, 2019.

Women's Wear Daily *reminded its readers of the Stutz years*—Moin and Clark, "L Brands Closing Henri Bendel."

CHAPTER 12

presuming a fifty-two-story mixed-use skyscraper . . . proceeds apace—Michael Young, "Demolition For Future 52-Story Skyscraper At 10–14 West 57th Street Moving Quickly, In Midtown," *New York YIMBY*, August 10, 2019, https://newyorkyimby.com/2019/08/demolition-for-future-52-story-sky-scraper-at-10-14-west-57th-street-moving-quickly-in-midtown.html.

Henri had donated the Camellia Lodge and its property to his life partner Abraham—Jeanette Plauché Parker, *Bendel Gardens: An Historic Treasure in Lafayette, Louisiana* (Lafayette, LA: Angers Graphics Press, 2021).

Judge Saloom recalled how as a boy he had seen Bendel—Author interview with Kaliste Saloom.

he was intrigued by the house, which he thought had a "mysterious air"—Parker, *Bendel Gardens: An Historic Treasure in Lafayette, Louisiana.*

She hazily recalled a visit to the house—Author interview with Elaine Cohen.

"For 41 years he could be found in the front of the store"—John Bendel notes, courtesy of Diana Bendel.

he took pride in the history of his great-uncle—Author interview with John Bendel.

"I became fascinated"—Author interview with Diana Bendel.

"Many of us probably wouldn't even know each other"—Author interview with Susan Gillette.

"a man renowned the world over as a genius of women's fashions"—Lorraine Goreau, "Lafayette Estate, Home of Fashion Arbiter Henri Bendel, to Be Sold," *Daily Advertiser* (Lafayette, LA)*,* March 19, 1950.

"His admirers attributed his success to quick perception"—Frances Anderson, "Henri Willis Bendel, 1868–1936: an appreciation" (unpublished manuscript, n.d.), print.

"It is with collaboration of the people I have surrounded myself by"—"The Success of Henri Bendel, Local Man, In Business, Fashion World, Is Told By New York Newspaper," *Daily Advertiser* (Lafayette, LA), April 14, 1925.

"When he was in Europe, I had it all to myself"—"September Song," *New York*, September 27, 1976, 78.

"The desire for beautiful things"—M. D. C. Crawford, "Definite Change For Better Is Noticed by Henri Bendel," *Women's Wear Daily,* Friday, December 20, 1935.

PHOTO CREDITS

The following abbreviations are used for sources from which several images were obtained:

Brooklyn Museum—Brooklyn Museum Libraries. Special Collections.
    ©Bath & Body Works Direct, Inc.
Harper's Bazaar-Hearst, ProQuest—*Harper's Bazaar* Hearst Magazine
    Media Inc. Image produced by ProQuest LLC as part of ProQuest®
    Women's Magazine Archive www.proquest.com. Further reproduc-
    tion is prohibited without permission.
Henri Bendel, LLC—Reproduced with permission of Henri Bendel, LLC
LOC—Library of Congress
MCNY—Museum of the City of New York
MET, Art Resource NY—© The Metropolitan Museum of Art, Art
    Resource, NY
NYPL—New York Public Library
PLI—Preservation Long Island, "Forker House" real estate brochure, via
    oldlongisland.com
ProQuest—Image produced by ProQuest LLC as part of ProQuest® Women's
    Magazine Archive www.proquest.com. Further reproduction is pro-
    hibited without permission.
Town & Country-Hearst, ProQuest—*Town & Country* Hearst Magazine
    Media Inc. Image produced by ProQuest LLC as part of ProQuest®
    Women's Magazine Archive www.proquest.com. Further reproduc-
    tion is prohibited without permission.
USMMA—Unites States Merchant Marine Academy
WWD—*Women's Wear Daily* Archive

Front Cover: Philadelphia Museum of Art, Henri Bendel, LLC

Front Flap: *Millinery Trade Review*, NYPL

Back Cover: (t) Brooklyn Museum, (b) Henri Bendel, LLC

Back Flap: (t) Henri Bendel, LLC, Izak Zanou, (b) Michael Lionstar

Epigraphs: Henri Bendel, LLC

TOC: (l) Henri Bendel, LLC, (r) Henri Bendel, LLC, Izak Zanou

CHAPTER 1: xiii Philadelphia Museum of Art; 3 *Harper's Bazaar*-Hearst, ProQuest; 4 Henri Bendel, LLC; 5 courtesy of Sally Robbins; 6 Brooklyn Museum; 7 Henri Bendel, LLC; 8 *Harper's Bazaar*-Hearst, ProQuest and estate of George Platt Lynes; 9 Steven VanAuken

CHAPTER 2: 10 J.H. Colton & Co., Center for Louisiana Studies at the University of Louisiana at Lafayette; 12 Wikimedia Commons; 13 Lafayette Parish Clerk of Court, Louis J. Perret; 14 (t) courtesy of Diana Bendel, (b) LOC; 15 Wikimedia Commons; 17 Jesuit Archive; 18 Lafayette Parish Clerk of Court, Louis J. Perret; 19 *Lafayette Advertiser,* LOC; 20 The Historic New Orleans Collection; 21(t) The Historic New Orleans Collection, (b) courtesy of Morgan City Public Library, Morgan City Historical Society

CHAPTER 3: 22 Sanborn Map Company, LOC; 24 Morgan City, Louisiana Historical Society; 25 No. 43. M.A. Collection. Ghering-van Ierlant, Rijksmuseum, Amsterdam. Wikimedia Commons; 26 *Lafayette Advertiser*, LOC; 27 (t) C&R Lavis, Eastbourne, Wikimedia Commons, (b) *Illustrated Milliner*, NYPL; 28 *Morgan City Daily Review*; 29 (all) courtesy of Jere Bacharach; 31 *Lafayette Gazette*, LOC

CHAPTER 4: 32 LOC; 33 *Lafayette Advertiser*, LOC; 34 *Illustrated Milliner*, NYPL; 35 (all) by the author; 37 *Nashville Banner*; 38 (t) Wikimedia Commons, (b) US Passport Records, National Archives and Records Administration; 40 (t) *New York World*, (b) NYPL; 41 NYPL; 42 NYPL; 43 (t) *New York Times*, (b) US Passport Records, National Archives and Records Administration

CHAPTER 5: 44 NYPL; 46 (t) NYPL; 46–47 Burton Welles, NYPL; 47 *Stage*, NYPL; 48 (tl) *Vogue* ©Condé Nast, (tr) LOC, (b) *Harper's Bazaar*-Hearst, ProQuest; 49 (all) *Illustrated Milliner,* NYPL; 50 *Illustrated Milliner,*

NYPL; 51 courtesy of Elizabeth Marchesani; 52 courtesy of Elizabeth Marchesani; 53 Ancestry.com; 54 courtesy of the family of Elene Davis and Lynn Davis Lasher; 55 WWD; 56 (t) courtesy of Sally Robbins, (b) Wikimedia Commons; 57 Brooklyn Museum; 58 Organ Historical Society; 59 Bendel family; 60 Wurts Bros., MCNY; 61 NYPL

CHAPTER 6: 62 MCNY; 63 Henri Bendel, LLC; 64 (t) *Illustrated Milliner,* NYPL, (b) *Harper's Bazaar*-Hearst, ProQuest; 65 Photographic Bureau of the New York Edison Co.; 66 courtesy of Lynn Davis Lasher; 67 Brooklyn Museum; 68–69 MET, Art Resource, NY; 70 Bendel family; 72 © Chalk & Vermilion, LLC, Artists Rights Society (ARS) New York; 75 *Harper's Bazaar*-Hearst, ProQuest; 77 NYPL; 79 *New York Sun*, LOC

CHAPTER 7: 80 *Harper's Bazaar*-Hearst, ProQuest; 82 *Vogue* ©Condé Nast; 83 *Harper's Bazaar*-Hearst, ProQuest; 84 (t) courtesy of Leslye Arsht, (b) Brit Huckabay; 86 Brooklyn Museum; 87 *Harper's Bazaar*-Hearst, ProQuest; 88 PLI; 89 courtesy of Lynn Davis Lasher; 90 PLI; 91 (t) PLI, (m) USMMA, (b) USMMA; 92 (all) PLI; 93 (all) PLI; 94 (all) Andrew Cronson; 95 (all) courtesy of Diana Bendel; 96 courtesy of Sally Robbins and Betty Ann Bernell; 97 Culver Pictures; 98 MCNY; 99 (t) *Harper's Bazaar*-Hearst, ProQuest, (b) LOC; 100 Brooklyn Museum; 101 *Town & Country*-Hearst, ProQuest; 102 *Harper's Bazaar*-Hearst, ProQuest; 103 *Harper's Bazaar*-Hearst, ProQuest; 104 (t) *Harper's Bazaar*-Hearst, ProQuest, (b) MET, Art Resource NY; 105 (all) Brooklyn Museum; 106 MET, Art Resource NY; 107 MET, Art Resource NY; 108 NYPL; 109 Brooklyn Museum

CHAPTER 8: 110 Brooklyn Museum; 112 *Town & Country*-Hearst, ProQuest; 113 courtesy of Elizabeth Marchesani; 114–15 (all) 1st Dibbs and Lauren Lepire of Timeless Vixen; 116 (t) *Vogue* ©Condé Nast, (b) *Harper's Bazaar*-Hearst, ProQuest; 117 (all) *Harper's Bazaar*-Hearst, ProQuest; 118 (l) NYPL, (r) *Town & Country*-Hearst, ProQuest; 119 *Harper's Bazaar*-Hearst, ProQuest; 120 *Vogue* ©Condé Nast; 121 courtesy of Elaine Cohen; 122 (all) Wurts Bros., MCNY; 123 *Harper's Bazaar*-Hearst, ProQuest; 124 Palm Beach Historical Society; 125 Brooklyn Museum; 126 (t) *Harper's Bazaar*-Hearst, ProQuest, (b) Brooklyn Museum; 127 courtesy of Sally Robbins and Lynn Davis Lasher; 128 © Patrice Cartier/Bridgeman Images; 129 *Town & Country*-Hearst, ProQuest; 130 (t) *Town & Country*-Hearst, ProQuest, (b) *Harper's Bazaar*-Hearst, ProQuest; 131 *Harper's Bazaar*-Hearst, ProQuest; 132 courtesy of Sally Robbins and Leslye Arsht; 133 *Vogue* ©Condé Nast

CHAPTER 9: 134 Pach Bros., *The Spur* magazine, courtesy of Sally Robbins; 136 *Morning Herald* (Gloversville and Johnstown, NY) via Newspapers.com;

137 Courtesy of the RISD Museum; 138–39 courtesy of Elene Davis and Lynn Davis Lasher; 140 Wikimedia Commons; 141 University Archives and Acadiana Manuscripts Collection, Edith Garland Dupré Library, University of Louisiana at Lafayette; 142 (t) Brit Huckabay, (b) State Library of Louisiana; 143 © *Palm Beach Post*–USA Today Network; 144 *Harper's Bazaar*-Hearst, ProQuest; 146–47 courtesy of Elene Davis and Lynn Davis Lasher; 148 (all) Mattie Edwards Hewitt, Pach Bros., *The Spur* magazine, courtesy of Sally Robbins; 149 (all) Stamford Museum and Nature Center; 150–51 (all) Mattie Edwards, Pach Bros., *The Spur* magazine, courtesy of Sally Robbins; 152 Leon Deran, Stamford Museum and Nature Center; 153 WWD, ProQuest; 154 Robert M. McBride and Co.; 155 *Harper's Bazaar*-Hearst, ProQuest, and courtesy of estate of Toni von Horn; 156 *Vogue* ©Condé Nast; 157 MCNY

CHAPTER 10: 158 Summer Greer, the Lafayette Museum; 160 courtesy of Leslye Arsht; 161 MET, Art Resource NY; 162 Brooklyn Museum; 163 Henri Bendel, LLC; 164 courtesy of Diana Bendel; 165 *Vogue* ©Condé Nast, Henry Bendel, LLC; 166 Twitchy Lamarr Vintage Shoppe; 168 University Archives and Acadiana Manuscripts Collection, Edith Garland Dupré Library, University of Louisiana at Lafayette; 169 Southwestern Louisiana Institute Photographs, 1923–1940, Edith Garland Dupré Library, University of Louisiana at Lafayette; 170 courtesy of Diana Bendel; 171 *New York Times*; 172 Wikimedia Commons

CHAPTER 11: 174 Victoria Pickering; 175 Henri Bendel, LLC; 176 Henri Bendel, LLC; 177 George Platt Lynes, *Vogue* ©Condé Nast; 178 *Harper's Bazaar*-Hearst from NYPL; 179 (tl) George Platt Lynes, *Vogue* ©Condé Nast, (tr) Horst P. Horst, *Vogue* ©Condé Nast, (b) Rene Bouche, *Vogue* ©Condé Nast; 180 *Harper's Bazaar*-Hearst, ProQuest; 181 *Vogue* ©Condé Nast; 182 courtesy of Diana Bendel; 183 Parsons School of Design; 184 Wilbur Pippin for the *New York Times* from Parsons School of Design; 185 Parsons School of Design; 186 AP Newsroom; 187 (all) C.P. Smith, courtesy of Robert Rufino; 188 (l) Museum of Fine Arts Boston, (r) Michael Cooper for *New York* magazine; 189 (t) Fairchild Archive/Penske Media/Getty Images, (b) photo courtesy of Charles Tracy Archive; 190 Fairchild Archive/WWD/Penske Media/Getty Images; 191 *Vogue* ©Condé Nast and estate of Richard Avedon; 193 courtesy of the estate of Gösta Peterson; 194 Eddy Kohli; 195 Henri Bendel, LLC; 196 Brian Jannsen, Alamy; 197 (t) Philip Scalia, Alamy, (b) ZUMA Press Inc., Alamy; 198 Horst P. Horst, *Vogue* ©Condé Nast; 199 Irving Penn, *Vogue* ©Condé Nast; 200 (t) Ron Galella Collection/Getty Images, (bl) David Lefranc/Gamma-Rapho/Getty Images, (br) Izak Zanou and Henri Bendel, LLC; 201 (t) Steven VanAuken, (b)

Summer Greer; 202 Patti McConville, Alamy; 203 (all) Steven VanAuken; 204 Paolo Mastrangelo, Flickr; 205 Fairchild, WWD; 206 (t) NYPL, (b) Charles Sykes, Shutterstock

CHAPTER 12: 208 Henri Bendel, LLC; 209 by the author; 210 by the author; 211 (all) Andrew Cronson; 212 (all) Stamford Museum and Nature Center; 214 Brit Huckabay; 215 Summer Greer; 216 Brit Huckabay; 217 (t) courtesy of Jane Cohen, (b) Museum of Fine Arts Boston; 218 (all) courtesy of Diana Bendel; 219 courtesy of Lisa Bernell Rostad; 220 MET, Art Resource NY; 221 MCNY; 222 WWD; 223, *Millinery Trade Review*, NYPL

Selected Bibliography: 230 Brooklyn Museum